The Worst
Baseball Pitchers
of All Time

The Worst Baseball Pitchers of All Time

Bad Luck, Bad Arms,
Bad Teams, and
Just Plain Bad

by
ALAN S. KAUFMAN
and
JAMES C. KAUFMAN

A CITADEL PRESS BOOK
Published by Carol Publishing Group

To Nadeen:
For inspiring her husband and son
to transform their dream into a reality

Copyright © 1995 by Alan S. Kaufman and James C. Kaufman

A Citadel Press Book
Published by Carol Publishing Group
Citadel Press is a registered trademark of Carol Communications, Inc.

Editorial Offices: 600 Madison Avenue, New York, N.Y. 10022
Sales and Distribution Offices: 120 Enterprise Avenue, Secaucus, N.J. 07094
In Canada: Canadian Manda Group, One Atlantic Avenue, Suite 105, Toronto, Ontario M6K 3E7
Queries regarding rights and permissions should be addressed to Carol Publishing Group, 600 Madison Avenue, New York, N.Y. 10022

Carol Publishing Group books are available at special discounts for bulk purchases, sales promotions, fund-raising, or educational purposes. Special editions can be created to specifications. For details contact: Special Sales Department, Carol Publishing Group, 120 Enterprise Avenue, Secaucus, N.J. 07094

Manufactured in the United States of America
10 9 8 7 6 5 4 3 2 1

Library of Congress Cataloging-in-Publication Data
Kaufman, Alan S.
    The worst baseball pitchers of all time : bad luck, bad arms, bad teams, and just plain bad / by Alan S. Kaufman and James C. Kaufman.
      p. cm.
    "A Citadel Press book."
    Originally published: Jefferson, N.C. : McFarland, © 1993. With new epilogue.
    Includes index.
    ISBN 0–8065–1653–4 (pbk.)
    1. Pitchers (Baseball)—United States. 2. Baseball—Records—United States. I. Kaufman, James C. II. Title.
[GV871.K38 1995]
796.357'22'0922—dc20

94–48362
CIP

CONTENTS

ACKNOWLEDGMENTS

◆ We are grateful to numerous people for their generous help in the preparation of this book. Nathan Stone spent many hours transcribing interviews, searching through back issues of *The Sporting News,* and critiquing drafts of several chapters. Pete Palmer conducted numerous time-consuming statistical analyses for us using his special data base for *Total Baseball,* and gave us invaluable suggestions by telephone and letter. John Phillips offered valuable leads for us to follow, and his detailed books provided definitive sources on a century of baseball in Cleveland. Steve Gietschier, archivist for *The Sporting News,* provided us with important information about many forgotten pitchers, while George Brace supplied us with their photographs. Former minor-league pitcher Dr. Cecil Reynolds shared many interesting anecdotes and memories of his playing days. Thanks also to players' agent Tony Attanasio; sports editor Dan Shryock, and others on the *Times-Advocate* staff; Dr. Steven Ross; Lee Johnson; and Harvey Packer.

The highlight of writing this book was getting to know former major leaguers. We are grateful to Rollie Fingers and Greg Riddoch for sharing their insights in personal interviews. And special thanks go to the following pitchers who agreed to fill out questionnaires and, in almost all cases, to be interviewed by telephone, although they knew that our book was about "pitchers who endured at least one season in which everything went wrong and they lost many more games than they won—as you did": Ray Benge, Milt Gaston, Frank "Lefty" Hoerst, Elon "Chief" Hogsett, Art Houtteman, Sid Hudson, Art Johnson, Si Johnson, Clay Kirby, Mike Parrott, Charley Schanz, and Carl Scheib.

Milt Gaston, Frank Hoerst, Si Johnson, Sid Hudson, and Mike Parrott were gracious and informative beyond any reasonable expectation; these fine, warm, intelligent men shared with us their passion for baseball, as well as their knowledge and memories. And when Clay Kirby died suddenly at age 43 of a heart attack just a few months after we had interviewed him, we felt as if we had lost a close friend.

◆　◆　◆

During the writing of this book, we consulted countless books, periodicals, monographs, newspapers, and other sources of information about baseball, past and present. The publications that we relied on the most heavily are the following: *Aaron to Zuverink* and *Aaron to Zipfel* (Richard Marazzi and Len Fiorito); *Baseball Anecdotes* (Daniel Okrent and Steve Wulf); *Baseball Digest; Baseball's Greatest Records, Streaks and Feats* (Harvey Frommer); *The Bill James Historical Baseball Abstract* (Bill James); *Great Baseball Feats, Facts & Firsts* (David Nemec); Media Guides, especially for the San Diego Padres; Bruce Nash and Allan Zullo's series of *Baseball Hall of Shame* books; *"On a Clear Day They Could See Seventh Place": Baseball's Worst Teams* (George Robinson and Charles Salzberg); Preston D. Orem's books chronicling baseball's beginnings via detailed newspaper accounts; SABR *Bulletin* (and other SABR publications, such as *Nineteenth Century Stars*); *100 Years of Baseball* (Lee Allen); *The Ballplayers* (Mike Shatzkin); *The Baseball Encyclopedia* (8th ed.); *The Baseball Record Companion* (Joseph Reichler); *The Crooked Pitch* (Martin Quigley); *The New York Times Book of Baseball History; The 99 Spiders* (John Phillips); *The Pitcher* (John Thorn and John Holway); *The Scouting Report: 1991* (John Dewan); *The Sporting News; Total Baseball* (1st and 2nd eds., John Thorn and Pete Palmer); *The Ultimate Book of Baseball* (Daniel Okrent and Harris Lewine); *Where Have You Gone, Vince DiMaggio?* (Edward Kiersh); and *Who Was Who in Cleveland Baseball in 1901–10* (John Phillips).

1

Introduction to the World of Skunks

◆ You've read tales of Walter Johnson, Lefty Grove, Sandy Koufax, and Nolan Ryan. What about Toad Ramsey, Egyptian Healy, and Crazy Schmit? Or Buster Brown, Chief Hogsett, and Mike Parrott? The best pitchers win Cy Young Awards, enter the Baseball Hall of Fame on the first ballot, and are portrayed in the movies by future U.S. presidents. The worst pitchers get less respect than General Custer and suffer a fate more demeaning than notoriety: They are forgotten.

We recently spoke to Hall-of-Famer Rollie Fingers and asked the former relief ace to name the worst pitcher he ever saw. Fingers pitched for 13 seasons in the American League (AL) and four in the National League (NL), but was stumped by our question. "I don't know who," he said. "The worst pitcher, I probably wouldn't even remember his name. I've got no clue who the worst pitcher would be."

We intend to correct this injustice by honoring pitchers who made a habit of losing. Some had one terrible season, whereas others could be counted on to lose with ridiculous regularity throughout their major-league careers. Some came back from the depths of defeat to become stars—several made it to Cooperstown—while others plunged from stardom to failure and still others drifted quickly out of the majors after getting shell-shocked on the mound.

There has been no blueprint for failure: Injuries, inept support from teammates, alcohol, lack of talent, and lack of effort can each claim its victims. But we're not trying to explain why pitchers have failed; we want to identify *who* have been the biggest failures of all time, the least effective hurlers in history. Who had the worst careers? Who suffered through the worst seasons? Who most resembled underwear king Jim Palmer on the mound against the Boston Red Sox during his "brief" but memorable comeback attempt in 1991, a year after his enshrinement in the Hall of Fame?

After four straight 20-win seasons, Oakland's Dave Stewart suffered through a miserable 1991 season, yielding more than five earned runs a game. In late August, he asked the Bay Area writers to write the truth. He told the *San Francisco Chronicle,* "I've been taught you're supposed to write when someone's bad. When I'm lousy, I'm lousy.... Do your job. Don't think I'll be angry if you tell it like you saw it." And that's just what we will do in this book: Write the painful truth.

To honor the worst pitchers requires an award—a skunk award—to be given to the worst pitcher each season since 1876, the year that the National League made its debut with eight charter ball clubs. And special skunk awards are needed to immortalize those hurlers who endured the most terrible careers of all time. Our skunk awards will go to those pitchers who ranked a notch below the rest. To those hurlers, past and present, who took too literally Alexander Cartwright's 1845 rule that the ball should be aimed at the bat—a mandate for pitchers of old to let batters hit their soft, underhand tosses. To those pitchers who threw as if they were unwittingly forced to follow the official rule instituted in 1871 for the first season of organized baseball: To pitch the ball precisely where the hitter wants it, whether high or low.

What Shall the Award Be Called?

An award should have a name to honor the person who best exemplifies its spirit. The World Series hero earns the Babe Ruth Award, and the outstanding pitchers of the year are likened to Cy Young. John Thorn and John B. Holway, when selecting the best pitchers of the year since 1876 in their book *The Pitcher,* presented Jim Creighton Awards to honor a forgotten hero, the first paid player and the first real baseball superstar: a man who revolutionized the art of pitching and who once played an entire season without making an out at bat. Creighton, pitching for the Niagaras of Brooklyn at age 17, used a slight wrist snap—a controversial pitch at the time—to perfect the sail and dip of his speedball. His style of throwing helped transform the pitcher from wimp to stud, from an unimportant player trying to hit the enemy's bat to the center-stage spotlight. Creighton's fame spread rapidly until his tragic death in 1862 at age 21 from an injury sustained while circling the bases for a home run. A true Roy Hobbs hero.

Who is the antithesis—the true skunk, the unnatural, the pitcher who is more likely to be portrayed by Danny DeVito than Robert Redford? Should it be a pitcher who once was great and then descended to the depths of skunkdom? Then Asa Brainard would surely have skunk credentials. Nicknamed the "Count," Brainard led the invincible Cincinnati Red

Stockings of 1869, the first professional baseball team, to 64 wins and a tie in front of more than 200,000 fans and earned an audience with President Ulysses S. Grant. Three years later, the great Asa—who gained fame for his grace in the box, blazing speed, and wicked twister— was 2–9 in the National Association (NA). In 1874, at age 33, Brainard was the worst pitcher in the nation's first professional league with a 5–22 mark for the Baltimore Canaries. His candidacy for lending the name Asa Brainard to the skunk award was further enhanced by his actions off the field. Following the 1870 season, this man with muttonchop

whiskers, who might have walked out of a Dickens novel, deserted his infant son and wife (the girl who once sewed Cincinnati's red stockings), leaving them both destitute.

But maybe the skunk namesake should never have achieved greatness; perhaps he should be a pitcher who was terrible for one or two seasons before disappearing from sight. The hapless Brooklyn Atlantics of the 1870s, once a powerhouse of the 1860s (they went undefeated while the Civil War was raging from 1863 to 1865, including a 75–11 slaughter of the undefeated Canadian champion), produced two pitchers who deserve to be mentioned. Jim Britt lost 64 games during his two seasons in the sun (1872–73), compiling records of 9–28 and 17–36. Not to be outdone, southpaw John Cassidy posted a 1–20 record in 1875 for a winning percentage of .048. In his debut against a tough Hartford nine, in front of an overflowing crowd of 3,000 screaming fans, he frustrated the opposing hitters who complained about his hard-to-hit pitches. Little did Cassidy

Above: **You could always count on Asa Brainard ("the Count") to win for the great Cincinnati Red Stockings in the late 1860s, but his pitching was as off-the-wall as Humpty-Dumpty after the National Association was formed (photo courtesy of George Brace).**

realize that his narrow 6–5 defeat by Hartford would be one of the few highlights of his brief and futile professional career.

Perhaps a real skunk is a pitcher who lasts no longer than a game or two, but still manages to leave his mark. In 1874, Dan Collins, of the Chicago White Stockings, compiled a nondescript 1–1 mark. He defeated the powerful Boston Red Stockings, although Boston manager Harry Wright threatened to protest the game because the ball was ripped (at that time the same ball was used for the entire game). How did Collins do without a ripped ball? He was rocked 38–1 by the New York Mutuals, who compiled 33 hits. Collins, who threw more wild pitches than the scorer could count, was mercifully replaced in the pitcher's box, to the relief of his frustrated catcher and the fearful hitters.

Should the skunk award be named for a pitcher who carved his name in history by having the rookie jitters not once, but twice? Cherokee Fisher was easily the worst pitcher in the inaugural season of the NA in 1871, enduring a 4–16 record for the last-place Rockford Forest Citys. Despite a drinking problem, Fisher was still around in 1876—the NL's first season—and he proceeded to compile a 4–20 mark for the Cincinnati Reds. Old Cherokee also surrendered the first home run ever hit in the NL, to batting champion Ross Barnes of the Chicago White Stockings. It was Barnes' only home run of the year.

Bill Stearns: A Skunk for All Seasons

The Cherokee Fisher Skunk Award has a nice ring to it, and the list of other candidates is impressive. The Asa Brainard Skunk Award, in par-

Above: **This is not a very good picture of Cherokee Fisher, but, then again, he wasn't a very good pitcher (photo courtesy of George Brace).**

ticular, would have been cloaked in irony because legend has it that a star pitcher became forever known as an "ace" when teams in the 1870s called their best pitchers "their Asas." But no one merits the skunk distinction more than does right-hander William (Bill) Stearns, a man who paired an ordinary name with an extraordinary pitching career.

Born in Washington, D.C., in 1853, Stearns pitched in the NA each year of its existence, compiling the following record in the first organized professional league:

Year	Team	Won	Lost	Winning Percentage	Estimated Earned Run Average
1871	Washington Olympics	2	0	1.000	2.50
1872	Washington Nationals	0	11	.000	6.91
1873	Washington Nationals	7	25	.219	5.02
1874	Hartfords	2	14	.125	4.50
1875	Washington Nationals	1	14	.067	5.36
	Total	12	64	.158	5.17

But Stearns' skunk behavior extended beyond his .158 winning percentage, the nearly 1,200 hits he gave up in about 700 innings, and the .323 average that the league battled against him. He also possessed little character. In 1873 he inexplicably failed to show up for a game with the Brooklyn Atlantics and was fired by the Washington Nationals. Given another chance in 1874 by Hartford, Stearns showed no favoritism: Once again he vanished without a word, this time near the end of the season. Stearns, who also had overdrawn his salary, was expelled by his new team for breach of contract. Yet the phoenixlike Stearns surfaced in 1875 with his former Washington team to close out an eminently forgettable career at age 22 with a 1–14 mark.

But Bill Stearns should not be forgotten. His misdeeds on and off the field—his special combination of inept pitching and boorish behavior—impelled us to "honor" him posthumously with a variety of Skunk Stearns awards.

•The award is given to the worst pitcher of the year from 1876 to 1992.

•It's given to the pitchers who suffered through the worst single seasons of all time.

•And it's given to the pitchers from every era who compiled the worst career statistics.

Jim Creighton was memorialized shortly after his death by a monument erected in a cemetery on the crest of a hill, a stone baseball resting softly at the pinnacle of the monument. Bill Stearns, who died at age 45 in 1898 in Washington, D.C., on a date (December 30) that would one day be Sandy Koufax's birthday, is now memorialized with a long-overdue but most deserved monument: a small stone skunk.

Selecting the Annual Skunk Stearns Award Winners

For the annual Skunk Stearns trophies, we opted to select a single pitcher per year, not one per league. Except for occasional seasons when we chose co-winners, our method guaranteed that each winner emerged center stage and shared top billing with no one—something that few skunks enjoyed during their careers. But just as there are no objective criteria for selecting winners of the Most Valuable Player or Cy Young Award, there is no sure way to choose the worst pitcher of the year. As in the Cy Young elections, some Skunk Stearns choices are clear-cut, whereas others are arguable. In making our selections, we used a blend of the following statistics and guidelines.

•*Losses minus wins.* Plain and simple: Subtract the number of wins from the number of losses. A hurler with 17 more losses than wins (a guy with a 6–23 mark, for example) would have the "disadvantage" over a pitcher who went 2–15—even though the second pitcher had a lower winning percentage. We gave a bit more weight to losses minus wins than to the other criteria when making our annual selections.

•*Earned run average.* We placed more emphasis on the ERA as of 1913, when it became an official NL statistic; the AL followed suit a year later.

•*Wins-above-team.* We adopted one of Pete Palmer and John Thorn's high-tech stats, wins-above-team (WAT). This index tells how many wins a pitcher earned over and above the number that the average pitcher would have won for the same team. In most skunk races, the candidates won *fewer* games than expected and had negative values for their WAT statistic. So we were really searching for pitchers who compiled the most compelling wins-*below*-team stats. When several pitchers had terrible records, we preferred to give a Skunk Stearns Award to a man who pitched for a pretty good team, not one who lost because his teammates were crummy. We didn't use the WAT before 1893 because it's meaningless when the whole staff has just two or three pitchers (sometimes just one!).

•When two more more pitchers seemed about equally deserving of the Skunk award, we favored the one who was handed the ball time and again (refusing to shirk his inevitable punishment) over the one who spent most of his time in the dugout or bull pen. Virtually all Skunk Stearns winners had at least 15 decisions, and most had 20 or more. In fact, we awarded skunks only to pitchers with fewer than 20 decisions when they were "dandruff" candidates—head and shoulders ahead of the field.

AN ILLUSTRATION OF THE METHOD:
THE 1991 SKUNK RACE

We'll use the 1991 Skunk Stearns race to illustrate our method of selecting the champion. The major-league worsts in the three categories, in order, are as follows:

Order and Name*	Losses minus Wins	Order and Name*	WAT
1T. Kirk McCaskill		1. Kirk McCaskill	−5.1
1T. Rod Nichols	9	2. Dennis Rasmussen	4.0
3T. Dennis Rasmussen	9	3. Allan Anderson	−3.9
3T. Jim Deshaies	7	4. Rod Nichols	−3.8
3T. Randy Myers	7	5. Randy Myers	3.2
3T. Greg Swindell	7	6T. Storm Davis	−3.1
3T. Ron Darling	7	6T. Ron Darling	−3.1

*T = tie.

Order and Name	ERA (minimum of 115 innings)
1. Tim Leary	6.49
2. Wade Taylor	6.27
3. José Mesa	5.97
4. Jeff Johnson	5.95
5. Mark Gubicza	5.68
6. Jeff Ballard	5.60
7. Jack Armstrong	5.48

Every pitcher on these three lists was a candidate for the 1991 Skunk Stearns trophy. Because of so many contenders, we narrowed the group to pitchers with (1) at least 15 decisions, (2) an ERA worse than the average for their league (4.09 AL, 3.68 NL), and (3) a WAT of −2.0 or less. The records of the six finalists are shown on the next page, ordered by the difference between their losses and wins (L–W).

Skunk Candidate	Team	Won–Lost	L–W	ERA	WAT
Kirk McCaskill	California: AL	10–19	9	4.26	−5.1
Dennis Rasmussen	San Diego: NL	6–13	7	3.74	−4.0
Jim Deshaies	Houston: NL	5–12	7	4.98	−2.5
Ron Darling	New York/Montreal: NL and Oakland: AL	8–15	7	4.26	−3.1
Allan Anderson	Minnesota: AL	5–11	6	4.96	−3.9
Jack Armstrong	Cincinnati: NL	7–13	6	5.48	−2.6

Of this group, McCaskill led the majors in 1991 with 19 losses, tied for the major-league lead with nine more losses than wins, and had the worst WAT; his ERA of 4.26 was unimpressive. The Angels finished at .500 in 1991 (the first cellar dweller to do so); they were a .534 team when Mc-Caskill and his .345 winning percentage stayed on the bench. McCaskill won five games fewer than the average pitcher would have won with the 1991 Angels (he was 10–19; the average pitcher would have gone 15–14). McCaskill is the odds-on winner of the Skunk Stearns trophy. Rod Nichols (2–11) and Tim Leary (4–10, 6.49 ERA) had too few decisions to be serious candidates.

None of the pitchers who fell just short of 20 decisions qualified as dandruff candidates. Jim ("Two Silhouettes on") Deshaies, Allan Anderson, and Dennis Rasmussen had about equally bad seasons, but none of these semiregular starters had stats that were head and shoulders ahead of the field.

McCaskill is one of the few Skunk Stearns contenders who took his regular turn every fifth day for most of the season, and he is the un-contested champion. His award comes courtesy of a mix of bad luck and bad pitching. The bad luck was an awful Angels' offense whenever he pitched; the team scored either one or no runs during the innings he was on the mound in 16 of his 19 losses. The bad pitching? His ERA for those 19 defeats was 6.02, and he was knocked out before the fifth inning eight times. McCaskill was 6–5 in early June, then skidded to a 4–14 finish. So naturally he signed a multiyear free-agent contract with the White Sox for nearly $2.5 million a year—and reportedly could have earned even more by staying in Anaheim.

During 1991, we began a "skunk watch" early in the season. Doug Drabek was 1–6 nearly six weeks into the season, and we envisioned a Cy Young-to-Skunk Stearns plunge. In early July, we found ourselves actively rooting for our favorites. The Braves' John Smoltz (2–11, 5.16 ERA) looked like a lock for the award at the All-Star break. We then suffered through his three-game winning streak, but watched in admiration as he finished the season 12–2 with a 2.63 ERA, followed by a 2–0 record in postseason play that included a pennant-clinching shutout against Pittsburgh and a near-miss in game seven of the World Series against the Twins.

At various times we rooted for most of the Cleveland staff and were distressed when Rod Nichols (1–10 with a 4.14 ERA in mid–August) was dropped from the starting rotation. We wanted him to get enough decisions to mount a challenge for the trophy.

August 30 was a skunk-watcher's paradise. Five skunk candidates started—McCaskill, Deshaies, Rasmussen, Myers, and Alex Fernandez—and each one lost. But the last month of the season lost some spark when Deshaies (who struck out eight straight Dodgers in 1986) was removed from the Houston rotation, along with his 75 mile-per-hour fastball, and McCaskill was dropped from the California starting five. Thank goodness for Stump Merrill, who sent left-hander Jeff Johnson out every fifth day no matter what. The Yankee rookie brazenly defied the odds as his ERA rose after each of ten straight starts. On Friday the 13th of September his ERA had more than doubled to 5.99. He finally snapped the string in his next start, a no-decision, but for a ten-game period he was 1–8 with a 10.51 ERA. Johnson transformed himself from a candidate for AL Rookie of the Year to a Skunk Stearns contender.

And we were enjoying a skunk-watch bonanza during 1992. When this book went to press as the regular season ended, the Phillies' Kyle Abbott (1–14, 5.13 ERA, WAT= −6.4) defeated the Indians' Jack Armstrong (6–15, 4.64 ERA, WAT= −4.4) for the Skunk Stearns trophy. Seattle's Erik Hanson (8–17, 4.82 ERA) and the Mets' Anthony Young (2–14, 4.17 ERA) each started the season poorly and flopped near the finish, but pitched too well in between to cop the trophy. Only a decision by Phils' manager Jim Fregosi to banish Abbott to the bull pen in August saved the rookie southpaw from mounting a serious challenge for the worst single season of all time.

And who knows what Houston's Ryan Bowen (0–7, 10.96 ERA) might have achieved in 1992 if he hadn't spent most of the season in the minors?

SOME PAST SKUNK WINNERS

Most of the award winners and contenders are the unknowns of baseball (the John Colemans, Harry Harpers, Lou Knerrs, and Jay Tibbses), but some skunks will surprise all but the most dedicated fan. The roll call of dubious honorees includes the inventor of the curveball and a few other Hall of Famers, the pitcher of the only perfect game in World Series history, a 30-game winner who received two Cy Young trophies, and the 297-game winner who invented the spitball. One two-time skunk pitched all 26 innings of the longest game in major-league history, while the only *three*-time Skunk Stearns winner (a redhead who had a "ruff" time in the 1920s) turned his career around and landed in Cooperstown. The most recent skunk repeater was given a raise after going 2–19 in the mid–1980s and earned $1.67 million in 1990—nearly $90,000 per defeat.

A Few Extra Awards

We wanted to honor more pitchers than just the ones who took home Skunk Stearns trophies, so we came up with a few more awards.

• *The Cherokee Fisher Rookie Award.* Most pitchers get one shot at being a rookie, but Cherokee Fisher had two: in 1871, the first year of the NA, and in 1876, the NL's inaugural season. He debuted in the first professional league with a 4–16 record for the Rockford Forest Citys; if we had awarded Skunk Stearns trophies to NA pitchers, Fisher would have won the first one hands down. As a rookie in 1876, he failed to win the first NL Skunk Stearns Award, but not because of a lack of effort, since he posted a 4–20 mark for the Cincinnati Red Stockings.

When you think of Fisher, you think of lightning—as in striking twice, not as in a nickname for his fastball. Though he lost out to Bill Stearns for our main award, is anyone more deserving than Fisher as the namesake of the rookie award?

• *The Asa Brainard Humpty-Dumpty Award.* Who else could better sponsor an award to be given to pitchers who had a great fall? In a few short years Brainard went from the ace of the unbeatable 1869 Red Stockings to a patsy in the NA and a cad to his wife and infant. An award bearing this Humpty-Dumpty's name will be given to the pitcher from each era who reached the pinnacle of success before taking a downhill plunge.

• *The John Cassidy Root Canal Award.* The left-handed John Cassidy pitched in a total of 32 games, mostly in the NA, although he had a two-game cup of coffee in the NL as well. Overall, he lost 21 of 23 decisions. Since our candidates for the worst careers had to have had at least 50 defeats, we wanted to bestow an award on the pitcher from each era who pitched relatively briefly but with sublime incompetence—someone whose major-league career was, like root canal, fairly short but strikingly painful. We had to look no further than John Cassidy to name the Root Canal trophy.

The "pain," of course, is figurative. To many ball players, any seasons spent in The Show were literally the best years (or months) of their lives. Art Johnson pitched one full year and parts of two others for the Boston Braves in the early 1940s and had a 7–16 record. But the tall left-hander told us that just playing in the majors was "a little boy's dream that came true—meeting and playing with and against idols like Casey Stengel, Carl Hubbell, and Mel Ott." Frank ("Lefty") Hoerst, who was 10–33 for the Phils in the 1940s, told us, "I loved what I was doing, so I don't see how you can fail when you do that."

•*The Joe Hardy Sell-Your-Soul Award.* Picture Joe Boyd, a middle-aged, overweight, balding real estate agent. In a flash, and with a little help from a Mr. Applegate, Joe Boyd is transformed into the young slugger Joe Hardy, who leads the ever pathetic Washington Senators over the Damn Yankees. Only in fiction? Not quite.

Baseball has been witness to many turnabouts that were nearly as sensational as the Joe Boyd–to–Joe Hardy metamorphosis. Sometimes there's a rational explanation for the sudden stardom. John Smoltz credited a Georgia sports psychologist for his abrupt about-face after the 1991 All-Star game. Often, though, the sudden stardom has no explanation. Did anyone really sell his soul to the devil to achieve astonishing fame? Who knows? But a number of pitchers throughout baseball history have deserved the Joe Hardy Sell-Your-Soul Award.

Selecting the All-time Skunk Stearns Award Winners

Which pitchers had the worst single season of all time? Which hurlers had the least effective careers? These questions are a bit more difficult to answer because they require comparisons across generations. Rules change; standards fluctuate. Player's ERAs have averaged 3.00 or less for the entire major leagues some years (in 1908, 1918, and 1968, for example). Yet in other years (such as 1926 and 1986) ERAs have averaged about 4.00, and in 1930 the average ERA approached five runs a game. So what does an ERA

Above: **John Cassidy won a single game in the National Association and repeated the feat in the National League. Unfortunately, he lost a total of 21 games (26 according to the *Baseball Encyclopedia*) (photo courtesy of George Brace).**

of 4.00 mean? It's crummy if it was done in 1908 and about average for a pitcher in 1986, but it's close to the league leaders in 1930. Most stats are relative, so if we wanted to compare pitchers across time we would need methods to take into account the fluctuating standards for measuring pitchers from one generation to the next.

Thorn and Palmer (*The Hidden Book of Baseball* and *Total Baseball*) provided some innovative procedures, such as the WAT stat we mentioned before, that allow direct comparisons of players from different eras. We borrowed some of their ideas and methods and blended them with a few conventional stats that don't change much over time. Taken together, we came up with the following five criteria for determining the worst single seasons, as well as the worst pitching careers, of all time. (We used only four criteria before 1893 because the WAT wasn't useful.)

Losses minus wins: a simple bottom-line stat whose meaning has remained constant over time.

Winning percentage: another bottom-line stat that has always identified the least-successful pitchers in any league at any time. Divide the number of wins by the number of decisions. Period.

ERA, adjusted for league and ballpark: a Palmer-Thorn stat that adjusts ERAs, enabling them to be compared across the decades. The average adjusted ERA for any season is always 100. Regardless of when a pitcher played ball, a value of 90 is bad and a value of 80 is terrible; the heroes of this book often wallowed in the 60s and 70s. Excluding pitchers with brief careers, the lowest lifetime adjusted ERA that we found in *Total Baseball* (2nd edition) was 51—by none other than Bill "Skunk" Stearns. (See the Appendix for details about this stat.)

WAT: As was mentioned previously, this Palmer-Thorn stat compares the number of games a pitcher won to the number the *average* pitcher would have won for the same team. (See the Appendix for more details.)

TPI: Also from Thorn and Palmer, the TPI reflects a combination of three aspects of a pitcher's job—pitching, fielding, and hitting. Pitchers with skunk credentials often earn TPIs below zero: They are not adept at preventing runs with their pitching and fielding and, in some cases, at knocking in runs as hitters. (See the Appendix for more details.)

Our goal was to come up with a rank ordering of the worst of the worst—the worst single seasons and the worst careers. To do so, we blended the various criteria, giving as much weight to the "old" stats as to the newfangled ones—giving us a surefire way to find the cream of the crap. Primarily because we used a few Palmer-Thorn stats, we chose as our definitive source the pitching records included in the 1991 edition of *Total Baseball*. (To obtain WATs, we used the first edition of *Total Baseball*, along with updates and new analyses provided by Palmer.)

Grouping Pitchers by When They Played

Theoretically, we could have used the five criteria to identify the worst pitchers of all time—from 1876 to 1991—because changes in rules and standards are largely taken into account by these yardsticks. Some changes, however, are too great to overcome by any statistical sleight of hand. From 1876 to 1892, the pitching distance fluctuated from 45 to 55 feet, the number of balls required for a walk varied from four to nine, and pitching staffs usually included only one to four "twirlers." For this experimental, pioneering era, we compared bad pitchers to each other, but not to latter-day pitchers. Still, we used the same criteria (except for WAT) and present our lists of "worsts" at the end of Chapter 2, which is devoted to the years 1876 to 1892.

We decided to use the five criteria to select the worst pitchers and the worst single seasons of the 20th century—from 1901 to 1991. The "dead-ball" era spanned the years 1893 to 1919, and Chapter 3 is devoted to this entire period. But we have excluded from our "worst-ever" lists those pitchers whose careers were mostly confined to the 1890s because baseball was not quite modern then.

In 1893, the baseball lords created, once and for all, a constant distance of 60 feet 6 inches to home plate and replaced the pitching box with a pitching rubber. But it took pitchers about a half-dozen years to adjust to the longer distance. The ball was indeed dead, and home runs were scarce, but there was no shortage of hits and runs. The NL sported a Danger Zone in the middle of the diamond; it was known as the pitcher's mound. The league's ERA jumped from about 3.3 in 1891–92 to about 5.0 in 1893–94. In 1894, batters hit .309, on the average, and pitchers had an overall ERA of 5.32! The league's ERAs stayed in the range of about 4.0 through the end of the century and didn't "round" to three runs per game until 1901.

But the 1890s pitchers' slow adjustment to the longer distance was not the only reason for not comparing them with the 20th-century pitchers. High ERAs became a way of life in the 1930s as well. Baseball in the latter part of the 19th century was just different. From the time the AA folded in 1891 until the AL began operation in 1901, baseball had a single league, the NL, and it was crammed with 12 teams. Even more disturbing was the NL's approval of two teams having the same ownership. The 1899 season was a travesty: The Brooklyn Superbas won the pennant by filling its roster with the best players from Brooklyn and Baltimore, while at the far-distant reaches of 12th place, the Cleveland Spiders became the worst team ever by supplying its best players to St. Louis and trying to make do with inept, but inexpensive, players.

Pitching in the early 1900s was not exactly the same as pitching in later

decades of the 20th century. Pitchers were often left in games to rot, and some lost an awesome number of games. Boston's 1906 NL doormats produced *four* 20-game losers. Their star, 16-game winner Irv Young (nicknamed, inappropriately enough, "Cy the Second" and "Young Cy") lost 25 games—and didn't even lead the league in losses. But similarities among pitchers of the 1900s and 1940s and 1980s obscure the differences. Bad pitching, by any name, is still bad pitching, and the Palmer-Thorn stats made it a legitimate enterprise to compare players across generations, even across a span as large as 1901 to 1991.

Babe Ruth ushered in the long-ball era in 1920, and Chapter 4 deals with the 1920–46 period. Another era dawned in 1947 when Jackie Robinson broke the color barrier; Chapter 5 treats pitchers who played mostly from 1947 to 1968. And Chapter 6 is devoted to the present era that began in 1969, when increased expansion led to four-division baseball.

In Chapters 2 to 6 we give out the annual Skunk Stearns Award, plus our various special awards. We also rank order the five worst pitchers of each era on the basis of their lifetime stats, along with the five worst single seasons of the era. In Chapter 7, we throw all the candidates from 1901 to 1991 into the hopper and come up with a rank ordering of the 25 worst pitchers of the 20th century, alongside a list of the 25 worst single seasons in this century.

For the career comparisons in each era and from 1901 to 1991, we considered only pitchers with at least 50 losses, excluding those who pitched terribly for only a couple of seasons. The *real* worst professional pitchers of all time never made it to the major leagues or lasted only a few games.

Above: **Chief Hogsett was 6–19 for the 1937 Browns and had a career ERA of 5.03, but he still clawed his way to more than ten years in the majors (photo courtesy of Chief Hogsett).**

We searched for pitchers who made it to the majors and who stayed around for a while, long enough to memorize the taste of defeat. Those pitchers — like Chief Hogsett, who pitched for 11 years, had a career ERA of 5.03, and was 6–19 for the 1937 Browns — are the true heroes of this book. The left-handed Hogsett was a sidearmer. He had a good change-up and curveball, poise, an easy and graceful delivery — and the highest career ERA of the century for pitchers who appeared in at least 1,000 innings. The Chief, known in his playing days as being extremely stingy with the spoken word, responded to our letter, at age 87, by writing this short message: "I never was a star — but I played with and against a lot of them. I am not in the Hall of Fame either but being a pitcher, perhaps I helped some of them get there."

2

1876–1892
Skunks in a Box

◆ The first half of the 1870s witnessed the birth of the National Association in 1871, a league that is forever labeled "minor" even though this first organized professional league was manned by players like Al Spalding, Cap Anson, and Tommy Bond, who went on to star in the National League. How different from baseball today was the game in the 1870s? In 1867, the sport had already been proclaimed by President Andrew Johnson as the National Game and a source of moral recreation. But the rules of the National Game were still in flux. In the NA's first season, the pitcher stood only 45 feet from home plate and not on a mound but in a "box" (really a rectangle, 6 feet wide by 4 feet long, painted in the middle of the diamond). He had to throw the ball underhand where the hitter requested it—whether high, low, or "fair" (between the hitter's shoulders and knees). Three balls were a walk, and three strikes were an out, but umpires weren't allowed to call the first pitch a ball or a strike (unless it was swung at and missed), and called balls and strikes didn't count until the umpire first warned the pitcher or batter that "I shall call the next one."

Not until 1872 was a pitcher allowed to snap or jerk the ball, a boon to curveballers like Candy Cummings. In 1876, just one year after the first running of the Kentucky Derby and during the United States' Centennial year, the first NL season began. The pitching distance was still 45 feet, but the pitching box was expanded to 6 feet by 6 feet. A walk was nine balls, and an umpire wouldn't call a third strike without first giving the batter a warning pitch. Catchers wore no glove or mask, stood several feet behind the batter, and did not have to catch strike three on the fly. Only underhand deliveries were legal, though Tommy Bond of the Hartford Dark Blues terrorized opposing batters with his fastball, using a controversial sidearm delivery. Unfortunately for Hartford's opponents, hit batters were not awarded first base.

Most of the eight charter teams in the NL had only one or two

Skunk Stearns Winners: 1876–1892

Year	Winner	Team	Won	Lost	Percentage	ERA	Adjusted ERA	TPI
1876	Dory Dean	Cin: NL	4	26	.133	3.73	59	–3.7
1877	Candy Cummings	Cin: NL	5	14	.263	4.34	61	–2.3
	Bobby Mathews	Cin: NL	3	12	.200	4.04	66	–2.0
1878	Sam Weaver	Mil: NL	12	31	.279	1.95	134	+2.8
1879	George Bradley	Troy: NL	13	40	.245	2.85	88	–0.7
1880	Will White	Cin: NL	18	42	.300	2.14	116	+0.4
1881	Fred Corey	Wor: NL	6	15	.286	3.72	81	–1.2
1882	John Lee Richmond	Wor: NL	14	33	.298	3.74	83	–1.3
1883	John Coleman	Phil: NL	12	48	.200	4.87	63	–8.1
1884	Bob Barr	Wash/Ind: AA	12	34	.261	3.94	79	–3.6
1885	Billy Serad	Buf: NL	7	21	.250	4.10	72	–3.4
1886	Stump Weidman	KC: NL	12	36	.250	4.50	84	–3.2
1887	Egyptian Healy	Ind: NL	12	29	.293	5.17	80	–3.7
1888	Toad Ramsey	Lou: AA	8	30	.211	3.42	90	–2.1
1889	John Ewing	Lou: AA	6	30	.167	4.87	79	–3.3
1890	Charlie McCullough	BB/Syr: AA	5	23	.179	4.88	79	–3.2
	Kirtley Baker	Pitt: NL	3	19	.136	5.60	59	–3.9
1891	Kid Carsey	Wash: AA	14	37	.275	4.99	75	–4.6
1892	George Cobb	Balt: NL	10	37	.213	4.86	71	–4.6

Note: Mil = Milwaukee; Wor = Worcester; Wash = Washington; Buf = Buffalo; Ind = Indianapolis; Lou = Louisville; BB/Syr = Brooklyn-Baltimore/Syracuse; AA = American Association.

pitchers. Grin Bradley pitched all 64 games played by the St. Louis Brown Stockings in 1876, completing 63. Spalding paced the Chicago White Stockings to the championship with a 47–12 mark, while the last-place Cincinnati Red Stockings managed only nine wins. The tail-enders' Cory Dean made the most of his only year in The Show: He won our first-ever award, heading our list of Skunk Stearns winners during baseball's early years (see table on opposite page).

Skunks and Fallen Stars in the New National League

Alexander Graham Bell patented the telephone in 1876, and General George Custer was slaughtered by the Sioux Indians the same year. Charles "Cory" Dean could have used Bell's invention to phone for help, since his battles in the pitching box during 1876 matched Custer's South Dakota experience. Dean, a 24-year-old right-hander from Cincinnati, was around long enough in the NL to lose 16 straight games and to capture the first Skunk Stearns Award. His record of 4–26 for the Cincinnati Red Stockings was spiced by the 397 hits he allowed—over 13 a game.

THE CHARMER

Dean was challenged for the trophy by his teammate, Cherokee Fisher, and by George "the Charmer" Zettlein of the Philadelphia Athletics. These two former NA pitchers each suffered through identical 4–20 seasons. For Fisher it was clearly a déjà vu experience, evoking memories of his rookie season in the NA, and etching his name forever on our Cherokee Fisher Rookie Award. The Charmer, however, had seen better days.

A 125-game winner in the NA, including a 36–14 mark in 1873, Zettlein was one of the hardest throwers of his time and pitched the first 1–0 shutout in league history in 1875. (At that time, shutting out a team was known, appropriately enough, as "skunking.") He had gained fame in June 1870 when he opposed Asa Brainard in what has since been billed as baseball's first truly great game—the Brooklyn Atlantics' win over Cincinnati, ending the Red Stockings' legendary 91-game unbeaten streak. (The contest featured a trick play that spawned the infield-fly rule, the first known switch-hitter, and a three-run rally by Brooklyn in the bottom of the 12th to snatch an 8–7 win.)

In 1871, the Charmer was among the best pitchers in the new NA, when—if not for Mrs. O'Leary's cow—he might have led Chicago to the pennant. Like the San Francisco earthquake that rocked Candlestick Park before the third game of the 1989 World Series, the Chicago fire of 1871 played an unexpected role in crowning the baseball champion. The White

Stockings were playing like champions when the raging Chicago fire destroyed the team's uniforms, equipment, and morale. The ball club was flat broke. There was no ballpark to play in, so they had to finish their remaining games on the road. (In 1989, former Commissioner Fay Vincent, by contrast, opted to wait for the Giants' ballpark to "recover" from the earthquake, rather than force the World Series into foreign territory.)

The Charmer, looking ludicrous in a borrowed uniform with a huge *A* on the chest, pitched well and scored his team's only run, but Chicago lost the championship game to the Athletics, 4–1. Zettlein may have still been smarting from a severe beating he got during the great fire, when he was unable to charm a mob who mistakenly identified him as a looter.

But don't get the impression that Zettlein was a saint. In 1875, he was thought to have fixed some NA ball games. The White Stockings' Board of Directors accused him of throwing a game in July, a 14–1 thrashing by Boston, and the Charmer was finally released by Chicago under a cloud of suspicion and innuendo. At the end of the season, Zettlein, who served under the command of Admiral David Farragut as a 20-year-old sailor during the Civil War, was named pitcher on an honorary team of "rogues" selected by the *Brooklyn Eagle*. His teammates on this first all-skunk team were players who were known to be controlled by gamblers.

Footnotes to the first Skunk Stearns race: Dean, Zettlein, and Fisher each pitched a grand total of one other game in the NL after 1876 (a loss by Fisher). Louisville rookie Johnny Ryan pitched the only game of his brief career in the NL's first season. In that contest, Ryan gave up 22 hits and uncorked 10 wild pitches in 8 innings.

CURVEBALL, SPITBALL, SKUNKBALL

The second Skunk Stearns competition was a tie between the original spitballer (Bobby Mathews) and the original curveballer (Hall of Famer Arthur "Candy" Cummings). Since the curveball is more palatable than the unsanitary spitball, it's not surprising that Mathews failed to make the Baseball Hall of Fame. However, as a 19-year-old in 1871, Mathews won the first game played in the NA, a 2–0 skunking of the Cleveland Forest Citys—the lowest-scoring game of the season and the first shutout in organized baseball. And Mathews became the all-time victory champion in 1885, when he surpassed Al Spalding's record of 253 wins (counting NA stats); he retained that title until 1888, when Pud Galvin became the first man to amass 300 wins. On the downside, Mathews was also the first man to lose 200 games. Nonetheless, his combined record between 1871 and 1887 shows a victory total of 297 (the *Baseball Encyclopedia* says 298), the most wins of any old-timer *not* in Cooperstown. If NA stats are excluded (as they usually are), who qualifies for the opposite distinction, the fewest number of major-league wins by a Hall of Famer? Cummings, with 21.

Possibly the first spitballer, Bobby Mathews shared the 1877 Skunk Stearns Award with Candy Cummings. Mathews won more games than any eligible pitcher not in the Baseball Hall of Fame (photo courtesy of George Brace).

Still, the Candy Man did have strong Cooperstown credentials. He was proclaimed by famed journalist and baseball historian Henry Chadwick as the best pitcher in baseball in 1871, when he pitched for the "Stars of Brooklyn," the top amateur team in the nation. Cummings then gained fame as a professional, averaging 31 wins for four years in the NA. Although known for his "twister," his fastball was likened to a rifle shot. Until Cummings teamed up with Nat Hicks in 1872, his catchers were plain scared to call for a "speedball."

In 1877, Mathews and Cummings each pitched poorly for a weak-hitting Cincinnati team, although they were not teammates. Mathews compiled a 3–12 mark for the Reds before the team folded in June and then pitched briefly for the Columbus Buckeyes in the International Association. Cummings (5–14) took the reverse route. He began 1877 as the pitching-president of the International Association, but quit the presidency of the minor league when his team (the Lynn Live Oaks) folded in July. He rejoined the NL and the regrouped Cincinnati nine, hoping to recapture his success of the previous season—a 16–8 record for Hartford that included a shutout against St. Louis in his NL debut. Instead, in 1877, the Candy Man pitched more like Dory Dean, the man he beat the previous year to complete the first sweep of a doubleheader.

Were Mathews and Cummings just victims of the inept Reds' attack? Maybe. But the third Reds' pitcher, nonentity Bobby Mitchell (6–5), nearly matched their combined win total in just 12 starts.

Bobby Mathews' Skunk Stearns season in 1877 seemed to mark the end of his career. The small (5 feet 5 inches) man with the huge moustache that hid half his face had lost the phenomenal two-year total of 72 games in 1875 (the NA's last year) and 1876; then he spent 1878 in the minor leagues. But the former boy star of the NA made a strong comeback in the 1880s, winning 90 games (against 48 losses) in three years for the Philadelphia Athletics in the new major league—the American Association (AA). Mathews, a lifelong bachelor of "careless habits and not too robust constitution," was an unsuccessful umpire after he retired from baseball and died in a Baltimore asylum at the age of 46.

For the slight (5 feet 9 inches, 120 pounds) Cummings, just 29 years old, his skunk season was the virtual end of his pitching career, and the journalists were ruthless. As the 1877 season drew to a close, the Cincinnati newspapers were merciless in their criticism of the 18 to 25 hits that he allowed routinely. One editorial claimed that Cummings' "presence on the team is demoralizing" and argued that fans will stop coming to see the Reds play "unless the evil is remedied." Cummings never pitched another game in the major leagues after the 1877 season. Pitching in the International Association in 1878, the former ace lost ten games and won only twice for a team that moved from Brooklyn to New Haven to Hartford before being expelled from the league. He finished his career in 1878 with the Cleveland Forest Citys and then opened a paint and wallpaper business in his native Massachusetts.

Both 1877 Skunk Stearns co-winners knew greatness during their careers, but in 1874, each was implicated and accused—but not tried or convicted—of fixing a game. In a game against Chicago, rumors were rampant that three gamblers who were traveling with the New York Mutuals had fixed the game. Mathews seemed in peak health, but claimed illness and departed suddenly after the fifth inning. His replacement, John Hatfield (who never pitched before or again in the NA), was a dud. Mathews produced a "doctor's excuse," but suspicion lingered about his quick exit. Cummings' brush with the seamy side of baseball concerned umpire Billy McLean, a well-respected ex-prizefighter who earned the name "King of Umpires." McLean insisted that Cummings was one of three Philadelphia players who fixed a game with Chicago; he claimed that the Pearls' John Radcliff offered him $175 to make calls in Chicago's favor and that Radcliff named Cummings as a coconspirator.

In any case, Cummings is remembered for inventing the curveball, not for the so-called fix. Mathews was also among the first to throw the curveball and was credited by his Mutuals' teammate Alphonse (Phonney) Martin with beating Cummings to the punch. Ironically, Martin's quotes about Mathews, recorded for posterity when Martin was 87 in 1932, helped secure Mathews' niche in history as the inventory of the spitball: "Mathews would wipe one side of the ball clean, and then moisten it with the tips of his fingers and let it go. The ball would break in a wide out-curve at times and again would drop and curve in."

Though Mathews allegedly started spitting on the ball at age 16, the pitch didn't make a dent in the majors until 1902. And credit for the spitball is often given to George Hildebrand, best known as an AL umpire.

So Cummings and Mathews invented pitches—maybe. There are always doubters, such as the cynics who claim that the only thing Cummings ever invented was a coupling device for railroad cars. (He really did invent it and had the royalties to prove it.)

Oddly, the real skunk of 1877 was Jim Devlin, who won 35 games for the Louisville Grays (against 25 losses) and led the NL in games pitched, innings pitched, and complete games. It was a good record, but this star pitcher would have approached 40 wins and might have led the Grays to a pennant if he hadn't sold out to New York gamblers. Devlin and three teammates were banned from baseball for life when the Grays' conspiracy to blow the pennant to Boston became public knowledge during the winter. Ironically, this highly publicized baseball scandal occurred in the same year that the newly elected U.S. President, Rutherford B. Hayes, took his oath of office in private and avoided the inaugural parade and ball

because of the crooked dealings that denied Samuel J. Tilden his rightful victory.

Devlin, previously known for his famous "drop" pitch and his iron-man durability (he completed 127 of 129 starts and pitched nearly 1,200 innings in his two NL seasons), was exiled for life by the quick and unyielding actions of William Chase, the Grays' vice president, and William Hulbert, the NL president and Devlin's close personal friend. (Hulbert even slipped Devlin a $50 bill with one hand, but his other one remained iron fisted.) For years after his banishment, the semiliterate and destitute Devlin, a pathetic figure who suffered from unsightly boils, showed up at the annual owners' meetings to beg for clemency, but the ban was permanent, serving fair warning to future players.

Although Devlin led the NL in losses in both 1876 and 1877, he also compiled 65 wins, despite shaky offensive support (no pitcher has even come close to the 14 shutout losses he suffered in 1876) and was on the verge of stardom when he sold out. His Louisville team left the league after 1877, as did the St. Louis Brown Stockings—a fallout of the scandal.

WILL WHITE

Will (Whoop-La) White and Jim "Pud" Galvin were among the premier pitchers of their day, but in 1880 they vied for the Skunk Stearns Award. Cincinnati's White (18–42), a former minister, defeated Buffalo's Galvin (20–35), the future saloon keeper. Both tumbled from their 1879 glory: White won 43 games and completed all 75 of his starts; Galvin had a 37–27 record that probably would have earned him the Rookie of the

Above: **Will White, the first major leaguer to wear glasses, must have had 40-40 vision—40 wins during three different seasons, but more than 40 losses during his Skunk Stearns year in 1880 (photo courtesy of George Brace).**

Year Award if such awards had been given then (Boston outfielder John O'Rourke might have been given the nod).

White, the first major leaguer to wear eyeglasses, had the satisfaction of knowing that his replacement in the box was worse. White rarely rested, but when he did, Blondie Purcell took over, almost guaranteeing a loss (he lost 12 straight and finished 3–17). Purcell had a two-year total of 7–34 that would have made Bill Stearns envious. Purcell was once fined $100 for cutting the cover of a ball to have a new one brought into play. If only Whitey Ford, Don Sutton, or Mike Scott could have traveled back in time, Blondie—who doubled as a mediocre outfielder—might have learned to use that cut ball to reverse his pitching fortunes.

The bespectacled White, with a fair complexion and a blond moustache, had the appearance of a schoolteacher or a mild-mannered businessman. In fact, he was both, teaching Sunday school at the YMCA during the baseball season and founding the Buffalo Optical Company (a thriving business to this day) after his overworked arm gave out at age 31. With his older brother Jim "Deacon" White, a veteran of the NA who lasted in the major leagues until 1890, Will formed the first brother battery when both played for Cincinnati. Deacon was the stuff of legends. In July 1873, he played all three outfield positions simultaneously for Boston in a 20–4 win over the amateur Portland Resolutes when only seven Red Stockings showed up for the exhibition game.

Will was a bit of an oddball, driving his own horse and buggy to the ball field. He disdained alcohol, tobacco, profanity, and screaming at umpires, but the former minister wasn't afraid to hit and intimidate batters. He was one of the main reasons the AA decided to award first base to a hit batter. And no one challenged his courage; if it was game day, give him the ball. His 680 innings pitched and 75 complete games in 1879 are out of reach for mortals (as are his 73 losses in two consecutive seasons).

The workhorse blew out his arm during his skunk campaign, but he recovered and became the pitching sensation of the NL's new rival, the AA. He led Cincinnati to the 1882 pennant with a 40–12 record, and from 1882 to 1885, he completed 201 of 204 starts—an eye-popping achievement, even in the days when relief was spelled g-a-r-b-a-g-e. But he destroyed his arm again, this time for good, in 1886.

Though a Skunk Stearns winner in 1880, White was 229–166 for his career and had one of the lowest career ERAs ever (2.28). Unlike other pitchers whose stars shone briefly but brilliantly, he was never invited to Cooperstown. White, a nonswimmer, drowned at the age of 56, suffering a heart attack while teaching his niece to swim.

Galvin lost out in the Skunk Stearns derby, but had one unenviable distinction: Despite his 360 wins, he lost 21 or more games for ten straight seasons and lost 308 times in all. He was an old-time Robin Roberts or

Fergie Jenkins, a pitcher with exceptional control who both won and lost an abundance of games. Cy Young had to pass Galvin to become the all-time win leader in 1903—and the all-time loss leader in 1911!

Ironically, in 1884, White and Galvin became the first two pitchers to achieve the 200-win plateau in the majors. Galvin hung on in the majors until 1892 and was still trying to get back in 1894, perhaps because he had 11 children to support (he once joked about forming a family team called the "Galvinized Nine"). But he was unsuccessful in the Eastern League and had little success that same year in his alternate plan to raise money: He was arrested for robbery, ironically by George Streif, a policeman who played major-league baseball during Galvin's glory years.

The Asa Brainard Humpty-Dumpty Award

George Bradley, nicknamed "Grin" for his ornery personality, ascended rapidly to brilliance only to sink like lead weight and earn our first Asa Brainard Humpty-Dumpty Award. As an NA rookie in 1875, the right-hander was 33–26 for the St. Louis Brown Stockings. His fame spread on June 5, when he pitched brilliantly to end the fabled 22-game winning streak of Al Spalding's Boston Red Stockings. The St. Louis crowd went into a frenzy, with hats flying, ladies shouting, and fans streaming onto the field. Several fans hoisted the strapping Bradley to their shoulders and ran with him to home plate, while others strained to grab his hands and legs. His legend continued to grow the next season when his won-lost record of 45–19 challenged Spalding's mark of 47–12 in the NL's first season. Bradley was awesome in July and August: He hurled the first major-league no-hitter, 2–0, for St. Louis against a tough Hartford team on July 5 and added three one-hitters against Louisville (twice) and Chicago. His 16 shutouts have been matched only once, by the great Alex (Grover Cleveland Alexander) in 1916.

If sportswriters voted for pitching awards in 1876, Spalding might have edged Bradley. He led Chicago to the pennant and was far more popular than the irascible "Grin." But even the great Spalding, who doubled as the White Stockings' manager, was impressed with Bradley. The former star of the NA, who perfected the art of changing speeds, hand picked Bradley as his successor in Chicago's pitching box. (Spalding started only one game after his incredible 1876 season.) The decision was not a good one. Bradley began his decline in 1877, winning only 18 games while losing 23, and spent the next year pitching in the minor leagues, mostly for Tecumseh of London. Although he led Canada's team to a 22–13 record before it disbanded, his return to the majors in 1879 following his demotion was not triumphant. Bradley (13–40) paced Troy—previously in the

International Association and still playing like minor leaguers—to a last-place finish. He gave up nearly 600 hits in fewer than 500 innings.

At the time that Thomas Edison's career was on the upswing (he invented the phonograph and electric light in the late 1870s), Bradley's was tumbling. He had a combined record of 31–63 and gave up over 1,000 hits during the 1877 and 1879 seasons. In his first five major-league seasons, he pitched for exactly one team per year, but never the same team twice. Bradley had one brief reversal of fortune, when he won 25 games in 1884 for Cincinnati in the Union Association, but he never won another ML game.

Honorable mention for the Asa Brainard Award goes to Joe Borden, who failed to last out a remarkable roller-coaster season in 1876. He won the first NL game—defeating the Athletics 6–5 for Boston—and is credited with hurling the first no-hitter in organized baseball a year earlier for the Philadelphia "Fillies" (formerly the Pearls) in the NA. Borden, who earlier had pitched under aliases to prevent prominent New Jersey family and friends from learning about his "shady" occupation, was bombed 20–3 in his second NL start by the same Athletics team he had beaten three days previously in the season opener. He seemed to take aim at opposing batters, his own catcher, and umpires (bruising most parts of Umpire Hodges' body and almost knocking off his hat in Louisville). Despite a respectable 11–12 record, he led the league with 51 walks at a time when it took nine balls to give a batter a free ride to first. The coup de grace: Borden, architect of the only no-hitter in NA history and winner of the first NL contest, wound up the 1876 season in the Boston outfield—not as player, but as the Red Stockings' groundskeeper!

Skunks During an Era of Expansion and Change

The Skunk Stearns winners from the early NL were mostly men of distinction, pitchers who experienced success, sometimes fantastic success,

Above: **George Bradley, nicknamed "Grin," was an irascible pitcher who tumbled from a 45–19 record in the NL's maiden season in 1876 to a 13–40 Skunk trophy just three years later (photo courtesy of George Brace).**

at other times in their careers. Not so for most of the Skunk Stearns winners from the early 1880s through the end of the era, when the award list reads like the Who's Who of bums. And that's not surprising considering the incredible expansion that occurred at that time, opening up jobs for the undeserving.

Indeed, no rule was inviolable during the 1880s, not even "three strikes and you're out." A decade that began with three men occupying the White House by the middle of 1881 also witnessed instability, change, and experimentation in baseball. The distance between the pitcher and home plate was increased from 45 to 50 feet before the start of the 1881 season, and an additional 5½ feet were added in 1887 when pitchers had to stand with their back foot touching the *back* of the pitcher's box. Even the size of the pitcher's box underwent an annual change in the mid–1880s, as if they were trying to get it right. And throughout the 1880s the number of balls for a walk fluctuated between nine and five before coming to a permanent rest at four in 1889.

Innovators experimented with night baseball as early as 1880, when the employees of two Boston department stores, Jordan Marsh & Co. and R. H. White & Co., played to a 16–16 tie under the illumination of 36 carbon lamps. In 1888, the major leagues toyed with evening baseball, when Indianapolis played exhibitions using gas lamps. Some changes were tried for a year and abandoned, such as using a bat with one flat side in 1885, counting walks as hits in 1887, and insisting on four strikes for a strikeout, also in 1887. Other changes simply represented the natural evolution of the game to its present form, such as the pitcher being allowed gradually to elevate his arm from his underhand and sidearm captivity to a powerful overhand throw. But the biggest change in baseball was expansion, to as many as three leagues and 33 teams in 1884; the AA was a full-fledged major league from 1882 to 1891.

New teams meant diluted talent, weak sisters in all leagues, and the emergence of stars of the brightest magnitude. But the thinning out of talent produced its share of skunks as well as heroes. At no time before or since the 1880s have so many pitched so poorly for so long. Two of these men, John Lee Richmond and Toad Ramsey, fell from grace in the tradition of Grin Bradley.

JOHN LEE RICHMOND

The 1882 season welcomed a new major league, the six-team AA, although that welcome was not extended by the NL. Had NL President William Hulbert survived, the transition to two major leagues might have been smooth. However, his unexpected fatal heart attack in April put Arthur Soden in the office of the president. The suspicious Soden allowed NL teams to raid players in the AA, a league derogatively referred to as the

"Beer and Whiskey League," alluding to the financial backing of the association's teams by men who made their fortunes in alcohol. The Beer and Whiskey League, with the ironic abbreviation AA, charged 25 cents admission to its team's games, half the going rate for NL games. But in 1882, it provided only half the quality: The NL swept all 21 spring exhibitions.

Six additional major-league teams meant extra candidates for the Skunk Stearns Award, but the NL held onto the trophy. Worcester's John Lee Richmond—a thin left-hander who pitched the major leagues' first perfect game in 1880 a few days before his graduation from Brown University—took the Skunk Stearns honors by tumbling to a 14–33 record. In 1879, at age 22, Richmond no-hit Cap Anson's White Stockings in an exhibition game, captained and pitched Brown to a 3–2 win over Yale for the College Championship, and pitched the final game of the major-league season for Boston. In that game, he defeated 47-game-winner Monte Ward of Providence, striking out five straight men (then a league record) and allowing just one hit in the last eight innings. After pitching in the major leagues for a single game, Richmond was already referred to by the *New York Clipper* as "the famous lefthanded pitcher of the Worcesters."

And all that was just a warm-up for 1880. Worcester graduated from the minor leagues to the majors by gaining admittance to the NL in 1880, largely because Richmond's pitching heroics transformed manager Frank Bancroft's team from mediocre to exceptional. Richmond didn't disappoint his fans, tying for the NL lead in games pitched, winning 32 times (versus the same number of losses), and pitching the first perfect game in major-league history. On June 12 the curveballer, whose ball broke sharply down to induce grounders, retired all 27 Cleveland batters that he faced, winning 1–0. He accomplished this feat even though he got no sleep the night before (because of pregraduation events at Brown) and did not have time to eat before the game (his train was late).

Richmond's perfect game was one of three shutouts that he pitched in a nine-day span. Ironically, the second perfect game was pitched five days later by Monte Ward, although neither game aroused much attention (some writers failed to mention that no one reached base). However, if any fans yawned, thinking that perfect games were about to become commonplace, they were mistaken. Cy Young pitched the third perfect game in 1904, in the AL, nearly a quarter of a century later. And the next perfect game in the NL? That didn't occur until Jim Bunning silenced the bats of the helpless New York Mets in 1964. Like Richmond, Bunning went on to win a Skunk Stearns Award a few years after his perfect game.

While he was on top, Richmond took full advantage of the moment and fell victim to an epidemic that permeated the pitching box in 1881 known as "attitudinizing." The newspapers of the day complained repeatedly about this strange, contagious behavior: Some of the best pitchers in the league began to pose as statues while in the pitching box to impress the fans, especially the ladies. But Richmond was unaware that his strutting and posing days were numbered. He pitched only one more complete year after his 1882 skunk season, losing seven of ten decisions for Providence in 1883. He attempted a comeback in the AA a few years later, but failed.

Still, Richmond was the first of a handful of pioneering left-handers in early professional baseball, breaking in at a time when a southpaw was a bit of a freak. And though Richmond's meteoric rise to stardom was followed by an equally sudden downward slide, he was well prepared for his plunge. He continued his studies at Brown, and like Burt Lancaster's Doc "Moonlight" Graham in *Field of Dreams*, earned his medical degree.

"TOAD" RAMSEY

Thomas "Toad" Ramsey drank himself out of a fine career and into a Skunk Stearns trophy in 1888, when he tumbled to an 8–30 disaster after having two near-identical, remarkable seasons (38–27 and 37–27) for the Louisville Eclipse in the AA. The left-hander from Indianapolis struck out 499 men in 1886, and only fellow southpaw Matt Kilroy, with 513 that same season, ever had more. These strikeout records drifted into obscurity when the pitching distance was moved back to 60 feet 6 inches in 1893.

In 1886–87, Ramsey was awesome, pitching two straight one-hitters in 1886 with only a day's rest between games. He struck out 16 in the first gem and followed that with 17 Ks in the 12-inning one-hitter that followed. The next season, Ramsey struck out 355 men to lead the majors, despite the new four-strike rule. Like Richmond, Ramsey was one of the pioneering lefties in early major-league baseball. In 1899, according to the recollections of Senators' manager Arthur Irwin, the Toad "confined his deception to the drop ball, a slow paced curve ball," and "was simply a clown as a fielder of his position."

The Toad was something less than a clown off the field. Louisville almost released him before the 1886 season began because he was drunk every day on the preseason southern trip. And in September that year, he finally broke down from too much drink. Instead of winning over 40 games and besting Kilroy as the all-time strikeout king, the Toad did not pitch on the team's final eastern trip (and the Eclipse lost every game).

But patrons in the dingy saloons throughout Louisville got to know Ramsey rather well, watching him play a French harp alongside teammate Reddy Mack's banjo. And the police got acquainted with the Toad also, arresting him for smashing a brunette who was brawling with his auburn-haired girlfriend.

In 1887, Ramsey again deprived Louisville of a 40-win season with suspensions in May and August. He even lost 10–4 to the hapless Cleveland "Remnants," a new AA team that was formed from other team's discards, when he pitched stone drunk. But things were going to be different in 1888, Ramsey vowed. Though he went on a drinking spree before the season and spent a few days in jail, the 23-year-old reported to the team in excellent shape. He even took a pledge to abstain from drink the day before the season when he and several teammates were reached by Pittsburgh evangelist Francis Murphy.

But the Toad couldn't keep that pledge or the next one, and he was suspended without pay more than once during the year. After colliding with a barrel of bourbon and not paying his debts, he wound up in jail once again in July. A sore arm over the summer didn't help. When the dust cleared, his record was 8–30, and the Skunk Stearns Award was his.

The Worst Season of Them All: John Coleman (12–48)

The list of Skunk Stearns winners reveals some paragons of inept pitching, starting with Dory Dean's (4–26) inaugural trophy in 1876 and extending through George Cobb's 10–37 disaster in 1892, his only year in The Show. But which season was the worst of the era, the one that might take its place alongside nearly any of Bill Stearns' seasons in the NA?

A table at the end of the chapter lists the five worst single-season marks in four categories: losses minus wins, winning percentage, adjusted ERA, and TPI. We assigned points based on these rankings and used the system described in the Appendix to crown our champion. John Coleman takes first prize, for his 12–48 farce in 1883, as can be seen in the table on the following page.

How bad was John Coleman? Hiram Maxim invented the Maxim machine gun in 1883, and Coleman could have used one that year. He pitched most of the games for the last-place Phillies and was obviously unable to retire NL batters by less violent methods. A schedule that was expanded from 84 to 98 games gave Coleman more opportunities to lose, and the 20-year-old native of Saratoga Springs, New York, did just that.

Coleman found more ways to lose than anyone since Bill Stearns, dropping 48 games against only 12 wins. He gave up 772 hits in 538 innings, allowed nearly 300 earned runs, and gave up nearly five earned runs a game—a light year away from the league average of about three. For the first time in 1883, the *Spalding Guide* computed statistics called "Runs Earned by Opponents," a forerunner of the ERA; baseball now had new ways to tell a man just how miserably he pitched.

Coleman's main saving grace for 1883 was that his winning percentage of .200 was considerably better than the Phillies' percentage when other

Worst Seasons, 1876–92 (15 or more losses)

Order*, Skunk, Year (Team)	Won	Lost	Percentage	ERA	Adjusted ERA	TPI
1. John Coleman 1883 (Phil: NL)	12	48	.200	4.87	63	−8.1
2. Art Hagan 1883 (Phil/Buf: NL)	1	16	.059	5.27	59	−3.4
3. Jack Neagle 1883 (Phil: NL) (Balt/Buf: AA)	5	23	.179	5.94	55	−5.0
4T. Dory Dean 1876 (Cin: NL)	4	26	.133	3.73	59	−3.7
4T. George Cobb 1892 (Balt: NL)	10	37	.213	4.86	71	−4.6

*T = tie.

pitchers stepped into the precarious pitching box: His "change" pitchers compiled a record of 5–33 for a winning percentage of .152. And who was Coleman's number one alternate in the box? The pitcher who had the second-worst season of the 1876–92 era: Art Hagan.

Hagan, another 20-year-old, lost 14 of 15 games for Philadelphia and lost two more games for Buffalo. His winning percentage of .059 is the third worst of all time for pitchers with 15 or more decisions. Together, the Coleman-Hagan tandem combined for a record of 13–64, almost matching Bill Stearns' lifetime mark of 12–64 in a single season!

Nearly everyone who pitched for the Phillies in 1883 was a skunk candidate. Hardie Henderson lost his only game as a Phillie, then moved on to the Baltimore Orioles and wound up with an overall mark of 10–33. Jack Neagle (5–23), who had the third-worst season, also played no favorites; he was 1–7 as a teammate of Coleman and Hagan for the NL Phillies and 4–16 for two teams in the AA. In 1883, Congress passed the Pendleton Act, creating the Civil Service Commission that opened up thousands of federal jobs—a good break for the whole Phillies' team, who obviously needed to find different occupations.

Another 1883 happening: Novelty games stretched from east to west. Fat teams ("Jumbos") played skinny teams ("Shadows"), while Philadelphia sponsored the Snorkey team (in honor of the handicapped hero in "Under the Gaslight"). Most Snorkeys were missing a hand, though one had a paralyzed arm and another was missing an arm. Twice they played the Hoppers—all one-legged or on crutches—with each team winning one.

Above: **The good news is that John Coleman accounted for 71 percent of the Phillies' victories in 1883. The bad news is that his 12–48 record may be the worst single season of all time (photo courtesy of George Brace).**

In May 1883, the Snorkeys triumphed 34–11. The Athletics won the 1883 AA pennant and were undoubtedly the best team in the City of Brotherly Love. But which team was second: John Coleman's Phillies or the Snorkeys?

The good news is that John Coleman earned more than 70 percent of his team's wins in 1883. The bad news is that he did it while compiling the worst single-season stats of his era, perhaps the worst of all time.

The Cherokee Fisher Rookie Award

Thanks mostly to expansion, many pitchers were given the opportunity to pitch in the majors when the low minors should have been their loftiest goal. Pick almost any number of wins, and you can find a rookie or two with Skunk Stearns credentials. One? How about Art Hagan (1–16) in 1883? Two? How about John Hamill (2–17) and Jim Brown (2–14) in 1884? Three? You can't do much worse than Dummy Dundon or Sam Moffett, both 3–19 in the early 1880s. Double digits? Why not Hardie Henderson (10–33) or John "Pa" Harkins (12–32)?

Like Carl Mays, whose submarine pitch killed Ray Chapman in 1920, Harkins is remembered mostly for beaning a batter. During Harkins' nightmare rookie season in 1884, he knocked future Baseball Hall-of-Fame pitcher Mickey Welch unconscious with a pitch. Within a two-week period, Welch was beaned by Harkins and hit twice by line drives, yet managed to strike out the first nine Cleveland batters to face him in a game—a record that stood until Tom Seaver struck out ten straight Padres in 1970. Welch was known forevermore as "Smiling Mickey."

Hardie Henderson followed his awful rookie season in 1883 with a 27–23 mark the next year, but retired with a 81–121 record, thanks mostly to wildness on and off the field (he was locked up in July 1884 for causing a drunken public disturbance at a house of ill repute). Henderson died in 1903 when he was hit by a trolley car. John Coleman, who beat out Henderson for the 1883 Skunk Stearns Award, suffered a similar fate about 20 years later when he was hit by a car.

Speaking of John Coleman, did we forget to mention that he was a rookie in 1883 when he lost 48 times? He was, and so were the four runners-up for worst season.

The Cherokee Fisher Award goes to John Coleman. Case closed.

The John Cassidy Root Canal Award

Is it possible to offer an award for terrible pre-1893 pitching and not give it to John Coleman? The best way is to give a trophy for which Coleman is not eligible, and that would be the John Cassidy Root Canal Award, for pitchers who pitched briefly and terribly during their stay in the majors. But even for this award, it's impossible to ignore Coleman. The winner of the trophy is Art Hagan, who was 1–14 for Philadelphia in 1883 as Coleman's occasional alternate in the pitching box. With Buffalo for two games in 1883 and three games the next season, Hagan lost four of five decisions for an overall major-league record of 2–18. His lifetime ERA of 5.36, when adjusted for league and ballpark, produced a value of 58, one of the worst ever (Bill Stearns' career mark was 51).

Art Hagan was a poor hitter, who nonetheless had a higher lifetime batting average (.127) than winning percentage (.100). No question, his major-league tenure was as painful as a root canal.

1884: The Year of the Skunk

Every once in a while baseball has a landmark year, a season that is filled with innovation, change, controversy, experimentation, and record-setting performances; 1884 was one such year. Following the leadership of St. Louis real estate millionaire Henry Lucas, a portly former amateur baseball player who strongly opposed baseball's reserve rule, a third major league, called the Union Association, was formed. Whereas the AA was to achieve parity with the NL during the mid–1880s and to last for ten years, the UA, derisively called the "Onions," was a one-year wonder whose quality was only marginally major league.

The unstable UA was paced by Lucas' almost unbeatable (94–19) St. Louis Maroons and included 12 different teams during the course of the season (only six of which played 90 or more games). Add to these come-and-go franchises the 8 NL teams and the 12 teams in the expanded AA, and one gets the most incredible dilution of talent in the history of baseball. Throw in the new rule permitting overhand pitching in both the NL and the UA (the AA allowed only throwing from the shoulder), and the stage was set for some strange happenings.

Records went by the wayside; some marks, like "Old Hoss" Radbourn's 59 wins (60 according to the *Baseball Encyclopedia*), will never be broken. "Smiling Mickey" Welch's 39 wins did not even place him among the elite during that season. Eight pitchers won 40 or more games in 1884, including four who pitched at least part of the season in the UA. But the downside of the dilution of major-league talent was a stream of negative pitching statistics that were never seen before and have not been seen since in the annals of baseball. The year of the skunk had arrived.

No fewer than 16 pitchers, most of them rookies, lost at least 12 games more than they won. Some of these Skunk Stearns candidates pitched their only major-league season in 1884, forgettable hurlers named Fleury Sullivan (16–35), Alex Voss (5–20), Sam Moffett (3–19, including 13 straight defeats), and John Hamill (2–17). Is it any wonder that Henry Chadwick published his popular book *The Art of Pitching* in 1885?

Ed "Jersey" Bakely led the UA with 30 losses (he won 16), pitching most of the season for the Philadelphia Keystones. However, winning games for a team that played like the Keystone Cops was not easy. The team made an enormous number of errors, with third baseman John Siegel once making six errors in seven chances. Bakely was considered the best player on the team when the Keystones folded in August, although he was once credited with 13 errors in a game (at a time when walks and wild pitches counted as errors). But the best Keystone player not only pitched and fielded poorly, he couldn't hit a lick (he batted .068 in 1884). The TPI blends pitching, fielding, and hitting into a single number, and Bakely's TPI in 1884 (−6.0) is the second worst in the long history of baseball. Only John Coleman's −8.1 was worse.

Bakely pitched for nine teams in *four* major leagues during his six-year tenure in The Show, including three Cleveland teams in three leagues from 1888 to 1890. An equal opportunity employee, Bakely lost between 22 and 33 games for the Cleveland nines in the AA, NL, and Players League (PL). He pitched the first game the NL Cleveland Spiders played in 1889; naturally, he gave up 16 hits and lost, 10–3.

However, in 1884 Bakely was not the main candidate for the Skunk Stearns Award, and neither was the previous year's winner Coleman, who improved to 5–17. That honor went to the following five Clydesdales: Bob Barr (12–34), John "Pa" Harkins (12–32), Larry McKeon (18–41), Jack Neagle (11–26) and Hank O'Day (9–28).

We chose Bob Barr for the trophy in a photo finish, even though he pitched for the two worst teams in the AA. He sandwiched his 12–34 season between records of 6–18 and 3–18, and it seemed unconscionable to let him escape without copping at least one Skunk Stearns trophy. Like an actor who finally wins an Oscar, Barr gets the 1884 Skunk Stearns Award to honor his consistent ineptness.

Incidentally, the UA disappeared after one season, and the AA went from 12 teams back to eight, so 1885 was a bit of a return to normalcy— that is, if using a bat with one flat side is normal. Also, it was in 1885 that the NL's New York team became forever known as the "Giants," when they seemed invincible—yet managed to lose the pennant to Chicago.

The Joe Hardy Sell-Your-Soul Award: Hank O'Day

Unlike most of the pitchers with skunklike credentials in 1884, Hank O'Day stuck around for quite some time and even made a name for himself as a pitcher and an umpire. Sometimes his name was an obscenity, as during his rookie year in 1884, but at other times, he was a hero. O'Day was a contender for the Skunk Stearns Award twice more in the 1880s, posting records of 8–20 and 16–29 in 1887–88 while pitching for the Washington Nationals. He continued in 1889 where he left off the previous year, going 2–10 for Washington during the first half of the season. But like another Washington player, Joe Hardy, O'Day may have sold his soul to the devil after switching to the New York Giants in midseason.

Hank O'Day had a long, distinguished career as an umpire following seven years as a perennial losing pitcher—he nearly lost 30 games twice—but for half the 1889 season, he was king of the hill for the world-champion New York Giants (photo courtesy of George Brace).

He arrived on the Giants' scene at about the same time that the team played its first game at the Polo Grounds in July 1889 and sparked them to victory in a feverish pennant race. The Giants' wouldn't have edged Boston for the pennant by one game without O'Day's 9–1 record down the stretch. And when aces Tim Keefe and Mickey Welch faltered in the best-of-11 World Championship Series against the AA champs, the Brooklyn Bridegrooms, O'Day and journeyman pitcher "Cannonball" Crane combined for five wins to pace a comeback from a 3–1 deficit. O'Day won both his games, including the 3–2 tense battle that clinched the series. The Bridegrooms, later to become the Dodgers, lost the World Series to a pre-1900 Shoeless Joe Hardy.

O'Day had a 23–15 record in 1890, his best ever, but his contract with the devil must have expired after that season. He never played another major-league game, although he did intersperse two years as a manager into his long umpiring career that ended in 1927. Like his record as a pitcher, his umpiring record had its highs and lows. The pitching star of the 1889 World Series umpired the first modern World Series in 1903 with Hall-of-Fame umpire Tommy Connolly and is generally remembered as a fine arbiter who was a stickler on technicalities. However, Hank O'Day also had his moment of skunkdom as an umpire.

Fred Merkle became known, undeservedly, as "Bonehead" in 1908, when his baserunning blunder (failing to run from first to second on a game-winning hit) ultimately cost the Giants the pennant. In fact, even veterans often made similar "blunders," and umpires never enforced the rule. O'Day, ever the stickler, called Merkle out when Johnny Evers appealed, although Evers might have been holding an illegal ball. (Giants' pitcher Joe McGinnity heaved the original ball into the stands when he figured out what was going on.) O'Day's call was supported by league officials, but not by Bruce Nash and Allan Zullo, who enshrined the unsung goat of the 1908 pennant race in the *Baseball Hall of Shame*.

As an umpire, O'Day did a lot of curious things, such as fining a player $25 and ejecting him for "violent and indecent language." Why was that a big deal? Because the player was Dummy Hoy, a mute. O'Day had learned sign language!

Possibly O'Day's best pitching record came in 1991, a century after he pitched his last game and more than a half century after his death. He went 3–0 in 1991 to improve his lifetime record from 70–110 to 73–110—just check the second edition of *Total Baseball*, published in 1991. As Pete Palmer tells it, careful scrutiny of old box scores revealed that O'Day was incorrectly listed as an outfielder a few times. In 1884, Tony Mullane was given a win that was rightfully O'Day's; that same year, O'Day was deprived of a shutout that for over a century had been curiously credited to Toledo teammate Curt Welch, an outfielder by trade. Another "found" victory from 1886 gave O'Day a neat three-game pickup long after he died. A final payment from the devil, perhaps?

There were several other candidates for the Joe Hardy Award, such as George Haddock and Charlie "Pretzels" Getzien. Haddock floundered with a 9–26 record for Buffalo in the PL in 1890, but was the class of the AA's pitchers the next season with a 34–11 record. He went from 20–47 during his first three seasons in the majors to 63–24 in the next two. Getzien, famous for his quick temper and fury with teammates who did not give him support, pitched for the Detroit Wolverines in the mid–1880s. He was 17–37 during his first two years in the major leagues and then did a complete about-face. He was 59–24 the next two years and helped turn the once pathetic Wolverines into the 1887 world champions.

These turnabouts are impressive, but we'll stick with O'Day for the Joe Hardy Award on the basis of his overnight transformation from perpetual bum to the one-man wrecking crew that put the Giants into the 1889 World Series and then helped put them on top of the baseball world. The next year, O'Day's teammates Keefe and Welch joined Pud Galvin in the 300-win club. In 1889, however, they took a backseat to a Joe Hardy clone.

1890—The Year of the Skunk's Revenge

If 1884 was the Year of the Skunk, then 1890 was the Year of the Skunk's Revenge. As in 1884, there were three major leagues in 1890, when the PL joined the established NL and AA. The PL was founded by the players as a protest against the NL. The players rebelled against the reserve rule, the owners' tyranny, and the classification scheme, which would have limited salaries to $2,500 and forced players to be graded on their ability (the kiss of death for skunk candidates). The NL players' union, known as the Brotherhood, helped found its own league. The union was headed by the Giants' Monte Ward—an ace pitcher-turned-star-shortstop, who earned his law degree from Columbia in 1885. The PL challenged the NL by putting seven of its eight teams in NL cities and stocking its teams mainly with NL players (four out of five NL regulars jumped to the PL).

Despite lofty goals, a few innovations (a livelier ball and an extra 1½ feet between the pitcher and the batter), and higher attendance, the PL lasted but one season. The PL's shaky finances and management forced it to consolidate with the NL; the AA was hurt the most and folded after the 1891 season. Four AA teams joined the NL, producing a 12-team NL in 1892. The majors went from three leagues in 1890 to one in 1892. But in 1890, when 24 teams ruled the land, the dilution of talent was more than a rumor; some strange things happened in the pitching box.

In 1889, Skunk Stearns winner Long John Ewing of Louisville, Kentucky, younger brother of New York's famed catcher Buck, was 6–30. Long John pitched the opener that year against Kansas City and faced the same team in the final game of the season; he lost both times, naturally. A year later, he was 18–12 and led the PL by striking out nearly five men per game. Teammate Red Ehret, 10–29 in 1889, became a 25–14 ace in 1890. Ehret, the "Germantown Wonder" with a blazing fastball, helped pace Louisville to a transformation that outdid the Minnesota Twins' and Atlanta Braves' rise from tail enders in 1990 to division winners in 1991. Louisville went from a 27–111 last-place team in 1889 to the AA pennant in 1890. Ehret was at his best in the World Series against the Brooklyn Bridegrooms (which ended in a tie), winning both his starts. Though he pitched until 1898, he never had another winning season.

Former skunks Egyptian Healy (from Cairo, Illinois, naturally) and Bob Barr were perhaps the most vengeful, since each won more than 20 games only one time in their underwhelming careers. Barr had a combined mark of 21–70 from 1883 to 1886 and didn't return to the majors until he saw all the Vacancy signs in 1890. He promptly won 28 games (although his total of 219 walks is among the ten worst marks of all time). Healy warmed up for the 1890 season with back-to-back-to-back seasons of 12–29, 12–24, and 2–15. Then he won 22 games and had the fifth-best ERA in the AA. Barr never won another major-league game after 1890, whereas Healy pitched poorly for two seasons and was gone for good. Healy, who became a policeman after his playing days and was only 32 when he died of "consumption," may have been the only Skunk Stearns winner to pitch poorly on four continents. He joined a group of players who toured the world in 1888–89, pitching in Europe, Asia, and Australia. The Egyptian never did get a chance to lose in Egypt because Africa wasn't on the itinerary.

The name Bob Barr became a synonym for loser. As the 19th century came to a close, nearly a decade after Barr retired, Barr was remembered by Deacon McGuire, a catcher who was in the middle of a record 26-year career (later matched by Tommy John and Nolan Ryan). McGuire was thrilled to be traded from the 11th-place Washington Nationals to the pennant-winning Brooklyn Superbas in the middle of the 1899 season. During early September of that year, he told the *Washington Post*, "For 10 years in a row . . . I played ball on teams of losers, my advent to the lobster class taking place in 1890, when I signed with the Rochester team of the American Association and caught Bobby Barr and other veterans." McGuire remembered Barr as a symbol of futility during Barr's only successful season!

Joe Hardy winner Hank O'Day was apparently still riding the long coattails of his 1889 soul swap when he won 22 for New York in the 1890 PL. Toad Ramsey followed up his 8–30 skunk campaign in 1888 with a

4–17 mark the next season (when he lost 9 of the 26 games that Louisville lost in succession during its record streak). How did he do in 1890, the Year of the Skunk's Revenge? He rebounded to a 24–17 mark for the St. Louis Browns. Neither O'Day nor Ramsey ever won another major-league game. Ramsey didn't even survive the 1890 season. Despite his 24 wins, the Browns' president Chris Von der Ahe offered to sell the alcoholic Toad to a sportswriter for a nickel, but finally just released him.

Here's a list of pitchers who exacted the most revenge in 1890:

Pitcher	Pitching Record in 1890			Pitching Record the Two Previous Seasons in Majors		
	Won	Lost	Percentage	Won	Lost	Percentage
Scott Stratton	34	14	.708	13	30	.302
Kid Gleason	38	17	.691	16	31	.340
Hank Gastright	30	14	.682	10	16	.385
Red Ehret	25	14	.641	13	31	.295
Hank O'Day	22	13	.629	27	40	.403
John Ewing	18	12	.600	14	43	.246
Toad Ramsey	24	17	.585	12	47	.203
Bob Barr	28	24	.538	15	52	.224
Egyptian Healy	22	21	.512	14	39	.264
Total	241	146	.623	134	329	.289

The Skunk Stearns Award for the Worst Career: John Coleman

We followed the same system for determining the worst careers from 1876 to 1892 that we used to identify the worst single seasons (see the Appendix). To compete for the worst career, all a pitcher had to do was lose at least 50 games. We bent the rules only once when making out the eligibility list, and that was for George Washington Keefe, who had only 48 defeats. The 20–48 Keefe was like Glenn Close's terrifying character in *Fatal Attraction*: He would not be ignored.

Keefe, who had trouble staying on the wagon, was involved in a bizarre four-game series that opened the only season of the PL in 1890. He was part of Buffalo's big four on the pitching staff that led an unlikely cast of misfits and has-beens to a decimation of Cleveland to the tune of 23–2, 15–8, 19–7, and 18–15. The law of averages caught up with the team quickly, when Buffalo went from first to last in two weeks and remained comfortably

Worst Seasons: 1876–92 (Minimum of 15 Losses)

Order, Name, and Year	Winning Percentage	Order, Name, and Year*	Losses minus Wins
1. Art Hagan (1883)	.059	1. John Coleman (1883)	36
2. John Hamill (1884)	.105	2T. George Bradley (1879)	27
3. Jack Wadsworth (1890)	.111	2T. George Cobb (1892)	27
4. Egyptian Healy (1889)	.118	4T. Will White (1880)	24
5. Dory Dean (1876)	.133	4T. Stump Weidman (1886)	24
		4T. John Ewing (1889)	24

Order, Name, and Year*	Adjusted ERA	Order, Name, and Year*	TPI
1. Jack Neagle (1883)	55	1. John Coleman (1883)	−8.1
2T. Dory Dean (1876)	59	2. Jersey Bakely (1884)	−6.0
2T. Art Hagan (1883)	59	3T. Jack Neagle (1883)	−5.0
2T. Kirtley Baker (1890)	59	3T. Lev Shreve (1888)	−5.0
5. George, the "Charmer"		5T. Bobby Mathews (1876)	−4.6
Zettlein (1876)	62	5T. Kid Carsey (1891)	−4.6
		5T. George Cobb (1892)	−4.6

Career Leaders: 1876–92 (Minimum of 50 Losses)

Order and Name	Winning Percentage	Order and Name*	Losses minus Wins**
1. John Coleman	.2421	1. Egyptian Healy	58 (78–136)
2. Jack Neagle	.2424	2. Stump Weidman	55 (101–156)
3. John "Chickenhearted"		3T. John Coleman	49 (23–72)
Kirby	.265	3T. Ed "Jersey"	
4. George Keefe	.294	Bakely	49 (76–125)
5. The Only Nolan	.307	3T. Bob Barr	49 (49–98)

Order and Name	Adjusted ERA	Order and Name	TPI
1. John Coleman	67	1. Stump Weidman	−11.4
2. Jack Neagle	72	2. John Coleman	−11.1
3. George Keefe	74	3. Jack Lynch	−9.5
4. John "Chickenhearted" Kirby	80	4. Billy Serad	−7.4
5. The Only Nolan	81	5. George Keefe	−7.2

* T = tie.
** W–L in parentheses.

in the cellar. Keefe had a typical season for him: 6–16 with a 6.52 ERA. He also gave up 280 hits and 138 walks in fewer than 200 innings.

A table at the end of the chapter shows the five worst career stats in several areas. A familiar name appears in the top three for each category: Good old John Coleman. The records of the worst pitchers (1876–92) are shown here.

Order and Name	Won	Lost	Percentage	ERA	Adjusted ERA	TPI
1. John Coleman	23	72	.242	4.68	67	−11.1
2. Stump Weidman	101	156	.393	3.60	89	−11.4
3. Jack Neagle	16	50	.242	4.59	72	−6.9
4. George Keefe	20	48	.294	5.05	74	−7.2
5. John Kirby	18	50	.265	4.09	80	−5.7

The records are not even close. In a rout that rivaled many of his defeats in the box, the worst pitcher in the early era of baseball was Coleman, the man who had the worst single season of the era as a rookie in 1883. Stump Weidman, who won 25 games in 1882 before putting up numbers like 4–21 and 12–36, finished second. Weidman beat out Boston's one-time 37-game winner and flamethrower, Jim Whitney (12–32), for the 1886 Skunk Stearns Award. Whitney, nicknamed "Grasshopper Jim" because of his peculiar gait, was once described "as having a head about the size of a wart."

The Skunk of 1887, Egyptian Healy, had the largest difference between losses and wins, but didn't qualify as one of the worst because he failed to crack the top five in any other area. Fred "Tricky" Nichols (24–44) fell short of the 50-loss criterion for eligibility, but would have challenged the leaders if NA stats counted. In 1875, as an NA rookie, the man who gained fame for a drop pitch had a record of 4–29 for the inept New Havens. He managed to stay in the majors until 1882, when a 1–12 record finally did him in. His overall record was 28–73, not too far from Coleman's credentials. Has anyone in professional baseball ever had worse debuts and swan songs than Nichols?

Probably not, but that does not diminish John Coleman's feats. Coleman followed his memorable rookie season with a 5–17 record in 1884 and then mostly played the outfield, starting only 11 games over the next six years. However, he went out in style as a pitcher in 1890, much the way he began his career: He gave up 28 hits and had an ERA of about ten in the two games he pitched in the NL, a league totally decimated by defections of its best players to the rival PL. He was a mediocre outfielder with a lifetime batting average of .257. As a pitcher, he never even approached mediocrity; he may have been the worst pitcher in major-league history.

Honorary Skunk Award: Tony Mullane

Why should Tony Mullane, who won 284 games in his career, win a Skunk Stearns Award? Because he single-handedly kept himself from election to Cooperstown, sabotaging his memory for posterity. Mullane retired with 285 wins (he had one taken away by *Total Baseball* that was rightfully Hank O'Day's) and missed winning 300 because of his own foolishness.

Mullane, a dashing ladies' man with a marvelous waxed moustache that made him resemble a nobleman, was known as "Count" and "the Apollo of the Box." Born in Ireland, the Count was suspended in 1885 for signing too many contracts and spent the season pitching for an independent ball club from Vermont. He had already won over 100 games in his first three full seasons in the AA—just before his suspension—and won over 30 games in both 1886 and 1887 following his reinstatement. He surely cost himself about 30 wins by missing the 1885 season. Actually, Mullane was lucky to escape with a suspension after signing a $3,500 contract with the Browns and then accepting a $2,000 advance from Cincinnati. The eccentric Chris Von der Ahe—"Der Boss President" of the Browns—was so enraged that he insisted on having Mullane arrested and jailed before he begrudgingly accepted his suspension. (Pitching contracts, by the way, were not the only legal agreements Mullane had difficulty honoring. Reporters had a field day discussing his divorce.)

The ambidextrous pitcher, who sometimes switched arms midbatter, was durable; he never suffered a serious arm injury and won more than 60 minor-league games after pitching his last major-league game in 1894. But he cost himself 30 wins in 1885 and another 10 in 1892, when he bolted Cincinnati rather than accept the midseason salary cuts imposed by the dictatorial NL. Mullane was the only pitcher to win more than 200 games in the AA, and he should have won 315 to 325 overall. Then he surely would have been elected to the Baseball Hall of Fame by the Veteran's Committee in the 1960s or 1970s with Galvin, Keefe, John Clarkson, and Welch—300-game winners all.

3

1893–1919
The Dead-Ball Era

◆ Amos Rusie, the Hoosier Thunderbolt, threw a ball that was considered to be so fast that his blazer took a backseat only to the speed of sound. He was the first true sports idol of the Big Apple; even the famed actress Lillian Russell asked to meet him. Rusie was fast, and Rusie was wild. He once beaned Baltimore shortstop Hughie Jennings, knocking the future Baseball Hall of Famer unconscious for four days. From 1890 to 1892 he walked more than 800 men, setting an all-time single-season mark with 289 bases on balls in 1890. Though he would one day be elected to the Baseball Hall of Fame by the Veterans' Committee, in the early 1890s Rusie was the potential executioner of every batter he faced. More than any other single reason, the powerful Indianan right-hander was responsible for increasing the distance between the pitcher and the batter to 60 feet 6 inches before the 1893 season.

Ironically, Rusie's control improved from the longer distance because the extra feet gave his curve the chance to break wickedly over the plate. He was a much-improved pitcher from the longer distance. In 1894, while NL pitchers had a 5.32 ERA, Rusie (36–13) led the league with a 2.78 mark that was nearly one full run better than the second-place finisher.

In contrast, Charley "Duke" Esper took a fall when the pitching distance was lengthened. From 1890 to 1892, he compiled a respectable 46–32 record, but in 1893 the 12–28 lefty became the winner of the first modern Skunk Stearns trophy (see the table of all winners for this period). His main claim to fame, however, stemmed from his running ability—or lack thereof. Esper pitched for a number of teams, including the legendary Baltimore Orioles of the mid-1890s. His Orioles teammates were reminded of a lame horse when they watched Charley Esper run. People with cramped leg muscles became known as suffering from a "charley horse"—courtesy of a long-forgotten skunk.

Unlike Rusie and Esper, a few pitchers were blissfully indifferent to

Skunk Stearns Winners: 1893–1919

Year	Winner	Team	Won	Lost	Percentage	ERA	Adj. ERA	WAT	TPI
1893	Duke Esper	Washington: NL	12	28	.300	4.71	98	-0.8	+0.4
1894	Jack Wadsworth	Louisville: NL	4	18	.182	7.60	67	-4.1	-3.4
1895	Mike McDermott	Louisville: NL	4	19	.174	5.99	77	-4.4	-2.4
1896	Les German*	Washington: NL	2	20	.091	6.43	68	-9.0	-2.7
1897	Red Donahue	St. Louis: NL	10	35	.222	6.13	72	0.0	-5.2
1898	Jim Hughey	St. Louis: NL	7	24	.226	3.93	96	-2.4	-0.9
1899	Jim Hughey	Cleveland: NL	4	30	.118	5.41	68	-1.9	-5.3
1900	Ed Doheny	New York: NL	4	14	.222	5.45	66	-4.6	-2.2
1901	Pete Dowling	Cleveland/Milwaukee: AL	12	26	.316	4.15	86	-4.4	-1.9
1902	Roscoe Miller	Detroit: AL, New York: NL	7	20	.259	3.98	87	-4.3	-1.6
1903	Patsy Flaherty	Chicago: AL	11	25	.306	3.74	75	-6.6	-2.9
1904	Happy Jack Townsend	Washington: AL	5	26	.161	3.58	74	-6.3	-3.5
1905	Kaiser Wilhelm	Boston: NL	3	23	.115	4.54	68	-8.9	-3.7
1906	Joe Harris	Boston: AL	2	21	.087	3.52	78	-8.6	-1.6
1907	Irv Young	Boston: NL	10	23	.303	3.96	64	-4.4	-4.0
1908	Jim Pastorius	Brooklyn: NL	4	20	.167	2.44	96	-6.6	-0.1
1909	George Ferguson	Boston: NL	5	23	.179	3.73	76	-6.1	-2.2
1910	Cliff Curtis	Boston: NL	6	24	.200	3.55	94	-7.0	-0.3
1911	Dolly Gray	Washington: AL	2	13	.133	5.06	65	-5.2	-2.0
1912	Walt Dickson	Boston: NL	3	19	.136	3.86	93	-6.9	-0.4
1913	Dan Griner	St. Louis: NL	10	22	.313	5.08	64	-1.5	-3.7
1914	Mysterious Walker	Pittsburgh: FL**	4	16	.200	4.31	74	-5.6	-2.0
1915	Rube Bressler	Philadelphia: AL	4	17	.190	5.20	57	-3.7	-4.1
1916	Jack Nabors	Philadelphia: AL	1	20	.048	3.47	83	-8.5	-2.1
1917	Burleigh Grimes	Pittsburgh: NL	3	16	.158	3.53	81	-5.2	-1.2
1918	Joe Oeschger	Philadelphia: NL	6	18	.250	3.03	99	-5.8	-0.6
1919	Harry Harper	Washington: AL	6	21	.222	3.72	86	-6.6	-1.5

*Les German was 0–0 in one game for New York (NL) in 1896.   **FL = Federal League.

the extra feet. Cy Young was 36–12 in 1892 and 34–16 the next season. Kid Nichols also never missed a beat, winning between 30 and 35 games each year from 1891 to 1894. Neither did Kirtley "Whitey" Baker, who was equally bad from any distance. The co-winner of the 1890 Skunk Stearns Award was 3–19 before 1893 and 6–19 after.

Coldwater Jim Hughey

We gave out Skunk Stearns Awards for nearly the first quarter century of baseball before someone was bad enough to win two trophies. In 1898 Jim Hughey won a skunk with St. Louis, and came back the next year to win one for the Cleveland Spiders. The 1899 Spiders have never been equaled for sheer incompetence—not even by the Mets in 1962—and Coldwater Jim Hughey, from Coldwater, Michigan, was the most inept of all.

Hughey wasn't even formally traded from St. Louis to Cleveland. The Robison brothers owned both teams and pooled the players to form two new teams: one that might contend for the pennant, and one that could be run on a shoestring. Despite the Spiders' glory in the mid–1890s when they were pennant contenders most seasons and beat the Orioles four games to one in the 1895 Temple Cup (the equivalent of a World Series featuring the top two finishers in the 12-team NL), Cleveland was awarded the booby team. The St. Louis Browns, renamed the Perfectos for the 1899 season in optimistic anticipation of a pennant, plucked future Baseball Hall of Famers Cy Young, Bobby Wallace, and Jesse Burkett plus eight other stars from the Cleveland roster. Jim Hughey, coming off a 7–24 Skunk Stearns season for St. Louis in 1898, was shipped to Cleveland, along with eight other low-paid duds. As godfather Michael Corleone might say, "the decision wasn't personal; it was strictly business."

St. Louis did not quite live up to the Perfecto name, finishing a distant fifth behind the pennant-winning Brooklyn Superbas. The Brooklyn Superbas lived up to their nickname, and not coincidentally because manager Ned Hanlon was the principal owner of both the Superbas and the Baltimore Orioles. Hanlon had great talent at his disposal and outdid the Robison brothers at their own game. And the players complained of the owners' collusion in the late 1980s!

And how bad were the 1899 Spiders? They were so bad that:

• Jim Hughey (4–30), the last player to lose 30 or more games in the major leagues, tied with rookie Charlie Knepper (4–22) for the team lead with four wins.

• Harry Colliflower lost 11 straight games after winning his debut, and that was only the *third*-longest losing streak on the team; Hughey closed the year with 16 straight losses, and Frank Bates did so with 14.

•The "crowds" in Cleveland often numbered about 100, impelling the Robisons to play nearly their entire remaining schedule on the road after July 1, a tactic that they also had used the previous year; the 1899 team was not even called the Spiders by the press, but the Cleveland Exiles, Waifs, Wanderers, Forsakens, Barnstormers, Castaways, or Tourists.

•The Spiders had only one winning streak as long as two games, and it was capped by Hughey's first win of the year, a 4–3 squeaker over Louisville.

•The team's pitching staff had an ERA of 6.37; no other team was above 5.00, and the league's ERA was 3.85.

•The Spiders finished with a 20–134 record, 84 games behind the first-place Brooklyn Superbas and an amazing 35 games behind the eleventh-place Washington Nationals.

•The team lost 24 straight games, won a contest on September 18, and finished with a string of 16 losses—a 1–40 record from the end of August until the season mercifully ended on October 15.

•The team lost 100 games before September rolled around.

The Spiders won seven games in May (but no more than four in any other month), and Hughey also enjoyed his best month, winning two games in a row and sporting a 2–3 record on May 25. Respectability seemed around the corner for the team and its workhorse pitcher, but neither one turned it. Both Hughey and the team plunged dramatically, since Coldwater Jim was continually in hot water from that point on, going 2–27. He lost in every imaginable way, although he did show flashes of competence in his two remaining wins, a 3–1 eight-hitter over the Perfectos in June and a 7–2 seven-hitter over the Orioles in July. He even had four hits in a June game against the Superbas; unfortunately, he yielded 17 and lost 10–6.

Above: **The 4–30 record of Jim Hughey, the first pitcher to win two Skunk Stearns Awards, symbolized the futility of the 1899 Cleveland Spiders (photo courtesy of George Brace).**

Hughey started the most games for Cleveland in 1899; pitched the most innings; and, despite 30 losses, was still the team's ace. Of the 14 pitchers who took the mound for Cleveland that season, only Jack Harper (3.89 ERA in 37 innings) had a lower ERA than Hughey's mark of 5.41. But Hughey was not your ordinary stopper. Staked to a 2–0 lead against Louisville in the April game that produced the Spiders' first 1899 win, he blew the lead and didn't get credit for the victory. He started the home opener on May 1, also a rare win by the team, but again he was long gone before the contest was decided. When Harper ended the Spiders' 24-game skid with his only victory of the year (he lost four) in the first game of a twin bill against Washington, Hughey promptly started another losing streak by squandering a 5–1 lead in the nightcap.

By combining Hughey's stats for his consecutive Skunk Stearns seasons, we get the following: an 11–54 mark (.169) with a 4.67 ERA. Shades of Bill Stearns. What could Hughey have done to resemble Cy Young instead of Stearns? Simple — just swap the *Y* at the end of his name for an *S*. The NL's best pitcher during the 1898–99 campaigns was Jim Hughey's near-namesake Jim Hughes, who was 23–12 as a Baltimore rookie in 1898 and the 28–6 ace of the Brooklyn staff in 1899. Hughey and Hughes had much in common in that each pitched for one of the NL's two-team syndicates and each was shuttled from one team to the other in search of a pennant — only Hughes earned wins, while Hughey specialized in losses. Hughes, by the way, was one of a handful of pitchers to hurl shutouts in his first two major-league starts — the first was a two-hitter, the second an 8–0 no-hitter against Boston. But he missed the 1900 NL season and pitched in an outlaw league in California instead because his new bride refused to move to Brooklyn.

Examine Jim Hughey's lifetime stats for the five major-league teams that employed him from 1891 to 1900, and you find a 29–80 record (.266 percentage) with a 4.97 ERA and a poor adjusted ERA of 80. Hughey completed exactly 100 games and never threw a shutout, the all-time mark of futility. Clearly shades of John Coleman, not Jim Hughes. Hughey's TPI in 1899 was −5.3, the worst of the entire 1893–1919 era. Only two pitchers from the previous era had lower TPIs, and the champion was Coleman with −8.1. Hughey's career TPI was −11.2, almost identical to Coleman's terrible value of −11.1. The resemblance between Hughey and John Coleman, the worst pitcher of the 1876–92 era, is striking.

According to the *Washington Post,* those who observed Hughey pitch during the 1899 season called him a mechanical pitcher who lacked ambition and judgment. That sounds about right. George Robinson and Charles Salzberg, whose 1991 book focused on baseball's worst teams, referred to Hughey as "a journeyman's journeyman," and that may be the finest compliment ever paid to the Stearns-Coleman clone. Although

Robinson and Salzberg were alluding to the great deal of traveling Hughey did during his career, the primary definition of journeyman, according to *The Dickson Baseball Dictionary,* is a "veteran ballplayer who is reliable but not a star; consistent rather than colorful." Well, at least he was consistent—so consistently bad, in fact, that Baltimore manager John McGraw blew his top at Orioles pitcher Jerry Nops for pitching hung over in the July game that produced Hughey's final win of the 1899 season. McGraw suspended Nops for a month without pay!

The only Cleveland pitcher to win as many as Hughey's four games in 1899 was Charlie Knepper, a hard-throwing, lanky (6 feet 4 inches, 190 pounds), right-handed rookie. During that season, Knepper kept reminding baseball writers of stars like fireballer Amos Rusie and 203-game winner Jack Stivetts (who was 0–4 for the Spiders in 1899). But in the end, Knepper finished the season at 4–22 with a 5.78 ERA. The pitcher he seemed to resemble most was ... well ... Jim Hughey.

Were Hughey and his supporting cast of pitchers merely victims of an incompetent offense and defense? To some extent, yes. The *Washington Post* said in late August that "a team of class B or college players could win more games." Was it a lack of effort? The *Post* stated in mid–September, "The Exiles are a pathetic galaxy to look upon. Loss, adversity, hard luck are written over their every action whenever they develop a flash of movement." But baseball observers still pinpointed the main problem as pitching. After Cleveland lost its 24th straight game, the *Post* said: "Joe Quinn can play second with the best, while [Harry Lochhead] covers short better than some older men in that position.... In McAllister, Cleveland has probably the best all-around [handyman] in the League. But the club's pitching staff is weak."

In short, the Spiders' players were fair to bad, but the pitching staff was truly disgraceful.

Asa Brainard Humpty-Dumpty Award: Russ Ford

A Ford pitching for the Yankees conjures up images of Baseball Hall-of-Fame lefty Whitey Ford piling up victories in the 1950s and 1960s. But the best season by a Ford in a Yankee uniform was probably turned in by a Canadian named Russ Ford in his 1910 rookie season. Whitey was magnificent in his 1961 Cy Young season with a 25–4 record and 3.21 ERA. But Russ was even better in 1910 with a 26–6 mark paired with a 1.65 ERA. Russ' 26 wins were topped by only one rookie ever, when Grover Cleveland Alexander went 28–13 for the Phillies the next season.

Russ had Whitey's craftiness and ability to doctor a baseball. He learned that scuffing a ball made it break sharply, something he discovered accidentally as a semipro pitcher after several stray pitches bounced off the stone wall that he and his brother were using as a backstop. Scuffing a ball wasn't legal in the majors then, but spitting on a ball was. So Russ, a man ahead of his time, displayed some of Whitey's clever deceit: He used emery paper to doctor the ball and simply made believe he was throwing a spitter. Unfortunately, Russ lacked Whitey's longevity and consistency. He defied the sophomore jinx by winning 22 in his second season, but then he took a fall, perhaps because of chronic soreness in his right arm. He led the AL with 21 defeats in 1912 and was almost as bad the next season. A comparison of Ford's first two seasons with his next two indicates why he is the winner of our Asa Brainard Award:

Years	Games Started	Won	Lost	Percentage	ERA	Adjusted ERA	Strikeouts	Shutouts
1910–11	66	48	17	.738	1.95	160	367	9
1912–13	63	25	39	.391	3.15	106	184	1

Ford's adjusted ERA tumbled from a superhuman value of 160 to a mortal 106 level as every aspect of his pitching game suffered. The right-hander, who threw one of the first good knucklers (and may have invented it) jumped to Buffalo in the new, outlaw Federal League in 1914; it was as if he had to prove that his Asa Brainard performance in the AL was no fluke.

He regained his form in 1914 with a 21–6 record (FL–leading .778 winning percentage, ERA of 1.82), only to have an FL pratfall in 1915, his last year in any major league (5–9, 4.52 ERA). He did well in the FL's first year, when it didn't even pretend to be a major league and had only a spattering of major-league has-beens (like Russ Ford) on its rosters. He was a bum once again in 1915, when the FL improved its image and ability level by signing some real talent like future Hall-of-Famers Joe Tinker and Mordecai "Three Finger" Brown.

Russ Ford earns the Asa Brainard Humpty-Dumpty Award for demonstrating his tendency to go splat not once, but twice, during a career that began as well as any pitcher in the Baseball Hall of Fame. Ford's main competition for the Humpty-Dumpty Award came from a pitcher who also had an incredible rookie season: Roscoe "Rubberlegs" Miller. Miller was 23–13 as a rookie for Detroit in 1901, the rookie season for the entire AL. No AL rookie has ever surpassed his 332 innings pitched or his 35 complete games. But he fell to a 6–12 mark for Detroit in 1902 and finished the season with the New York Giants. His 1–8 record for the Giants gave him a 7–20 record for the year, good enough for the 1902 Skunk Stearns Award.

Joe Hardy Sell-Your-Soul Award: Red Donahue

Francis "Red" Donahue made a brief pitching debut for the New York Giants in May 1893, the same year that Robert Louis Stevenson's *The Strange Case of Dr. Jekyll and Mr. Hyde* was published in the United States. Donahue's pitching career was a Jekyll-Hyde affair that started deep in skunk territory, ascended rapidly to stardom, and finished in mediocrity. His turnaround in the late 1890s from a Skunk Stearns winner to a 20-game winner was so astounding that he earns our Joe Hardy Award. The right-handed Donahue posted back-to-back seasons of 7–24 and 10–35 with the NL's St. Louis Browns in his first two full years in the majors, losing the Skunk Stearns Award to a more deserving Les German (2–20) in 1896, but capturing the 1897 trophy when his 35 losses set a record for the 60 foot 6 inch distance that has never been challenged.

It's true that the St. Louis teams he pitched for were terrible—the 1897 squad finished 29–102—and his improvement coincided with his 1898 change to the much-better Philadelphia Phillies. But Donahue was truly terrible for the Browns, not just a victim of bad luck. His ERAs were around 6.00, and his TPI of −5.2 in 1897 is the second worst from the 60 foot 6 inch distance. When he reached the 20-win circle in 1899, reporters credited his medium-paced curve and change-up and his exceptional knowledge of hitters. He won more than 20 games three times in a four-year period, twice with the Phillies and once with the St. Louis Browns in 1902. Could he really have gained so much new knowledge of the hitters, or did he sell his soul? Consider the evidence:

Years	Won	Lost	Percentage	ERA	Adjusted ERA	Shutouts	TPI
1893–97	17	60	.221	6.02	73	1	−9.4
1898–1902	95	59	.617	3.15	114	10	+4.3

Donahue closed out his career as an ordinary pitcher from 1903 to 1906, compiling a 53–56 record; however, for a five-year stretch in the

middle of his major-league stay he was a top-notch starter. No one who saw him pitch in the latter half of the 1890s could have predicted the startling reversal of fortune on the mound for the notorious hot-weather pitcher—except, perhaps, the man from Hades. (It is interesting that no Phillie has pitched a no-hitter in Philadelphia in the 20th century. The last man to do it was Donahue, when he beat Boston 5–0 in 1898. Tommy Greene pitched a 1991 no-hitter for the Phils—in Montreal.) Even Donahue's success off the field began to escalate in 1898. A traveling shoe salesman in the off-season, he earned $1,500 during the winter of 1898 selling "soles." Not bad, considering that the highest-paid ballplayer in 1899 was Cy Young at $4,000.

St. Louis fans weren't kind to Donahue when he returned to St. Louis to pitch for the Browns, especially when he stopped flashing his 20-win form. In 1903, they booed him relentlessly, and he had an open feud with them. The fans had soured on NL players who jumped to the AL for big bucks, and the press was no better. Local reporter Harold Lanigan wrote: "No two pitchers who get the money and are supposed to be the 'real thing' were ever the gold bricks that Donahue and [Jack] Powell are."

But Donahue kept his flair for humor and was called a "comedy pitcher"; he even considered a career on the stage. His fondest baseball memory was as an 18-year-old, when he pitched for King Mike Kelly's comedy baseball troupe. Donahue, who idolized Kelly, echoed the words of veterans of every era when he said in 1899, "Somehow there are no stars playing ball today."

But stars continued to emerge, and one of them was the unlikely

Above: **No pitcher from the 60 foot 6 inch-distance can top Red Donahue's 35 defeats in 1897 (33 according to** *Baseball Encyclopedia***), yet this Joe Hardy winner came back to post three 20-win seasons (photo courtesy of George Brace).**

runner-up to Donahue for the Joe Hardy Award: Ol' Stubblebeard, Burleigh Grimes, a man likened by some to the devil himself. The old spitballer, who loaded up the ball with saliva mixed with the slippery elm he chewed, looked like the devil on game days, thanks to a one-day-old beard (he didn't shave because the elm irritated his skin). He was menacing to opposing hitters, once knocking down a player in the on-deck circle who looked too eager to bat, and he extended his meanness to teammates, managers, and reporters. He refused to speak to Wilbert Robinson, his Dodger manager in the 1920s, who used a clubhouse boy to tell Ol' Stubblebeard when it was his turn to pitch.

But during Grimes' first two seasons in the majors with the Pirates, he didn't scare anyone. He was 2–3 in 1916 after being called up from Birmingham to close out the season and won the Skunk Stearns Award in 1917 with a 3–16 mark. Pittsburgh was bad in 1917, finishing in the cellar, 20.5 games behind seventh-place Brooklyn, but Grimes was worse. He won five games fewer than expected for a pitcher on his inept team (as indicated by his WAT of −5.2); his ERA of 3.53 was well below the NL average of 2.70 and his team's average of 3.01.

In Grimes' first game with Pittsburgh in 1916, he was tied 1–1 in the seventh with a man on first. An aging Honus Wagner implored the rookie to get the batter to hit it to short. Grimes did, and Wagner kicked the easy double-play grounder into center, with the runner scoring and the batter winding up on third. But with or without good fielding, Grimes' early pitching was rotten.

Yet after a five-player trade in 1918 that sent Casey Stengel to the Pirates and Grimes to the mediocre Brooklyn team (the Pirates finished ahead of the fifth-place Dodgers in 1918), Grimes took his first step toward a 270-win Hall-of-Fame career by going 19–9 with a 2.14 ERA. Almost overnight, he went from a 5–19 pitcher with the Bucs in 1916–17 to a 134–89 ace for Brooklyn from 1918 to 1924—from a .208 winning percentage to .601. The man who lost 13 straight games during his Skunk Stearns season in 1917 won 13 straight games ten years later. Quite an improvement for the man who threw the last legal spitter in the majors and who hit into a triple play and two double plays in one game at Chicago in 1925.

Joining Grimes as a runner-up for the Joe Hardy Award is Earl Hamilton, who pitched the first no-hitter in the St. Louis Browns' history in 1912. Hamilton had pitched in the AL from 1911 to 1917, compiling a 61–91 record, and his career seemed like history when he went 0–9 for the Browns in 1917 and was released. Yet he surfaced in the NL the next season with the Pirates, for whom he pitched six games, completed every one, and sported a 6–0 record with a gawdy 0.83 ERA. Though he was never again unbeatable, he pitched in the NL until 1924 and was a .500 pitcher in the senior circuit (55–56), not the .400 pitcher he had been in the AL.

The John Cassidy Root Canal Award: Jack Nabors

He came in second to Kaiser Wilhelm for the worst single season despite floundering through a 1–20 year in 1916, but how can we deny Jack Nabors the John Cassidy Root Canal Award? Nabors was 0–5 as a rookie in 1915 and closed out his brief career with two relief appearances (and no decisions) in 1917. His final tally was 1–25, an .038 winning percentage, and a 3.87 ERA (which was not too good in those days, translating to a terrible adjusted ERA of 75). At 3–30 a decade earlier, Boston Red Sox skunk Joe Harris was a bonafide Root Canal contender, but there's no way to dismiss Nabors' credentials — not when he had a worse record than John Cassidy (2–21)!

Nabors pitched for some awful Philadelphia Athletics' teams. He debuted the year after Connie Mack disposed of his high-priced veterans, rather than knuckle under to the new salary structure caused by the FL challenge. Although Mack was quoted several times as minimizing the money angle and emphasizing dissension among the players as the reason for dismembering his pennant-winning 1914 Athletics' squad, the bottom line seems to be the buck rather than the bull that Mack was throwing. The 1915 team plunged to last place and the 1916 team (36–117) lost 20 games in a row, lost a record 19 games in a two-week span, and had the worst winning percentage (.235) in AL history.

Jack Nabors and the future manager of the San Francisco Giants, Tom Sheehan, set an all-time record for futility by roommates. Sheehan, known in later days for his storytelling ability and his keen eye as as scout, had a 1–16 record in 1916 as the pair checked in with a combined 2–36 mark. Nabors lost 19 straight to tie Bob Groom's record set in 1909.

The story of the roommates' desperate 1916 saga can be summed up by a twin bill at Boston. Sheehan pitched a one-hitter in the first game, but lost 1–0 when the Red Sox squeezed out a run on a walk, the hit (by first baseman Doc Hoblitzell), and an error by shortstop Whitey Witt. The second game seemed to be heading toward a 1–0 no-hit win for Jack Nabors and revenge for the roommates, when disaster struck in the ninth. Again, a walk, a hit, and a Whitey Witt error produced a run. The winning run was now on third with one out, thanks to an error by the Athletics' catcher, but he didn't stay on third long because Nabors promptly threw the pitch way over the batter's head into the grandstand. The Athletics lost 2–1.

Nabors reportedly told Sheehan (who told Jack Orr) that he heaved the ball away on purpose because, "I knew those guys wouldn't get me another run, and if you think I'm going to throw nine more innings on a hot day like this, you're crazy." Well, if a guy's going to lose nearly every time he pitches, he may as well have some creative excuses. With Whitey

Witt as the shortstop, though, a pitcher didn't need too many excuses. If Ozzie Smith is the Wizard of Oz, then Witt was surely the Tin Woodsman: He made 78 errors at shortstop in 1916, barely eclipsing a .900 fielding percentage. Yet when Witt was asked by *The "All Stars" All-Star Baseball Book* to name deserving Hall of Famers, he listed only one player: Whitey Witt!

Nabors, for some unearthly reason, was given the opening day assignment in Boston in 1916, but Babe Ruth won the game 2–1. And although Nabors won the A's second home game of the season, 6–2, that would prove to be he only win ever to grace his name in the majors. True, he had bad luck. Half his defeats were by one or two runs, and 14 times the Athletics scraped up two or fewer runs; he even lost a two-hitter to the Browns. But he was also bad. He was the losing pitcher in the A's 20th straight defeat on August 9, when the Tigers raked him for 9 runs and 16 hits. (Not to be outdone by his roommate, Sheehan was the losing pitcher nearly a month later for the A's 100th loss.)

Nabors started 30 games, nearly as many as his teammates Bullet Joe Bush and Elmer Myers. Though Bush (15–24) and Myers (14–23) joined Nabors in the 20-loss club, they also found ways to enter the victory column from time to time. Early in the season, Myers (who would give up Ty Cobb's 3,000th hit five years later) won three games in a week, and Bush not only pitched a near-perfect no-hitter against Cleveland in late August (a leadoff walk followed by 27 straight outs), but finished second to Ruth in the AL with eight shutouts.

Both Nabors and Sheehan discovered that great pitching in the minor leagues doesn't equate to success in the major leagues. Sheehan, a paltry 17–39 during six spread-out seasons in the majors, still shares the AA's record for wins, notching 31 for St. Paul in 1923. And Nabors was a hotshot, pitching a 13-inning no-hitter in 1914 in the Georgia-Alabama League and sporting a 12–1 minor-league mark when Connie Mack brought him to the A's in 1915. After Mack finally gave up on him in early 1917, Nabors went on to pitch another no-hitter for Denver of the Western

Above: **Jack Nabors had only one victory to go with his 25 losses in the big leagues (photo courtesy of George Brace).**

Association. He enlisted in the army in 1919; was ravaged by the Spanish flu, a worldwide epidemic; and succumbed to tuberculosis in his Alabama home a day after his 36th birthday. Our Root Canal Award winner wasn't much of a pitcher or a hitter (.106 average) and had a rotten life.

Honorable mention for the Root Canal Award goes to Ike Butler, who was 1–10 for the Baltimore Orioles in 1902, the AL team that would move to New York the next season to become the Highlanders and later evolve into the Yankees. That was Butler's only season in the majors, but he was a glutton for punishment. He pitched in 1903 for Portland in the Pacific Coast League and set a PCL record with 31 defeats. The record lasted for only one season, when it was tied—by the very same Ike Butler.

Harry Heitmann, a Brooklyn Dodger pitcher for a moment one July day in 1918, also gets honorable mention. The 21-year-old right-hander made one major-league appearance, a start that lasted one-third of an inning. He gave up four hits and four earned runs and promptly took his ERA of 108.00 to a recruiting station, enlisted in the navy, and never pitched again in the majors.

Cherokee Fisher Rookie Award: Joe Harris

The half-dozen worst rookies between 1901 and 1919 emerged during a six-year period that stretched from 1904 to 1909. This group includes Joe Harris, who had a three-game cup of coffee in 1905 before starting his real rookie season in 1906, plus a bunch of hurlers who pitched their first major-league game in rookie seasons that were chock-full of defeats:

Year	Rookie	Team	Won	Lost	Percentage	ERA	Adjusted ERA
1904	Beany Jacobson	Washington: AL	6	23	.207	3.55	75
1905	Harry McIntire	Brooklyn: NL	8	25	.242	3.70	78
1906	Joe Harris	Boston: AL	2	21	.087	3.52	78
1908	Joe Lake	New York: AL	9	22	.290	3.17	78
1909	Dolly Gray	Washington: AL	5	19	.208	3.59	68
1909	Bob Groom	Washington: AL	7	26	.212	2.87	85

Bob Groom had a rookie season to remember, highlighted by a record 19 consecutive losses. Although Jack Nabors later tied Groom's streak in his memorable 1–20 season, no one has ever lost more consecutive games in a single season. Groom, who was known to pay too much attention to base runners, gained some measure of fame as a 24-game winner in 1912.

He also pitched a no-hitter on May 6, 1917, in the second game of a doubleheader against the White Sox, duplicating the Browns' Ernie Koob's feat of the previous day.

But it's hard to overlook his 7–26 rookie season. Hard, that is, until you study the record compiled by Joe Harris. The Boston Red Sox right-hander, who was born in nearby Melrose, Massachusetts, never got to make the local fans proud. In 1905, the year that Alfred Fuller sold his first brush, Harris posted a reasonable 1–2 record during his brief introduction to the majors and even had a good 2.35 ERA. But his rookie season in 1906 (and his final season in 1907) was a story of total failure. In 1906, he had a memorable 2–21 year to earn a Skunk Stearns Award, and in 1907 he closed out his major-league tenure with a 0–7 mark for a lifetime 3–30 record and a whopping career WAT of –12.4. He lost 14 straight games in his Skunk season, had eight shutouts pitched against him, and couldn't even get a win when he allowed just one run in 23 innings against the Philadelphia A's on September 1. Rookie Jack Coombs, who would later win 31 games for the A's, matched Harris inning for inning and finally bested the Skunk Stearns champion 4–1 in the 24th when Harris yielded three runs. During Harris' 2–21 rookie season, he shared the mound with several notables, including a 13–21 Cy Young, for a Red Sox team that lost 20 straight games and finished dead last. That mark earned Harris the Cherokee Fisher Rookie Award. Despite Groom's heroics in losing 26 games, Harris' mark stands out as the worst rookie season since John Coleman dropped 48 games for the Phillies in 1883—and as the worst of the 20th century.

While the Boston rookie was losing almost every game in 1906, Teddy Roosevelt was trying to simplify spelling with words like "tuf," "notis," and 'takl," an experiment that was squashed by the press' sarcasm and the public's outcry. But no matter how you spell it, Harris wuz a totl loozr. Enuf sed? Not quite, because Harris' debut is not even his ultimate claim to fame.

Above: **Joe Harris was 3–30 in three major-league seasons in the early 1900s, but his "Harris Jinx" may last into the next century (photo courtesy of George Brace).**

Joe Harris and the Harris Jinx

Joe Harris has one legacy that is his alone. He was the first Harris ever to pitch in the major leagues, and he began the Harris Jinx, which, stated simply, stipulates that no pitcher named Harris will ever be successful in the major leagues. Consider the evidence, based on the lifetime records of the 15 Harrises (including one Harriss) who pitched at least one game in the major leagues through 1992. (The Harrises are listed in order of their first year in the majors. The five Harrises with fewer than ten decisions—Bubba, Herb, Buddy, Bill T., and current Oakland prospect Reggie—are lumped together as "All other" Harrises):

Pitcher	Years Played	Won	Lost	Winning Percentage
Joe Harris	1905–07	3	30	.091
Ben Harris	1914–15	7	7	.500
Slim Harriss	1920–28	95	135	.413
Bill M. Harris	1923–38	24	22	.522
Bob Harris	1938–42	30	52	.366
Mickey Harris	1940–52	59	71	.454
Lum Harris	1941–47	35	63	.357
Greg "BoSox" Harris	1981–92	63	75	.457
Greg "Padre" Harris	1988–92	31	30	.508
Gene Harris	1989–92	3	9	.250
All other Harrises		8	5	.615
Total		358	499	.418

It's a grim picture. Lum Harris—though equipped with a good fastball, a fair knuckler, and occasional control (he yielded the fewest walks per game in the major leagues in 1944)—was the only other Harris to earn a Skunk Stearns Award; he was 7–21 in 1943, losing 13 straight games and leading the majors in defeats. Lum's lifetime winning percentage of .357 ranks him among the worst of the 20th century. As a manager in the 1960s and early 1970s, he won the first NL Western Division crown in 1969, only to be swept three straight by the Mets. Though he fared better as a manager than as a hurler, he was nonetheless a sub–.500 manager for his career (.488). And all that losing seemed to spill over to his behavior. He used to wander around the Atlanta outfield before games, in search of coins that fans threw on the field. He told *The Sporting News* with a grin, "It's usually just pennies. I'll find maybe 15 or 20 cents a night." Way to go, Lum!

Slim Harriss also extended his ineptness to other domains. The only Harris to lose more than 100 games, Slim had his hand (really his foot) in no-hit history. He opposed Howard Ehmke on the mound on September 7, 1923, in Philadelphia when Harriss' A's faced the Red Sox. Ehmke no-hit Philadelphia 4–0 that September afternoon, but it shouldn't have happened. Harriss smashed a drive over shortstop that rolled to the wall with two out in the sixth and easily made it to second. The problem was, he never touched first and was declared out when the ball was thrown by the shortstop Johnny Mitchell to first base. The first baseman's name? Joe Harris, naturally, but not the same Joe Harris who started the jinx in the first place.

If not for an official scorer, Harriss' running mishap would be part of common baseball lore. Four days after Ehmke no-hit the A's, he pitched a one-hitter. The only hit he allowed was a ground ball that was mishandled by the Red Sox third baseman. Had the official scorer called it an error, Ehmke would have beaten Johnny Vander Meer to the punch by 15 years. And Slim Harriss (who was later traded for Ehmke) would have been part of every retelling of the double no-hit story.

Still, Slim secured his niche in the Harris history book with his pitching, not with his baserunning. He lost 40 more games than he won; only 14 pitchers have exceeded that total in this century. He also led the AL in losses twice and came close to a Skunk Stearns Award in 1922 when he was the worst in the AL with a 9–20 record and 5.02 ERA, but was edged for the Skunk Stearns Award by the NL's Joe Oeschger (6–21, 5.06).

Bill M. Harris' professional career extended from the early 1920s to the mid–1940s; he won nearly 300 games and in 1936 pitched two no-hitters. The trouble is that the no-hitters were pitched for Buffalo in the International League, and 257 of his victories came in the minors. As a major leaguer, he was able to win in double digits only once, when he was 10–9 for the 1932 Pirates. The other Bill Harris, Bill T., also did his best pitching in the minors, hurling a perfect game in the Southern Association for Mobile in the early 1950s. In the majors, he pitched two games for the Dodgers, finishing his career at 0–1. The oddity: He pitched one game in Brooklyn in 1957, the year before the Dodgers moved to Los Angeles, and he pitched the other game in Los Angeles in 1959. Another Harris, Russell, was a superstud in the minors, going 27–3 (.900) in 1952 for Ozark in the Alabama-Florida League, the highest winning percentage in the minors that season. But he never made The Show.

The most successful Harris was probably Mickey, a southpaw who made the 1946 All-Star team when he finished 17–9 and pitched the Red Sox into the World Series. He also led the AL in saves (15) and games pitched (53) in 1950 for the Senators, finishing second in the major leagues to Jim Konstanty, the NL's Most Valuable Player, in both categories.

Despite his moments of brilliance, Mickey—plagued by arm injuries—showed his Harris form by finishing 12 games below .500 for his career, by losing both of his starts in the 1946 World Series, and by managing only six other saves in addition to the ones he earned in 1950.

Mickey had a lifetime WAT of −10.6, meaning that he lost almost 11 games more than expected, given the quality of the teams he played for—not quite what you'd expect from someone who was hailed as the second coming of Lefty Gomez when he arrived in the major leagues.

In 1989, the Expos made an awful trade with Seattle to obtain Mark Langston for what turned out to be less than single season. The Expos gave up three potentially outstanding pitchers: Randy Johnson, Brian Holman, and Gene Harris. Two of the three made good. Anyone who knows about the Harris jinx could have predicted the outcome. Since joining the Mariners, the 6 foot 10 inch Johnson pitched a no-hitter, Holman pitched a one-hitter, and both have become studs on Seattle's strong, young starting staff (although Holman missed the 1992 season with injuries). Harris, who proved equally unsuccessful as a starter and as a reliever, ended 1992 with a lifetime record of 3–9. He was placed on the disqualified list early in 1991 for leaving the Mariners without permission and wasn't brought up to Seattle until September. And 1992 was no better. On May 1, Harris gave up three homers in one inning in a 15–1 blowout by the Orioles, and less than a week later he walked out on the Mariners for the second straight year. And for the second consecutive year, he tried to land a job as a cornerback in the National Football League. Instead, Harris landed on the disqualified list again and has yet to impress an NFL scout; no doubt the NFL is fearful that the former defensive back at Tulane University will bring the Harris jinx to pro football. But the Padres remain fearless: San Diego's general manager Joe McIlvaine obtained the disqualified would-be cornerback on May 11, giving Seattle a minor league outfielder.

Another active Harris is the Boston Red Sox Greg, an ambidextrous journeyman with a .457 winning percentage who has pitched for seven teams since 1981. A good relief pitcher for the Rangers in the mid-1980s and a solid Boston starter (13–9) in 1990, he demonstrated that the Harris jinx extends beyond the pitching mound. It can also settle in the brain. In 1987 he injured his elbow during a game, but not while pitching or even warming up. He hurt it by flicking sunflower seeds, aiming them at a friend sitting in the stands! It happened between starts, and he missed two starts because of it. "It sounds ridiculous," he said. Not if you know about the Harris jinx.

Who is the most likely Harris to break the Harris jinx once and for all? One possibility is the Athletics' prospect Reggie Harris. Oakland plucked him from Boston's farm system and thought enough of the hard-throwing right-hander to keep him around during the 1990 season even though he contracted hepatitis that spring; they didn't want to return him to the Red Sox. He showed promise by winning his only decision and yielding only 25 hits in 41⅓ innings. But he was a bust in 1991. He spent a few days with the A's in April, gave up four earned runs in three innings, and earned a one-way ticket to the minors. And 1992 was an instant replay. Coming into spring training, he had a good shot at the A's starting rotation, but his wildness and bulging waistline earned this perennial prospect another trip to the minors—where he stayed.

The best bet to smash the Harris jinx is the Padres' Greg, who has a wicked curveball and a penchant for injuries. After spending most of the first half of 1991 on the disabled list, he almost became the first Harris (and the first Padre) to pitch a no-hitter when he faced the Mets on Bastille Day. He gave up a ground-rule double to Mackey Sasser leading off the eighth. Greg needed relief help and escaped with a combined one-hit win, 2–1. He continued his outstanding starting pitching and was one of the top pitchers in the majors after the All-Star break. "I think he's the star of the future for the Padres," former San Diego manager Greg Riddoch told us.

Which doesn't mean he's immune to the Harris jinx. In September, when three Atlanta Braves pitched the first combined no-hitter in NL history, who was on the flip side of the event? The Pads' Greg, who absorbed the 1–0 loss.

But he took steps in 1991 to end the jinx. He and his namesake thumbed their noses at the Harris stranglehold on August 10, 1991. They started the day with a combined total of no complete games in 27 starts that season. Then, the Red Sox's Greg went out and pitched a four-hit complete-game 7–1 win over the Blue Jays; the Padres' Greg did him one better with his first shutout, a 1–0 six-hitter against the Reds. He repeated the 1–0 feat five days later with a three-hitter against Atlanta.

Perhaps inspired by the Padres' Greg, the other Greg turned around a 1991 season that started off 1–5 and dipped to 6–11 in late July by reeling off five straight victories (including two in fewer than 24 hours); he finished the year at a respectable 11–12. In 1993, the right-hander may finally get the chance to pitch left-handed to left-handed batters. The Red Sox's pitching coach Rich Gale (who retired in 1984 with a career ERA of 4.54) thinks the idea makes sense.

The Padres' Greg Harris, meanwhile, was 9–5 in the last half of the 1991 season; he had a 2.23 ERA, while averaging 6½ strikeouts and fewer than two walks per game. But just when hope was on the horizon to smash the Harris jinx, 1992 began. Greg was getting rocked regularly whenever he managed to stay on the mound and off the disabled list. And when he pitched well, he still suffered from the Harris jinx as Randy Myers blew two four-run leads in the ninth. At one point early in the 1992 season, Myers had a 0.00 ERA and was 5-for-5 in converting saves for non–Harris pitchers, but compiled a 19.64 ERA in relief of Greg. Later in the season, while Harris was languishing on the disabled list, Myers compiled a streak of 16 consecutive saves. Greg came off the disabled list, and Myers promptly blew a win for Harris in late August against the Pirates.

Now that the Padres have Gene Harris, they sport a pitching staff with a double dose of Harrises. Heaven forbid! If Myers doesn't thwart Greg Harris' bid for stardom, maybe Gene will. In 1992, the three active Harrises—Gene and the two Gregs—had a combined 8–19 record. Old Joe Harris' jinx just may be safe for a while.

The Worst Single Season from 1901 to 1919: Kaiser Wilhelm

Before awarding Skunk Stearns trophies to the pitchers with the worst single season, the worst career, and the worst rookie year, we decided to narrow the field to pitchers who played primarily or exclusively from 1901 to 1919. It took pitchers from 1893 until the end of the century to adjust to the longer pitching distance. Pitchers in the NL had an average ERA of about 3.30 in 1891 and 1892, but that average skyrocketed to the 4.50 to 5 range as soon as the pitching distance was stretched, and it didn't return to the pre–1893 norm until the start of the 20th century. Since 1901 also coincided with the formation of the AL and the end of the 12-team NL (and was just a year after the pentagon-shaped home plate replaced the old diamond-shaped one), it was the logical point to begin selecting the worst pitchers of the era. Besides, if we had included the 1890s, the 1899 Cleveland Spiders' pitchers would have run off with nearly all the awards. Even Joe Harris would have lost the Cherokee Fisher Rookie Award to Cleveland's Frank Bates, a pitcher we'll tell you about later in the chapter.

The five worst single seasons are listed for the following five categories in a table at the end of the chapter: losses minus wins, winning percentage, adjusted ERA, WAT, and TPI. Kaiser Wilhelm made four of the five lists, with Jack Nabors and Joe Harris winding up on three. Lefty Rube Bressler appeared on only two lists, but he topped them both; he had the worst adjusted ERA and TPI of his era. Bressler is best known as a .300-hitting outfielder, but he earned a negative niche in baseball history as a 4–17 pitcher in 1915. Ironically, that pathetic performance followed an impressive rookie season for the 1914 pennant-winning Athletics when he spiced a 10–4 mark with a 1.77 ERA. He was named "Rube" by those who thought he'd enter the southpaw fraternity pledged by Rube Waddell and Rube Marquard. Instead he joined the pitching partnership of Wilhelm, Nabors, and Harris.

In Chapter 7, we list the pitchers who had the worst single seasons of

Despite stiff competition, Kaiser Wilhelm's 3–23 record in 1905 was the worst season of his era (photo courtesy of George Brace).

Worst Seasons: 1901–19 (15 or more losses)

Order, Pitcher Year (Team)	Won	Lost	Percentage	ERA	Adjusted ERA	WAT	TPI
1. Kaiser Wilhelm (1905) (Boston: NL)	3	23	.115	4.54	68	−8.9	−3.7
2. Jack Nabors (1916) (Philadelphia: AL)	1	20	.048	3.47	83	−8.5	−2.1
3. Joe Harris (1906) (Boston: AL)	2	21	.087	3.52	78	−8.6	−1.6
4. Rube Bressler (1915) (Philadelphia: AL)	4	17	.190	5.20	57	−3.7	−4.1
5. Happy Jack Townsend (1904) (Washington: AL)	5	26	.161	3.58	74	−6.3	−3.5
6. Fred Glade (1905) (St. Louis: AL)	6	25	.194	2.81	91	−7.8	−1.1

the 20th century (1901–91) based on rankings for these same five cate-gories. The results of that competition won't be revealed until Chapter 7, but the following pitchers from the 1901–19 era all had seasons that ranked among the 15 worst of the century. They are listed on the next page in the order in which they finished.

Wilhelm had the worst season during the 1901–19 period, with Nabors and Harris close behind. Though Wilhelm was 5–3 as a promising rookie for Pittsburgh in 1903, he followed that season with two straight years as a 20-game loser for the Boston Braves, including his memorable 3–23 campaign in 1905. He never came close to a winning record in the majors, stringing together losing season after losing season. Yet, like Root Canal winner Jack Nabors and Tom Sheehan, Nabors' roommate on the A's, the Kaiser was a minor-league star.

In fact Wilhelm, known in those days as "Little Eva," was a bit of a folk hero in Birmingham. After losing 23 of 26 decisions in 1905, he was sent to the minors for a couple of years. In 1906, Wilhelm pitched a perfect game against Mobile and pitched the Barons to the Southern League pen-nant. During his stay in Birmingham, he added to his legend by striking out 16 in a game against Little Rock and by hurling 61 consecutive score-less innings. The man who was once referred to as "the greatest all-round hurler a Birmingham club ever owned" by the *Birmingham News* clawed his way back to the majors in time for the 1908 season. He promptly lost 22 for Brooklyn and had a 22–42 record for the newly named Dodgers from 1908 to 1910—remarkably similar to the 22–46 mark he compiled during his first three-year stay in the majors from 1903 to 1905.

Little Eva Wilhelm surfaced in the majors once more, in 1914 with Baltimore of the FL, and went 12–17 before a dead arm put a merciful end to his major league pitching career. As coach and then manager of the last-place Phillies in 1921, Wilhelm decided that as a 47-year-old, he could pitch better than his woeful pitching staff. He let himself pitch eight innings in four games. Bad move. The NL batted .393 against Wilhelm and had an on-base percentage of .452.

The Worst Career of the 1901–19 Era: Happy Jack Townsend

Career leaders in the five categories are shown in a chart at the end of the chapter, with William "Dolly" Gray topping two lists: winning percentage (based on a 15–51 record) and adjusted ERA. Gray was nicknamed for the then-popular Spanish-American War ballad "Goodbye, Dolly Gray," and when he pitched, it was usually good-bye, Dolly Gray. As a rookie in 1909 the left-hander walked a record eight men in one inning against the White Sox, including an amazing seven straight. In that fateful second inning, Gray forced in five runs and gave up six runs in all, but he somehow managed to complete the game and shut out Chicago the rest of the way.

To Gray, the 6–4 defeat was just one more loss, but to the *Washington Star*, the fiasco "looked like a military drill. Each batsman went to the plate . . . and then sedately marched to first."

Gray was joined on the worst career list by a few others with colorful names. We've already met Kaiser Wilhelm, but what about Buster Brown, plagued by wildness and terrible teams, who pitched in the majors from 1905 to 1913 and never had a winning record? Or Bill Bailey, a lefty who would have saved his teammates much grief if he had heeded the words to "Won't You Come Home, Bill Bailey?"

And don't forget Virgil "Ned" Garvin, a stringbean at nearly 6 feet 4 inches and 160 pounds, who was referred to as "two pounds to the inch." He started before 1900, but did most of his bad pitching in the 20th century. Garvin filled his life with misadventures, including the shooting and wounding of a Chicago saloon proprietor in 1902. He consistently had good ERAs, but his WAT of −17.6 is one of the worst of all time. He had a gem of a fadeaway (an earlier version of the pitch Carl Hubbell would later improve upon and rename "screwball"); some have credited Garvin with teaching the pitch to Christy Mathewson, although Matty gave credit to an unknown lefty, Dave Williams.

No one belied his nickname more than Happy Jack Townsend, who finished first, second, or third in all our categories except adjusted ERA.

Dolly Gray crammed a 15–51 record into just three years in the majors and gave Happy Jack Townsend the only real competition for worst pitcher of the era (photo courtesy of George Brace).

Townsend easily beat out Dolly Gray, the Kaiser, and Bill Bailey for the Skunk Stearns Career Award from 1901 to 1919.

The records of the five worst hurlers from this era, in order, are as follows:

Worst Career: 1901–19

All-time Skunk	Won	Lost	Percentage	ERA	Adjusted ERA	WAT	TPI
1. Happy Jack Townsend	35	82	.299	3.59	85	−18.3	−8.5
2. Dolly Gray	15	51	.227	3.52	75	−13.3	−5.0
3. Kaiser Wilhelm	56	105	.348	3.44	83	−13.8	−8.1
4. Bill Bailey	38	76	.333	3.57	80	−12.7	−8.1
5. Harry McIntire	71	117	.378	3.22	83	−14.6	−8.3

Happy Jack, proud owner of a scorching fastball, was born in Townsend, Delaware, where he honed his pitching skills on a farm by fllinging stones at apple trees. Townsend probably missed most of the trees. He was plum wild and walked 12 in a nine-inning game against Detroit in August 1902, an AL record that stood until 1915—the same year that the Yankees wore pin-striped uniforms for the first time—when the Athletics' Bruno Haas set the all-time record with 16 in his second, and last, major-league start.

The NL record for walks? Fourteen, set by Mathewson of the Giants in 1906 against Boston. Does the great Matty, one of the best control artists ever, hold a bases-on-balls record? No, it was younger brother Henry in the only major-league game he started. Bruno Haas, by the way, also has some trivia attached to his name: He played halfback in the new National Football League in 1921.

Townsend had the worst WAT in the 1901–19 era, while Case Patten had the worst TPI. The two were teammates with the Washington Senators from 1902 to 1905. While Happy Jack went 5–26 for the atrocious 1904 Washington team to set an AL record for defeats that still stands, Patten managed to win 14 (he dropped 23, but was the hard-luck victim of nine shutouts). Although Patten's bad luck has been well chronicled, his runaway first-place finish in the negative TPI derby suggests that he had at least a tad of trouble with his hitting, fielding, and ability to prevent runs from scoring.

Together, the Palmer-Thorn twins of WAT and TPI notoriety gained infamy among their Washington teammates by hiding white mice in their pockets and inflicting them on unsuspecting players.

Happy Jack Townsend was 7–37 in 1903–04 and was the worst pitcher of his era (photo courtesy of George Brace).

Jack Wadsworth: The Worst Pitcher of All Time?

Jack Wadsworth won the 1894 Skunk Stearns Award when he was 4–18 for Louisville, but otherwise slipped through the cracks of our system. He pitched in the majors on and off from 1890 to 1895, too long a stay to challenge Jack Nabors for the Root Canal Award; indeed, his career was more like progressive gum disease. He didn't pitch in the 20th century, so he wasn't eligible to compete for the worst pitcher of his era; in any case, his lifetime total of 38 defeats left him short of the 50 minimum needed to qualify. But Jack Wadsworth, who was 2–16 in 1890 while the pitching box was 50 feet from home plate and 4–22 from the time that the pitching distance was set at 60 feet 6 inches, may have been the worst pitcher who ever pitched more than 350 innings in the majors.

Wadsworth's lifetime record for three NL teams—Cleveland, Baltimore, and Louisville—was 6–38. His .136 winnings percentage trailed Bill Stearns' mark of .158 in the NA. Wadsworth's career ERA of 6.85 adjusts to 64 when league and ballpark factors are taken into account. Even John Coleman, by far the worst pitcher from 1876 to 1892, managed an adjusted ERA of 67. And in just two full seasons and parts of two others, Wadsworth compiled a WAT of −12.1 and a TPI of −7.5. These are both *cumulative* stats that are worthy of bad pitchers who stayed in the big leagues for ten years. In reverse, they are the equivalent of a pitcher winning 200 games or a hitter knocking 300 home runs in just half a dozen years.

Wadsworth gave up 524 hits and walked 199 in just 367 innings. The reward for his best season was the 1894 Skunk Stearns trophy. That year he allowed 28 singles in a mid–August game, a mark that has remained safe from all challengers, including the Indians' Bock Baker, who gave a good Wadsworth imitation in 1901 when he yielded 23 one-base hits in his debut. Other Wadsworth clones from this era: A physician named Doc Parker, who pitched one game in the 20th century, a complete game for the 1901 Reds in which he gave up 26 hits and 14 runs; Merle Adkins, of the 1902 Boston Pilgrims (later the Red Sox), who yielded 12 hits in one *inning*; and Al Mamaux, of the 1919 Dodgers, who gave up ten runs to Cincinnati in the thirteenth inning after pitching 12 scoreless frames. Well, Mamaux wasn't quite a Wadsworth clone, since old Jack never pitched 12 straight shutout innings in his life.

How Can We Ignore Frank Bates and Crazy Schmit?

Frank Bates and Crazy Schmit sound like they came from Hitchcock's *Psycho* instead of the 1899 NL, but Bates and Schmit were as instrumental as Coldwater Jim Hughey in contributing to the Cleveland Spiders' woes. They shouldn't be deprived of their rightful place in the sun.

Bates pitched impressively for the 1898 Spiders after the team bought his contract from Dayton late in the season. Cleveland was, according to the *Washington Post,* "experimenting with some new twirling timber." The experiment seemed successful when Bates went 2–1, winning his first two decisions before dropping a one-run decision to Louisville on the last day of the season.

But in 1899, Bates crumbled along with the rest of the Spiders. Shattered is probably a better word, since he walked 110 and struck out only 13. Opposing batters hit .349 against his tempting serves and had an on-base average of .436, similar to Wade Boggs' career totals in both stats. Bates finished at 1–18, a .053 percentage; his adjusted ERA of 54 is one of the worst ever.

Bates started the 1899 season in St. Louis, but took the baseball shuttle to Cleveland in early June, when the Robison brothers decided that he fit in better with the Robisons' *B* team in Cleveland than the *A* team in St. Louis. Bates started his first game for Cleveland on June 7 and quickly lost a handful of games before capturing what would prove to be his only win in 19 decisions for the Spiders. And what a win it was!

On July 1, defending champion Boston had a 7–0 lead against Bates going into the bottom of the ninth with Vic Willis on the mound. Willis, a fastballer who was destined to finish the 1899 season at 27–8, couldn't hold the lead. And reliever Parson Lewis couldn't save the win after Boston scored two runs in the top of the 11th. The line score of Bates' moment of glory:

Boston	010	203	100	02	9
Cleveland	000	000	007	03	10

Bates' only win of the season, a 17-hit complete game in which the Spiders scored only one earned run, was as big a long shot as anything in baseball history.

Unlike Bates, who pitched a few good games the year before, the hard-drinking southpaw Schmit never gave the illusion of competence. Nicknamed Crazy by his teammates because he was deemed the most eccentric player of his time, Frederic M. "Germany" Schmit had much in common with Jack Wadsworth: Neither man could pitch from any distance. Crazy was 2–13 before 1893 and 5–23 from 60 feet 6 inches, for a combined mark of 7–36. His career winning percentage of .163 was reminiscent of the lifetime mark of Bill Stearns.

Cleveland signed Schmit in late June 1899, even though he hadn't pitched in the majors for six seasons. He was literally a clown, having traveled for a few months in 1890 with J. Palmer O'Neill's troupe of baseball comedians, the Pittsburgh Wanderers. According to the *Washington Post*, the energetic Schmit had "a boiler-shop voice that was employed in disturbing the peace" during baseball games, and he served up "lobster-gaited" slow balls. How slow were Schmit's tosses? Following a 14–3 pasting by Washington on September 15, the *Post* ridiculed the slow curve, Schmit's only pitch, by describing the Crazy man as the "manipulator of a roundhouse scroll that wafts up to the plate with the nonchalance of a dapper youth flaunting through Burlington Arcade . . . an inviting, appetizing toss."

Schmit finished the season 2–17. Like Bates' one win, Schmit's pair of victories for Cleveland involved an oddity: He won the games consecutively in early August to tie for the longest winning streak by a Spiders pitcher in 1899. (Of course, every Spider victory was a bit of an oddity that season.)

Schmit's second win, a 14-hit–15-walk complete game against the Chicago Orphans, didn't come easy; he squandered most of an 8–0 lead and held on for dear life to win 10–9.

Was Schmit really crazy? Perhaps not, but what exactly did he mean when he told a reporter after a 21–6 shellacking: "If they look me up in the family Bible, they would find that I'm old enough to know, as the soubrette warbled in the fakerina sketch." Schmit was filled with such quotes, although the *Washington Post* insisted that he was not as zany as he pretended. To his Cleveland Spider player-manager Joe Quinn, Schmit was "one of the most original characters that ever broke into the League. He's so full of ginger that it oozes out of his pores." The Australian-born Quinn, who managed a team that barely had a pulse and who doubled as an undertaker in the off-season, may have been easily impressed by life of any sort.

While pitching for a Macon, Georgia, minor-league team, Schmit was accused by a fan of throwing a brick at him. The judge acquitted Schmit on the basis of his unorthodox defense: As a professional baseball player, "if I had thrown a brick at him, the guy would be dead." Sure. And what about the 12 Chicago players he walked in a June game while pitching for Pittsburgh in 1890? It was lucky for Schmit—the 19th-century Rob Dibble—that the judge didn't read *The Sporting News* (first published in 1886), or the crazy man might have served serious time.

The Spiders added Bates and Schmit to its staff in June, but neither made it to the end of the season. Bates was known to refuse all advice, preferring to pitch his own way. It didn't work. He was given his ten-day notice, as was the custom, after he was clobbered 19–3 by Cincinnati on

September 5. He gave up 22 hits and 8 walks and hit 2 batters for good measure. Schmit received his pink slip nearly three weeks later.

Only Schmit pitched in another major-league game, going 0–2 in the new AL in 1901. Bates left with a 3–19 legacy and a 14-game losing streak.

Honorary Skunks: Some 1890s Hurlers

We have awarded a few honorary Skunk Stearns Awards to pitchers who, like Bates and Schmit, played most or all their careers in the 1890s and lost a crack at our single-season and career awards for the 1901–19 period.

Les German. German won a Skunk Stearns trophy in 1896 for his 2–20 record with Washington, a team that was not so bad and even numbered 25-game winner Win Mercer among its staff. He won nine fewer games than expected for a Senators pitcher that season, producing a WAT of 9.0, the lowest ever from the 60 foot 6 inch distance. German couldn't do anything right that year. A career .260 hitter, his batting average of .070 was lower than his .091 winning percentage. The year 1896 also marked the Broadway debut of the Cherry Sisters, who gained notoriety because audiences loved to hate them. Florenz Ziegfeld installed a fishnet across the stage to protect them from the rocks, shoes, and turnips that people threw. German, with a lifetime mark of 34–63 and an ERA of 5.49, could have used a similar net whenever he pitched.

Bill Hart. A printer by trade, Hart played in the majors from 1886 to 1901, spanning the first two eras of baseball. He didn't pitch often enough or poorly enough in the 1876–92 era to gain mention in Chapter 2, and his worst seasons from the 60 foot 6 inch distance were overshadowed by others. He had back-to-back years of 12–29 and 9–27 for the NL's St. Louis Browns in 1896–97, but came away empty from the Skunk Stearns derby, thanks to Les German (2–20) and Red Donahue (10–35). But Bond Hill Billy, who claimed that he started throwing a spitball in 1896 (and was likely among the first to use it), should not be forgotten. At 66–120, he lost 54 more games than he won, a number matched by few.

Hart pitched a one-hitter in the Pirates' 1895 home opener, and he won Cleveland's first AL game in 1901. But the smiling, well-liked Hart's glory never lasted long. He was released by Pittsburgh in September 1895 and didn't make it through Cleveland's inaugural season either. He finished 1901 as an AL umpire—and was still on Cleveland's payroll while umpiring their games! And how slow was his slowball? After what would be his final major-league victory in July 1901, a reporter wrote, "Some days it is slower than others. It was slower today—slower than any other day since 1872.... Frequently it would stop until the batter was off his guard, and then sneak across the plate."

Kid Carsey. Carsey also spanned the first two eras of baseball, winning the Skunk Stearns trophy as a 14–37 rookie for Washington in 1891 and pitching until 1901. Although he followed his first-year disaster with four straight winning seasons for the Phillies, including a 24–16 record in 1895, Carsey had a lifetime TPI of −13.7, the second worst *ever.* He went out as he came in, compiling a 4–22 record in 1898 and 1899, including a 1–8 stint with the Spiders. A junkballer with a "dinky and sluggish slow curve," he was part of Cleveland's most painful loss of the 1899 season when he failed to hold a 10–0 lead.

Bill Magee. Magee played for six NL teams from 1897 to 1902 and pitched poorly for every one, walking more than twice as many men as he struck out. His 29–51 record is good compared to his 4.93 ERA, which adjusts to a value of 75—one of the worst ever. While pitching for Washington in late September 1899, Magee was ejected by umpire Cy Swartwood for "making faces." Team captain Dick Padden claimed that the pitcher was just breaking in a new chaw and blasted the umpiring staff for having "as much spinal column as is required to run a cockroach." But Magee had good reason to make faces at the umpires or at anyone for that matter. Twelve days earlier he had lost to the Cleveland Spiders to break their record 24-game losing streak. Magee was the only pitcher to lose to the Spiders in their last 41 games of the season! And he managed to lose to them *three* times in 1899 (they won only 20)—and for three different teams.

Honorary Skunks: Eddie Cicotte and Lefty Williams

The Black Sox pitchers can't escape mention in a book about Skunks, but that's all we'll do: mention them. Eddie Cicotte—master of the spitter, emery ball, screwball, knuckler, and slider, according to Ray Schalk, his catcher—blew the 1919 World Series with style and subtlety (1–2, 2.91 ERA), whereas Lefty Williams blew up like a hot-air balloon. Williams ignored Schalk's sign for his money pitch, the curveball, three times in one inning in the second game he pitched, and he never made it out of the first inning in this third start, thanks to his batting-practice fastballs. In all, Williams was 0–3 with a 6.61 ERA, rivaling Swede Risberg (an .080 batting average plus an iron glove) for devotion to the cause. The veteran Cicotte, who was 29–7 in 1919 and had 208 lifetime wins, threw away a bid to the Baseball Hall of Fame. Lefty, only 27 when banished after the 1920 season, won 45 games his last two years and cut short an All-Star career. Both earn honorary Skunk Stearns Awards.

Worst Seasons: 1901–19 (Minimum of 15 Losses)

Order, Name, and Year*	Statistic
Losses minus Wins	
1. Happy Jack Townsend (1904)	21
2. Kaiser Wilhelm (1905)	20
3T. Fred Glade (1905)	19
3T. Joe Harris (1906)	19
3T. Bob Groom (1909)	19
3T. Jack Nabors (1916)	19
Winning Percentage	
1. Jack Nabors (1916)	.048
2. Tom Sheehan (1916)	.059
3. Joe Harris (1906)	.087
4. Kaiser Wilhelm (1905)	.115
5. Walt Dickson (1912)	.130
Wins-Above-Team (WAT)	
1. Kaiser Wilhelm (1905)	−8.9
2. Joe Harris (1906)	−8.6
3. Jack Nabors (1916)	−8.5
4. Fred Glade (1905)	−7.8
5. George Bell (1910)	−7.6
Adjusted ERA	
1. Rube Bressler (1915)	57
2T. Oscar Jonse (1905)	62
2T. Elmer Myers (1917)	62
4. Dan Griner (1913)	64
5T. Tom Fisher (1904)	65
5T. George Bell (1908)	65
Total Pitcher Index (TPI)	
1. Rube Bressler (1915)	−4.1
2. Irv Young (1907)	−4.0
3. Case Patten (1907)	−3.8
4T. Kaiser Wilhelm (1905)	−3.7
4T. Vive Lindaman (1907)	−3.7
5T. Dan Griner (1913)	−3.7

*T = tie.

Career Leaders: 1901–19 (Minimum of 50 Losses)

Order and Name*		Statistic
Losses minus Wins**		
1. Buster Brown	52	(51–103)
2. Kaiser Wilhelm	49	(56–105)
3. Happy Jack Townsend	47	(35–82)
4. Harry McIntire	46	(71–117)
5. Long Tom Hughes	44	(131–175)
Winning Percentage		
1. Dolly Gray		.227
2. Happy Jack Townsend		.299
3. Cliff Curtis		.315
4. Buster Brown		.331
5T. Mal Eason		.333
5T. Bill Bailey		.333
Wins-Above-Team (WAT)		
1. Happy Jack Townsend		−18.3
2. Ned Garvin		−17.6
3. Harry McIntire		−14.6
4. Kaiser Wilhelm		−13.8
5. Dolly Gray		−13.3
Adjusted ERA		
1. Dolly Gray		75
2T. Jim Pastorius		78
2T. Gus Dorner		78
4. Bill Bailey		80
5. Elmer Myers		81
Total Pitcher Index (TPI)		
1. Case Patten		−12.7
2. Happy Jack Townsend		−8.5
3. Harry McIntire		−8.3
4. Gus Dorner		−8.2
5T. Bill Bailey		−8.1
5T. Kaiser Wilhelm		−8.1

*T = tie.
**W–L in parentheses.

4

1920–1946
The Long-Ball Era

◆ There's little argument that 1919 marked the end of one baseball era and 1920 began a new one, although it's hard to pinpoint the exact moment of the shift. To some, the event is marked by two related events: the Black Sox scandal and the start of Kenesaw Mountain Landis' iron-fisted reign as the first baseball commissioner in 1920. But more important than baseball ethics in the changing eras was the eruption of the long ball, a process that started in 1919 but was not in full swing until 1920. That eruption was accelerated by the ban of the spitball in the winter of 1919–20 and by Ray Chapman's death at the hands of Carl Mays and the traditional dirty gray ball in August 1920—a horrifying event that started the practice of playing with a clean, fresh ball instead of waiting for the ushers to retrieve well-worn foul balls from the stands. All these events helped bring about the new era, but everything takes a backseat to the exploits of one man: Babe Ruth, who was at the center of the home-run volcano. And at his side were two pitching skunks who shared second billing in baseball's transformation.

The Babe tied for the AL home-run lead with 11 in 1918 as a pitcher and part-time outfielder for the Red Sox and began 1919 with a bang in the second inning of an exhibition game against the Giants on April 4. Facing string-bean right-hander Columbia George Smith in Tampa for his first time at bat that spring, Ruth hit a ball so hard and so far that *New York Tribune* reporter Bill McGeehan claimed "it came down coated with ice." The Giants' right fielder Ross Youngs took a few sportswriters on a scavenger hunt to the place where he had retrieved the ball, and this group, organized by Fred Lieb, concluded that the ball came to a stop 625 feet from home plate. Boston's manager Ed Barrow estimated 579 feet, while John McGraw authoritatively claimed it a 587-foot homer. The exact distance didn't matter; Babe Ruth became the nation's passion at a time when it desperately needed diversion. World War I had recently ended, the Spanish flu had killed more than half a million Americans, and most of the U.S. workers seemed to greet the 1919 year by going on strike.

Fans flocked to ballparks, enraptured by Ruth and fantasizing home runs. And though the Babe delivered during the exhibition season—hitting four in one game against the Baltimore Orioles, perhaps the greatest minor-league team ever—his bat went on strike once the season began. As the end of May approached, he had only two home runs—and one was an inside-the-park job that could easily have been scored a single and three-base error. But on May 30, Ruth changed all that with one swing of the bat. He hit a prodigious shot in Philadelphia off the Athletics' hurler Scott Perry and never looked back. Ruth went on a power rampage that didn't stop until the abbreviated 140-game postwar season came to a close. When the dust cleared, Ruth had become the first truly modern ball player. His 29 home runs shattered the AL record of 16 set in 1902 by Socks Seybold and eclipsed Ned Williamson's NL mark of 27 set in 1884—a season with such diluted talent that we labeled it the "Year of the Skunk" in Chapter 2.

Ruth hit four grand slams in 1919, *still* the Red Sox's record. But he saved the best for 1920, his first year as a Yankee, when he nearly doubled his home-run mark by hitting 54. The new era had begun. Just as Amos Rusie's blend of power and wildness forced the pitching distance to be stretched to 60 feet 6 inches to usher in a new era in 1893, the powerful Ruth almost single-handedly changed the face of baseball in 1920. We say "almost" because he got some help from a couple of hurlers with Skunk Stearns credentials—Columbia George Smith and Scott Perry.

Smith, traded by the Giants to the Phillies fewer than two months after Ruth's mammoth blast, tied for the Skunk Stearns trophy in 1921 with Roy Wilkinson when Tweedle Dee and Tweedle Dum had identical seasons: 4–20 with ERAs of about 5.00. Smith's four wins that year included a 4–0 shutout of the Braves in which he gave up a dozen hits. Columbia George wasn't a one-shot wonder, though; he also competed for the title of worst pitcher of the era, with a 41–81 record and lifetime winning percentage of .336.

Perry was a runner-up for our Asa Brainard Humpty-Dumpty Award. He began his career like a star on the rise, winning 20 and leading the AL in complete games and innings pitched for the last-place Athletics in 1918. He stumbled to records of 4–17 and 11–25 the next two seasons, coming in a close second in both Skunk Stearns derbies, first to Harry Harper (6–21) and then to Speed Martin (4–15). But Perry's fate, like Columbia George Smith's, was being on the wrong end of a Ruth blast that turned the dead-ball era into the long-ball era. And Perry was involved in the politics of the time when he got in the middle of a "Who owns Perry?" dispute between the Boston Braves and Connie Mack's Athletics. The Braves thought that Perry's 20-win season was a portent of things to come and remembered a technical claim they had to him. Though Perry wound up as the booby prize when the Athletics were allowed to keep him (his 25 defeats remain a franchise single-season record), there was an amazing amount of fallout from the incident. NL President John Tener resigned, and AL President Ban Johnson—once the darling of the owners—incurred their wrath, which paved the way for his downfall. The authority of the National Commission, then the major league's governing body, was drastically weakened, speeding Landis' ascendancy to the commissioner's throne.

The Philadelphia Connection

The list of Skunk Stearns winners from 1920 to 1946 (see the table on page 80) includes such familiar names as Baseball Hall-of-Famers Jesse Haines and Red Ruffing and Cincinnati star Paul Derringer, along with some unknowns like Lefty Weinert and Ken Chase. Derringer won his Skunk for a 7–27 reord in 1933 and lost over 20 games the next year, but the blazing fastballer flip-flopped his career by winning 20 or more games four different times and retiring with 223 victories. Speaking of flip-flops, the highlight of the list is surely the three trophies won by 273-game winner Ruffing, something he accomplished in a five-year span, but that no one else has ever done. We'll come back to that devilish feat in a bit, but right now let's focus on the second highlight of the list: the flood of flops from Philly.

Starting with Columbia George Smith in 1921 and continuing through Lou Knerr in 1946, no fewer than a dozen pitchers from Philadelphia claimed Skunk Stearns trophies, eight Phils and four A's. The year 1936 was the quintessential season when we awarded Skunk Stearns trophies to both the A's Gordon Rhodes and the Phils' Joe Bowman, each 9–20 and posting nearly identical stats in every department.

In other seasons, Philadelphia hurlers finished 1–2 in our balloting. Dick Barrett (8–20) beat out Phillies' teammate Charley Schanz (4–15) for the 1945 Skunk Stearns Award because Barrett had a much higher ERA. We spoke to 72-year-old Schanz, now living in California, about his playing days. He had a good rookie season (13–16, 3.32 ERA) for the last-place Phils in 1944 and was easily the team's ace. He tumbled in 1945, coinciding with a bout of yellow jaundice ("The food wasn't wholesome, and I was sick and weak"), though it's hard to blame a liver infection for his failure to win more than six games in any year after his first.

The bespectacled, burly right-hander threw sinkers and sliders and got a lot of ground balls, but obviously that wasn't enough. So he did a bit of experimenting that proved fruitless: "I tried the spitter, but I could never get the damn thing over," Schanz told us. He was always confused with

Skunk Stearns Winners: 1920–46

Year	Winners	Team	Won	Lost	Percentage	ERA	Adj. ERA	WAT	TPI
1920	Speed Martin	Chicago: NL	4	15	.211	4.83	66	−5.6	−2.3
1921	Roy Wilkinson	Chicago: AL	4	20	.167	5.13	83	−7.4	−1.6
	George Smith	Philadelphia: NL	4	20	.167	4.76	89	−6.4	−2.0
1922	Joe Oeschger	Boston: NL	6	21	.222	5.06	79	−5.4	−2.0
1923	Lefty Weinert	Philadelphia: NL	4	17	.190	5.42	85	−4.6	−1.2
1924	Jesse Haines	St. Louis: NL	8	19	.296	4.41	86	−4.5	−1.7
1925	Red Ruffing	Boston: AL	9	18	.333	5.01	91	+0.6	−1.0
1926	Paul Zahniser	Boston: AL	6	18	.250	4.97	82	−2.2	−1.3
1927	Jack Scott	Philadelphia: NL	9	21	.300	5.09	81	−1.6	−1.5
1928	Red Ruffing	Boston: AL	10	25	.286	3.89	106	−4.8	+1.5
1929	Red Ruffing	Boston: AL	9	22	.290	4.86	88	−4.1	−0.7
1930	Claude Willoughby	Philadelphia: NL	4	17	.190	7.59	72	−4.9	−3.1
	Dutch Henry	Chicago: AL	2	17	.105	4.88	95	−7.2	0.0
1931	Pat Caraway	Chicago: AL	10	24	.294	6.22	68	−4.0	−4.3
1932	Milt Gaston	Chicago: AL	7	17	.292	4.00	108	−1.3	+0.8
1933	Paul Derringer	St. Louis/Cincinnati: NL	7	27	.206	3.30	103	−8.6	+0.3
1934	Si Johnson	Cincinnati: NL	7	22	.241	5.22	78	−4.9	−3.0
1935	Ben Cantwell	Boston: NL	4	25	.138	4.61	82	−7.1	−1.2
1936	Gordon Rhodes	Philadelphia: AL	9	20	.310	5.74	89	−1.7	−1.6
	Joe Bowman	Philadelphia: NL	9	20	.310	5.04	90	−1.9	−1.3
1937	Chief Hogsett	St. Louis: AL	6	19	.240	6.29	77	−2.7	−2.5
1938	Hugh Mulcahy	Philadelphia: NL	10	20	.333	4.61	84	+0.9	−2.2
1939	Vern Kennedy	Detroit/St. Louis: AL	9	20	.310	5.80	84	0.0	−2.0
1940	George Caster	Philadelphia: AL	4	19	.174	6.56	68	−6.2	−4.0
1941	Ken Chase	Washington: AL	6	18	.250	5.08	80	−5.8	−2.2
1942	Lefty Hoerst	Philadelphia: NL	4	16	.200	5.20	64	−3.0	−3.0
1943	Lum Harris	Philadelphia: AL	7	21	.250	4.20	81	−3.4	−1.9
1944	Roger Wolff	Washington: AL	4	15	.211	4.99	65	−4.9	−2.7
1945	Dick Barrett	Philadelphia: NL	8	20	.286	5.38	71	−0.6	−3.1
1946	Lou Knerr	Philadelphia: AL	3	16	.158	5.40	66	−5.0	−2.9

Shown here as a member of the Red Sox in 1950, Charley Schanz, the long-time minor leaguer and near-skunk in 1945, spent most of his major-league career with the futile Phillies of the 1940s (photo courtesy of Charley Schanz).

lefty Bobby Shantz because of their similar names, but no one confused near-skunk Charley with Bobby, the AL's 1952 Most Valuable Player, when they toed the rubber.

Schanz had the following capsule summary of his Phils' teammate Dick Barrett, who edged him for the 1945 Skunk Stearns Award: "He was

Though best known for pitching all 26 innings of a 1–1 tie against Brooklyn, Joe Oeschger also won two Skunk Stearns trophies—one in the Dead-Ball Era and one in the Long-Ball Era (photo courtesy of George Brace).

a good guy, didn't make many friends. When he was on the mound, he was all business." Too bad Barrett's business failed.

Two Phils had great nicknames—Claude "Weeping Willie" Willoughby, co-winner in 1930, and Hugh "Losing Pitcher" Mulcahy, the 1938 Skunk Stearns winner. Weeping Willie rarely finished what he started during his skunk season, so the Phillies' team captain Fresco Thompson once brought a lineup card to the umpire with the pitcher's slot listing the inevitable: "Willoughby—and others."

Losing Pitcher Mulcahy—so nicknamed by the Philadelphia press because the ticker line scores of his games, sent via Western Union, invariably ended with "L. P. Mulcahy"—averaged 10 wins and 19 losses from 1937 to 1940. He shocked the baseball world by being picked for the 1940 NL All-Star team and ended July with a 12–10 record. He was on the verge of shedding his humiliating nickname when disaster struck in the form of a 12-game losing streak. He managed to win his last start of the season, but his 22 losses led the NL. He surprised no one when he chose to escape baseball for a year, rejecting a deferment to join the military in the spring of 1941. But the United States declared war on Japan a few months before his planned discharge, and Mulcahy became the first major-league player to enter World War II. True to his luck, he was one of the last to leave.

And it wasn't just the Skunk Stearns winners who brought shame to Philadelphia. There were an unusual number of "Skunks for an Inning" from the City of Brotherly Love. Three Phillies suffered through nightmares in the 1930s and 1940s: Reggie Grabowski gave up 11 hits in the ninth inning of a 1934 contest; Hal Kelleher, a Phillie from 1935 to 1938, once gave up 12 runs in a single inning; and Charlie Bicknell surrendered four home runs and 18 total bases in one fateful inning in 1948. The Phils and Athletics also competed with each other for being on the wrong end of history-making events. The first major-league night game was played on May 24, 1935, in Cincinnati. In a matchup of mid–1930s Skunk Stearns winners, Paul Derringer of the Reds beat Joe Bowman of the Phillies 2–1. Not to be outdone, the Athletics hosted the first AL night game at Shibe Park five years later and promptly lost to Cleveland, 8–3, in ten innings.

The 12 Philadelphia Skunks can almost add Joe Oeschger to their ranks. The man who nearly all baseball fans have heard of because he, like Leon Cadore, pitched all 26 innings of the longest major-league game ever played (a 1–1 tie between Boston and Brooklyn in 1920), was a two-time Skunk Stearns winner. He won his first award in 1918, when he was 6–18, and his second in 1922, when he dropped 13 straight en route to a 6–21 mark. He was a Phillie, naturally, when he won his first trophy, but had moved to the Braves when he became the first pitcher since the Spiders' Jim Hughey to win two trophies. He was traded by the Phils to the Giants and then from the Giants to the Braves, all during 1919. And who did the Phils get for Oeschger? None other than Columbia George Smith in a skunk-for-skunk deal.

Oeschger pitched a single-game record of 21 straight scoreless innings in that marathon 1–1 tie; hurled another complete game in a 20-inning 9–9 tie against Burleigh Grimes in 1919, became just the fourth major-league

He wasn't a Skunk winner, but Ray Benge was part of the contingent of pitchers from Philadelphia teams that reliably posted losing records during the long-ball era (photo courtesy of Ray Benge).

pitcher of the century to hurl a perfect inning (three strikeouts on nine pitches, against the Phils, of course) in 1921, was a 20-game winner in 1920, roomed with the legendary Jim Thorpe, graduated from Stanford University, and was once traded for Casey Stengel. But posterity has not been kind to him, even before we honored him twice with Skunk Stearns Awards. The 1988 edition of the *Baseball Encyclopedia* listed his year-by-year and career stats without a flaw and got his date and place of birth correct, but it credited his record to Robert Arthur "Joe" O'Farrell. Robert Arthur "Bob" O'Farrell caught over 1,000 games, but there was no Joe O'Farrell. And in the 1988 *Baseball Encyclopedia,* there was no Joe Oeschger. Even in the team-by-team stats in a different part of the encyclopedia, J. O'Farrell was named whenever J. Oeschger was supposed to appear. Oeschger disappeared without a trace, not to be found until the 1990 edition corrected the error, in the ultimate insult ever paid to a skunk.

What were the opposing hitters like for a Philadelphia pitcher in the long-ball era? "All tough & no easy," wrote Ray Benge, a Phillie from 1928 to 1932, in response to our questionnaire. Benge (101–130) pitched a shutout in his first major-league start for Cleveland in 1925; had some good seasons; and once struck out 13 in a game, then the Phillies' record. But he had an 8–18 record for the Phillies in his first full major league season in 1928 and followed that up with the highest ERA on the team's staff the next year (6.29), so he still qualifies as a bit of an expert on Phillies' failures. Plus, his parents (Texans, not Pennsylvanians) must have had ESP when they gave him his unusual middle name: Adelphia. If only they'd named him Phil instead of Raymond!

The John Cassidy Root Canal Award: Frank Hoerst

When it comes to brief careers, it should surprise no one that a Phillie was at the bottom of the barrel for the long-ball era—6 foot 3 inch Frank "Lefty" Hoerst (rhymes with *worst*). Hoerst pitched for Philadelphia from 1940 to 1947, minus a 3½-year time-out to serve as a gunnery officer in the navy, and compiled a .233 winning percentage (10–33) with a 5.17 ERA; he walked one man for every two innings he pitched. Hoerst was 8–26 when he joined the navy and 2–7 after the war and is the clear-cut winner of our John Cassidy Root Canal Award. Si Johnson told us that he remembered his Phillies' teammate as a "big left-handed pitcher who wasn't too fast for one thing and didn't have too much stuff."

We had an interesting telephone conversation with the candid and friendly 73-year-old Frank Hoerst. He told us, "a lot of people used to say 'oh boy, oh boy, Hoerst had a terrible record in '42—before he was away in the service he lost 16 games.' And I'd say, 'Wait a minute, if I'd stayed for the whole season, I'd have lost 20 games.' And they'd say, 'What's so good about being a 20-game loser?' And I'd say, 'I would have been famous, like Bucky Walters who lost 20 for the Phils. He was traded to Cincinnati, and became the Most Valuable Player in the league.'" Well, Hoerst's 4–16 mark in 1942 didn't gain him much fame, but it earned him our Skunk Stearns Award.

Hoerst made the majors because "the Phillies needed pitching very badly and I had an absolutely sensational year for Pensacola in the Southeastern League," he told us. "I won about 18 games just in the last three months of the year." But with the Phils he never topped the four games he won in 1942. "I was known back then as a Dodger killer," he said, referring to a nickname he earned in 1941 as a 3–10 hurler who beat the World Series–bound Dodgers twice. "I think I stayed in the big leagues because I pitched well against the Dodgers. I had a few good games against the Cubs. But I could memorize every game I won because they were so few."

Lefty Hoerst's first victory in the majors caused a near-riot. "I was just a kid, we were playing Pittsburgh, and we were getting beat seven or eight to nothing. It was bad. I was just mopping up the game and we scored eight or nine runs in the ninth inning—that was my first win. Frankie Frisch managed Pittsburgh. He and an umpire by the name of George Magerkurth were always at odds, and Frisch just dashed out of the dugout when we scored the winning run in the ninth and laid down on home plate outstretched and he wouldn't move. I tell you, it was quite a scene."

None of his wins came easy. "I was a standard fastball pitcher," he said. "I had a fair curve. The slider was used, but back then we called it a half-assed curve. I think my greatest weakness was that I didn't have the talent. It wasn't the lack of work because I always worked hard at my job. I just didn't have enough skills as some other people, but I tried to make use of what I had."

Lefty couldn't pinpoint the worst game he ever pitched "because there were too many to remember. But the most embarrassing was that I was ready to go away in the service, and they gave me a Frank Hoerst day— and I couldn't get the Cardinals out in the first inning. Those are the things that can be embarrassing, when your friends and neighbors are all there and you blow it all." One of the last games he pitched before leaving for the military was a two-hitter on September 2 that he managed to transform into a loss when he walked four batters in the eighth inning and made a poor throw to home plate; Johnny Podgajny didn't provide much relief when he hit two batters with the bases loaded.

Lefty has remained a close friend of Hugh "Losing Pitcher" Mulcahy, who was part of Hoerst's career from start to finish.

"I'll never forget the fact," Lefty told us, "that when I joined the Phillies I'm out there feeling like a bump on a log. You know, what do I do next out here? Nobody's teaching me. Nobody's guiding me, and Hughie Mulcahy came over to me and introduced himself and said, 'Look, it looks like you don't know what the hell to do,' and he says, 'Just follow me,' and I felt comfortable and I felt great."

Lefty Hoerst was the model of consistency in 1941–42, when he combined for a 7–26 mark: Each season his ERA was 5.20, and opposing batters had a .357 in base percentage (photo courtesy of George Brace).

Nine years later, while wallowing in the minors, he knew it was time to leave baseball. "I quit very suddenly," Hoerst said. "As a matter of fact it was on a phone call with my good friend Hughie, who had been my roommate both with the Phillies and with Memphis. He called me one day and said, "I'll pick you up on the way to spring training.' This would be in Memphis in '49 and I said, 'Keep going Mul—I'm not going.' Two days later I went to work for a brewery."

Hearst knows he was a good basketball referee: "I refereed for about 20 years—high school, college, NBA. It was great to be getting paid to do something that you like to do and keep in shape, and I did a great job at it."

And he knows he was not much of a pitcher. We asked him how much he would earn if he were pitching today, in the age of megabucks?

"$1 over the minimum," Lefty said. And who was the worst pitcher he ever saw? "Me."

The Joe Hardy Sell-Your-Soul Award: Red Ruffing

When it comes to Joe Hardy winners, the all-time champion is Charles "Red" Ruffing, a man who could legitimately challenge the fictional Joe Hardy for the honor. As a Red Sox hurler in the 1920s, he won an unprecedented three Skunk Stearns trophies, averaging an 8–19 record from 1925 to 1929. Had he kept up that pace, Ruffing would have beaten Mulcahy to the nickname "Losing Pitcher." But a trade to the Yankees in May 1930, and a possible visit from the devil, changed all that. Ruffing's losing ways stopped overnight. He had already started off 1930 in the usual way and was 0–3 when he joined the Yankees, but he won 15 of 20 decisions with New York. Even his hitting improved dramatically, from .273 to .374. One of the best hitting pitchers ever, Ruffing's combined batting average of .364 in 1930 is second among pitchers only to Walter Johnson's .433 in 1925.

How drastic was Ruffing's turnabout? Take a look at his record with the Red Sox versus the Yankees (he was also 3–5 in 1947 with the White Sox for an overall mark of 273–225):

Team	Won	Lost	%	ERA	Adj. ERA	WAT	TPI
Red Sox (1924–May 1930)	39	96	.289	4.61	94	−11.7	−2.1
Yankees (May 1930–1946)	231	124	.651	3.48	115	+15.5	+30.0

The fastball pitcher with a one-pitch repertoire made a turnabout that defied rational explanation. He was much *worse* than his inept Red Sox teams, winning nearly 12 fewer games than the average pitcher would have won for the same team; yet he was considerably better than the average hurler on the top-notch Yankee teams. In fact, the powerful right-hander teamed with Lefty Gomez on the mound to help make the Yankees so great. Ruffing had four straight 20-win seasons from 1936 to 1939, winning two-thirds of his starts. At about the same time (1938–41), a young

Bob Feller won 93 games in four years, but couldn't match Ruffing's mark; neither could Sandy Koufax in his glory years. And despite being in continual pain from a coal-mining accident as a teenager that cost him four toes on his left foot, Ruffing won seven and lost two in World Series competitions.

So what happened after Red Sox owner Harry Frazee traded Red Ruffing to New York for utility-man Cedric Durst a decade after he gave the Yankees a gift called Babe Ruth? How did one man change so much so fast? Longtime Senators' first baseman Joe Judge, who played against Ruffing for years, was quoted as saying, "We always thought Red was dogging it with the Red Sox." That doesn't sound like the Ruffing who was always esteemed by the press and described so often as a fierce competitor. As a player, he put himself through a hellish conditioning regimen even though it meant intense pain in his left foot. As a senior citizen, with the help of his wife Pauline, he heroically battled two strokes, 13 years in a wheelchair, and the ravages of cancer before going down fighting at the age of 80.

Ruffing was once challenged by Athletics' pitcher George Earnshaw, first by verbal taunts, then by a ball in the neck. Ruffing ignored Earnshaw, except to fan him on three pitches, and then proceeded to make the A's hitters (Foxx, Cochrane, and others) dance, sprawl, and scramble in the dirt for the rest of the game. Even at age 36, Ruffing stood his ground against a maliciously playful Luke Appling, who deliberately fouled 24 of Ruffing's pitches in a single time at bat before drawing a walk.

Cedric Durst played one season in Boston before calling it quits, causing Frazee—a man who had already peddled Ruth, Carl Mays, Herb Pennock, and Everett Scott to the Yankees to help finance his theatrical productions—to be crucified once more for ruining the Red Sox. But if you take a look at Ruffing's record in Boston, it's hard to fault Frazee. More incomprehensible was the Yankees' interest in a pitcher who stunk against the entire AL and was at his worst against New York, losing 14 of 15 decisions. (The career record of our Joe Hardy winner against the Yankees was 1–16, counting his 0–2 mark with the White Sox.) But Yankee manager Miller Huggins liked Ruffing's strength and durability and told Ruffing one afternoon in 1929 not to let the Red Sox make an outfielder out of him because, "Someday you may be with us." Huggins died that year, but his prophecy came true eight months later.

Ruffing was an individualist, no question about that. The March 1988 issue of the *SABR Bulletin,* the newsletter of the Society for American Baseball Research, listed about three dozen celebrated holdouts—from Charley Sweasy, who wanted an extra $200 from the Cincinnati Red Stockings in 1870, to Dick Allen, who wanted more money from the 1972 Chicago White Sox. The reasons for the holdouts are listed as well, and these

cago White Sox. The reasons for the holdouts are listed as well, and these are invariably "more money," "cut in pay," or "disliked contract." Only one man's reason had nothing to do with salary: Red Ruffing, who held out in 1937 because he "wanted to see the Coronation."

Despite his damaged foot, Ruffing served in the armed forces for two years during World War II, a hitch that many believe cost him 300 wins and an automatic ticket to Cooperstown. By the time he was elected to the Baseball Hall of Fame in a special run-off ballot in 1967, his last year of eligibility, Ruffing was a bitter man. Yet perhaps he should have won 300 games even with his patriotic two-year absence from the major leagues. At least that's what Pete Palmer's stats suggest. Palmer believes that runs translate to wins; pitchers who get a lot of runs ought to win more games than those who pitch for teams with rotten offenses. This reasoning makes sense. On the basis of the scoring power of the Red Sox and Yankees during the seasons Ruffing pitched for them, Palmer calculated that the right-hander called Rufus by the media ought to have won 303 and lost 195—a 30-game swing from his actual won-lost record. Palmer calculated that only two pitchers in modern history lagged by as much as 25 to 30 games from their expected win total—Ruffing and Bert Blyleven, although Blyleven was in mid-career when Palmer did his study.

Ruffing got a lot of runs, but even with the Yankees, he gave up a bundle. In fact, no one has ever given up as many runs as the 2,117 he yielded in his career, and no pitcher in the Baseball Hall of Fame has a higher career ERA than Red's 3.80. Bob Feller said that Ruffing was skilled at pacing himself, going at top speed only when the chips were down. Ruffing

Above: **Red Ruffing, the future Hall of Famer, had little to smile about as a three-time Skunk Stearns winner for the Red Sox, although a trade to the Yankees and a possible bargain with the devil changed all that (photo courtesy of George Brace).**

would win 9–7 or 3–2, whatever it took to get into the win column. According to Palmer's stats, Ruffing may have paced himself out of 30 or so wins.

Tommy Lasorda may bleed Dodger blue, but no one was more devoted to a team than Red Ruffing was to the Yankees. He closed out his career with the White Sox in 1947, but his heart was still in New York—even though the Yankees dropped him in a heartbeat when he broke his kneecap the year before. Though still technically on Chicago's roster, he paid his own way to New York and worked for free in September 1947 to help the Yankees during the World Series. He told *The Sporting News*: "I'm a little worried about the Yankees' hitting. If I can get in uniform and do anything to help their batting eyes by letting them tee off on some of my fat pitches, it will make me feel better all during the off-season." Considering Ruffing's lifetime record against his old mates, batting practice must have seemed like old times. Or it may have reminded him of the 1940 All-Star game, when the NL treated him like a batting practice pitcher by jumping off to a 3–0 lead before he retired a batter in the first inning.

And Ruffing must have had a little more déjà vu in 1962. Everyone knows that Casey Stengel was the first manager of the amazin' Mets, but how many fans recall the name of the Mets' first pitching coach? Red Ruffing, though only for the legendary 1962 season. He nurtured and trained a staff that included Skunk Stearns winner Craig Anderson and featured a 10–24 Roger Craig, an 8–20 Al Jackson, and an 8–19 Jay Hook. Though the scene was New York, the Mets' big three must have evoked memories of his years with the Red Sox; their won-lost records match almost precisely the marks he posted to win his own three Skunk Stearns trophies (10–25, 9–22, 9–18). But, ultimately, Ruffing is remembered for the good times. He faced Lefty Grove in the opening game of the 1939 season in Yankee Stadium against the Red Sox in what proved to be an historic occasion. Lou Gehrig was playing in his 2,123rd consecutive game, and last opener, for the Yankees and would leave the lineup for good seven games later. A young Boston outfielder, Ted Williams, made his major-league debut in that same game, striking out twice against Ruffing before lacing his first hit, a double off the right-field fence. It was the only time that Gehrig's and Williams' names appeared in the same box score.

In his autobiography, Williams recalled his thoughts about Ruffing as he watched him warm up that day: "A big guy, I mean *big*, but a real easy-going style, like he didn't give a damn. When he came in with it, though, the ball whistled." The Spendid Splinter was furious after Ruffing struck him out in his first two times at bat, both times on high fastballs. A teammate came over to taunt the rookie, and Williams snapped, "Screw you. This is one guy"—pointing to Ruffing—"I *know* I am going to hit, and if he puts it in the same place again I'm riding it out of here." Ruffing did, and Williams' double missed the bleachers by a foot.

But 1939 was one of Ruffing's finest years as a Yankee; it ended with a 2–1 triumph over Paul Derringer in the World Series opener, setting in motion a four-game sweep of Cincinnati. After failing so miserably in Boston, Ruffing won 231 games for New York, the team record until Whitey Ford set the standard with 236. Bill James, in his *Historical Abstract*, asked, "If you drag down the level of a bad pitching staff, how can you possibly raise the level of a good pitching staff?" He added, "I have yet to hear an explanation that would explain . . . Ruffing." Maybe a Faustian bargain isn't so farfetched.

The Asa Brainard Humpty-Dumpty Award: Sad Sam Gray

Sad Sam Gray not only had to suffer through most of his career with the St. Louis Browns, but his sudden, rapid decline after a half-dozen seasons at the top made him the runaway winner of our Asa Brainard Humpty-Dumpty Award. Gray's career was the exact inverse of Red Ruffing's: Sad Sam starred in the 1920s, but fell apart as soon as the bell tolled 1930. His flop coincided so precisely with Ruffing's rise that one may wonder if the devil didn't just buy Ruffing's soul, but went ahead and swapped it for Gray's. How else can you make sense out of Gray's pre–1930 performance, when he showed amazing tenacity? The eccentric curveballer started off a 1926 game for the Athletics with 15 straight balls, yet won the contest 3–1 on a two-hitter, and he finished 16–8 in 1925 despite a broken thumb on his pitching hand and his wife's sudden death.

The right-hander was traded after the 1927 season from Connie Mack's second-place A's to the Browns, but he still won 20 games his first season in St. Louis and followed his 20–12 mark with an 18–15 record in 1929. Then, coinciding with the Wall Street crash, the roof fell in on Gray. Gray went from the AL co-leader with four shutouts in 1929 to a 4–15 record in 1930 and a league-leading 24 losses in 1931. His 11–24 record that season challenged, but fell just short of, Pat Caraway's (10–24) claim to the Skunk Stearns throne. As the Great Depression hit the United States in the 1930s, Sam's career just became sadder and sadder. The vital statistics on Gray's two-faced career:

Years	Won	Lost	Percentage	ERA	Adjusted ERA	WAT	TPI
1924–29	82	60	.577	3.64	115	+7.3	+8.3
1930–33	29	55	.345	5.05	96	−8.2	−2.2

Ruffing and Gray debuted within a month of each other in 1924. At the end of the 1929 season, which one seemed bound for the Baseball Hall of Fame? Neither, but a betting man would have put a lot more money on Gray than on Ruffing. If you combine Gray's 1920s record with Ruffing's records for the 1930s and 1940s, you get a colorful pitcher named Red Gray with a career mark of 316–189 and an automatic first-ballot ticket to Cooperstown. But if you add Ruffing's Red Sox record to Gray's 1930s stats, you're looking at the notorious Sad Sam Ruffing, a 68–151 pitcher who would be the leading candidate for our Skunk Stearns of the Century award in Chapter 7.

We've already mentioned Scott Perry as a runner-up for the Asa Brainard Award when he fell from winning 20 games as a rookie for a last-place team in 1918 to an 18–48 record the rest of his career. Another runner-up is Horace "Hod" Lisenbee, who once gave up 26 hits in one game for the A's against the White Sox in 1936. But that was nearly a decade after Lisenbee starred as a rookie in 1927 for the third-place Washington Senators, when he not only led the staff with an 18–9 record and the league with four shutouts, but he beat the Yankees of Murderers' Row fame five times. Though he gave up the Babe's 59th home run that year, who could have predicted that he would win only two games the next year and have a 19–49 record after his rookie season—almost a carbon copy of Scott Perry's career.

And Russ Van Atta, also an Asa Brainard contender, followed the same pattern—a good rookie season, followed by sudden, continual disaster. In his major-league debut for the 1933 Yankees, he pitched a shutout and went 4 for 4; he was 12–4 that year. Then, he had five straight losing seasons for the Yankees and Browns (21–37 overall) and retired with a lifetime ERA of 5.60.

Cherokee Fisher Rookie Award: Ike Pearson

We've just given awards to pitchers whose careers went in opposite directions. Ruffing started at the bottom of a well and wound up in Cooperstown, while Gray fell into the well and drowned. Our next award goes to a man who kept going to the well, only to find out that it was always dry—"Mississippi Ike" Pearson, one of the most consistent pitchers in major-league history. The right-hander spent virtually all his career with the Phillies and was 2–13 as a rookie in 1939 with a 5.76 ERA, to win our Cherokee Fisher Rookie Award. He didn't get any better; he couldn't get any worse. The University of Mississippi graduate was rushed to the majors without the benefit of minor-league experience and simply maintained his rookie pace for the rest of his career. His won-lost record:

Year	Won	Lost	Percentage
1939	2	13	.133
1940	3	14	.176
1941	4	14	.222
1942, 1946, and 1948	4	9	.308
Career	13	50	.206

No pitcher in baseball history with 50 or more decisions ever compiled a lower winning percentage. Pearson undercut Mike McDermott's .226 (12–41 from 1889 to 1897) and Dolly Gray's .227 (15–51 from 1909 to 1911) with percentage points to spare and was at his worst as a starter. Pearson, the relief pitcher, was a modest 6–10 with eight saves. But Pearson, the starter, had a 7–40 record (.149) in the 54 games he started. His schizophrenic performance was most evident in 1941, when he led NL relievers with a 2.07 ERA in 36 appearances, while posting a 4–4 record with six saves; he also started ten games and lost them all.

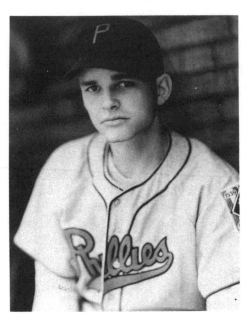

In the most amazing pairing of roommates since Jack Nabors and Tom Sheehan went a combined 2–36 for the A's in 1916, Pearson shared a room with Lefty Hoerst with the Phillies in 1940. Lefty, winner of our John Cassidy Root Canal Award, teamed with Ike for a deadly career mark of 23–83. Ten-game winner Hoerst was evidently impressed with Pearson's 13 career wins, though. "I thought Ike was a good pitcher," he said, without a trace of sarcasm. Si Johnson had a more realistic appraisal of Pearson: "He'd pitch pretty good ball for a while. Then he'd get into a slump or whatever would happen, I don't know, but then he couldn't do

Above: **"Mississippi Ike" Pearson had the worst winning percentage in history (.206) for pitchers with at least 50 decisions (photo courtesy of George Brace).**

nothing. He just wasn't consistent at all; he'd have a good game and then he'd have three or four bad ones."

Pearson joined the U.S. Marine Corps after the 1942 season, taking a 10–47 record into the war. He commented then: "I want to be on a first-place team." His postwar record of 3–3 with the Phils and Chicago White Sox lifted his percentage above .200, but he pitched mostly in the minor leagues after the war, calling it quits in 1951. Could Ike do anything well? Hoerst told us that Pearson was a great hitter—in golf.

Pearson received stiff competition for the Cherokee Fisher Award from the Athletics' Roy Moore, who debuted in 1920 with a 1–13 record and 4.68 ERA. He lost his first 13 before he finally earned his only win, but we gave Pearson the rookie award because of his one-run-higher ERA.

Worst Single Season for the Era: Ben Cantwell

The home-run avalanche during the long-ball era produced some awful seasons for a handful of shell-shocked hurlers. Five different pitchers had the worst stat in the five categories that we've used to define pathetic pitching, as shown in a table at the end of the chapter. And most of these leaders posted world-class numbers. Ben Cantwell (4–25) lost 21 more games than he won, to tie with Happy Jack Townsend for the century's worst mark. Paul Derringer's WAT of −8.6 was the third worst of the 20th century, while Lefty Hoerst's adjusted ERA of 64 and Dutch Henry's .105 winning percentage each cracked the top ten. But the prize goes to Pat Caraway, a 6 foot 4 inch bean pole with a fair curveball, who was known for his strange, accordionlike windup that nearly doubled over his frame just before he let go of the ball. Caraway's TPI of −4.3 was the worst of the century for pitchers with at least 15 losses.

Cantwell made three of the five lists of worsts for his era, as did Dutch Henry and Roy Wilkinson. Although Paul Derringer was on only two lists, he ranked first and second, making him a formidable contender for the

Order, Pitcher, and Year*	Won	Lost	Percentage	ERA	Adj. ERA	WAT	TPI
1. Ben Cantwell (1935)	4	25	.138	4.61	82	−7.1	−1.2
2. Paul Derringer (1933)	7	27	.206	3.30	103	−8.6	+0.3
3. Pat Caraway (1931)	10	24	.294	6.22	68	−4.0	−4.3
4. Dutch Henry (1930)	2	17	.105	4.88	95	−7.2	0.0
5T. George Caster (1940)	4	19	.174	6.56	68	−6.2	−4.0
5T. Roy Wilkinson (1921)	4	20	.167	5.13	83	−7.4	−1.6
5T. Jimmy Ring (1928)	4	17	.190	6.40	67	−3.7	−3.8

*T=tie.

In 1933, Ben Cantwell won 20 games and led the National League in winning percentage. The next two years he was a combined 9–36, including a memorable 4–25 in 1935 (photo courtesy of George Brace).

worst pitching season of his era. The long-ball era's worst seasons are listed below in order; all ranked among the 25 worst of the century.

Ben Cantwell is the champ. In 1927, he had a 25–5 record (.833 winning percentage) for Jacksonville in the Southeastern League, the highest minor-league percentage that year for pitchers with 20 or more decisions. He earned a promotion to the Giants in August and was traded to the Braves the next season. It was in Boston that he nearly reversed his minor-league record, when he compiled the worst season of his era. But Cantwell enjoyed his moments in the sun in the major leagues before he plunged into skunk territory. He was a top-notch relief pitcher for the Braves in 1932, leading the NL with 12 relief wins and earning a spot in the 1933 starting rotation. He didn't disappoint, leading the league with a .667 percentage (20–10) and trailing only King Carl Hubbell in wins. Then the bottom dropped out when he sunk first to a 5–11 record in 1934 and then to his landmark 4–25 season, spiced by 13 straight losses.

'Oom Paul Derringer's 7–27 record in 1933 (0–2 for the Cardinals, then 7–25 for the Reds after being included in a trade for Leo Durocher and Dutch Henry) was the second worst of the era. But Derringer impressed his own bosses, even in defeat. After putting the finishing touches on his 7–27 mark, he was given a $1,500 raise by Reds' owner Powell Crosby, not too shabby in those days. And the high-kicking fireballer with an over-the-top delivery later had the great satisfaction of reversing his record with the Reds; he was 25–7 in 1939, to lead Cincinnati to the first of two pennants in a row. The control artist also had three other 20-win seasons and 223 lifetime wins and won the first major-league night game in Cincinnati in 1935. In 1940, he was the winning pitcher in the All-Star game and won the fourth and seventh games of the World Series to bring the Reds their first world's championship since their tainted 1919 title. But he was also a good loser. After Red Ruffing defeated him 2–1 in the opening game of the 1939 World Series, Derringer hurried to the umpires' dressing room and told a shocked Bill McGowan, "That's the greatest job of calling balls and strikes I've ever seen. You didn't miss a single call all afternoon."

Derringer came full circle from the 20-year-old who tried so hard during his first spring training to convince the Cardinals of their wisdom in signing him: He added an extra inch to his high leg kick—and promptly got the spikes of his left shoe caught in the webbing of his glove!

Pat Caraway, on the way to a 10–24 record in 1931, was also embarrassed on the pitching mound. His niche as the owner of the third worst season of the era and the worst TPI of the century was cemented during a four-day stretch in late July. He pleaded with White Sox manager Donie Bush to take him out of the July 23rd game at Boston, but Bush let him suffer through 11 runs in 4⅔ innings. However, that pounding paled in comparison to the berating Bush gave Caraway between innings of that game. And then, three days later, the lefty was rocked mercilessly by the Yankees in a 22–5 loss, the worst defeat in White Sox history. Caraway was a respectable 10–10 as a rookie in 1930 and accomplished an awesome feat: He struck out Joe Sewell, the hardest man in history to fan, twice in a single game (that occurred on May 26, and Sewell didn't strike out again the rest of the year, finishing with 3 Ks). But Caraway never recovered from the 1931 bombardment; he was gone the next July after losing six of eight decisions and posting a 6.82 ERA.

The Worst Pitchers of the Era:
Ike Pearson, Si Johnson, and Milt Gaston

No pitcher dominated the lists of worst career stats for the 1920–46 era (see the table at the end of this chapter). Milt Gaston lost 67 games more than he won, an all-time record, while Si Johnson had the worst TPI and Ike Pearson had the lowest winning percentage. But no pitcher from this era ranked among the elite in more than two categories.

Les Sweetland had the worst adjusted ERA for pitchers from the long-ball era and holds the single-season record for worst-ever ERA for pitchers appearing in at least 150 innings — 7.71 for the Phillies in 1930. However, Sweetland lost the Skunk Stearns trophy that season to co-winners Dutch Henry of the White Sox and Phils' teammate Claude "Weeping Willie" Willoughby, owner of the second-worst ERA of all time (7.59).

Rube Walberg had a WAT of −19.6, the worst value ever recorded. However, he was eliminated from our worst-pitcher derby because he retired with a winning record, 155–141, mostly with the top-notch Athletics teams of the late 1920s and early 1930s. His negative WAT means that he should have won about 20 more games than he did: The average pitcher on the high-quality teams he pitched for would have come away with a record of 175–121. Of course, when Walberg rested, Lefty Grove often took the mound. After nine years together on the Athletics, Rube couldn't even escape Lefty when he was sent to the Red Sox after the 1933 season; Grove went with him in the deal.

The worst thing for a pitcher's WAT is to be on the same staff with a superstar or two, since his WAT is based on how his team does without him. So Walberg was hurt by Grove's habit of winning nearly 70 percent of his decisions. Pete Palmer recomputed Walberg's WAT in an "as if" fashion — as if Lefty Grove wasn't on his team; Palmer told us that Walberg's WAT was still terrible. Walberg's main problem was control, since he walked more men than he struck out for five straight years. He also holds the record for giving up the most career home runs to Babe Ruth — 17.

As we did with the worst single seasons of the era, we selected the worst careers of the era by examining how well the pitchers fared in the competition for worst pitcher of the 20th century (a story told in gruesome statistical detail in Chapter 7). Three pitchers from the long-ball era, all 6-foot right-handers, were bunched together in that race in a virtual triple deadlock: Si Johnson, Ike Pearson, and Milt Gaston. So we called the race a three-way tie. The records of the *five* worst from the era are shown on the opposite page; all ranked among the 25 worst of the 20th century.

We introduced "Mississippi Ike" Pearson, winner of the Cherokee Fisher Award and told how Hugh "Losing Pitcher" Mulcahy got his nickname; now it's time for Johnson and Gaston and a bit about Russell.

The Worst Pitchers of the Long-Ball Era

Order and Pitcher*	Won	Lost	Percentage	ERA	Adj. ERA	WAT	TPI
1T. Si Johnson	101	165	.380	4.09	92	-9.6	-11.6
1T. Ike Pearson	13	50	.206	4.83	79	-11.1	-6.1
1T. Milt Gaston	97	164	.372	4.55	97	-13.3	-2.7
4. Jack Russell	85	141	.376	4.46	97	-17.0	+0.8
5. Hugh Mulcahy	45	89	.336	4.49	89	-2.0	-4.9

*T = tie.

SI JOHNSON

When you think of a pitcher named Johnson, it doesn't matter how popular that surname is. Only one man comes to a baseball fan's mind: Walter Johnson. But if the Big Train is the epitome of pitching success, than Silas K. Johnson is the inverse, the flip side of success. Walter bowed out of the majors in glory in 1927, retiring with more than 400 wins. Si tiptoed into the NL the next season. Both men were hard throwers who had long careers and often pitched for poor teams. But the resemblance stops there; Walter won 20 or more games a dozen times; Si lost more games than he won, usually many more.

We had a marvelous telephone conversation with the 84-year-old Si Johnson, a man with a robust voice, clear thinking ability, and obvious pride in his baseball past. Si had fond, sometimes humorous, recollections of the bad times as well as the good. We asked if he remembered the worst games he ever pitched.

"I pitched a lot of them that weren't too good, I can tell you that," he said. "I know one day, I left some passes for a couple of friends of mine; I was pitching. They didn't come in until the second inning. I was gone by then; the New York Giants got nine runs in the first inning. So after the game they said, 'I thought you were going to pitch.' I said, 'You've got to come out early to see me work!'"

Johnson concedes that he had to overcome wildness. He told the *Sports Collector's Digest*, "When I first came up I was pretty wild. I had a fair curve, a decent change of pace. But my best pitch was my fastball, of course. I could throw real hard, but I had no idea where the ball was going. As I got a little older I developed more control." Yet, even as a 21-year-old, Si believed in himself. Pat Patterson, his first manager at Rock Island in the Valley League in 1928, told Johnson he was just wasting his time. Si pleaded for a chance to pitch a whole game, and he won a 3–0 exhibition game against Quincy of the Three-I League. He then won six straight games for

Rock Island before losing, with a 19–10 record, and pitched three games for the NL Reds that year.

Johnson blames his losing record in the major leagues mostly on the bad teams he played for. "I had a lot of close ball games," he told us. "It seems like I was on the mound when we just didn't get any runs to work with. In Cincinnati, you had to come pretty close to pitching a shutout to win. I know, once in a while, I'd get a one run lead or something, get ahead one to nothing, and the players that sat on the bench, they'd say, 'It's your lead Si, hang onto it.' Well, it's pretty rough to go nine innings trying to pitch a shutout, you know. And a lot of times it's not just the hitting. We didn't have the best fielding club."

Only two Cincinnati Reds won Skunk Stearns Awards during the 20th century—Paul Derringer in 1933 and Si Johnson in 1934. (It's a good thing for Reds' players and fans that Prohibition ended in 1933.) Si remembers Derringer: "Paul and I were great buddies. Yeah, he was a terrific pitcher, but he was a hard-luck pitcher, too. He lost 20-some games one year, so did I, when we were on Cincinnati. But, we both had that same trouble—you're not going to win without runs, and we didn't have any."

Yes, Si pitched for bad teams his whole career, teams that couldn't hit or field worth a lick and that finished in the cellar during 7 of his 17 seasons. And he had some great moments that made his father, a former semipro catcher, proud: two consecutive one-hitters against the Braves when he pitched for the Reds early in his career, five straight opening-day starts, and three strikeouts of Babe Ruth four days after he hit three home runs against Pittsburgh.

Si recalled the day he fanned Ruth three times: "That was 1935, and I was a starting pitcher," he told us. "Babe was on his way out, just about through. I pitched to Babe when he was in his prime, too, and he hit some out of sight off of me. But that day, he struck out three times on fastballs right down the middle of the plate. Ordinarily, he'd lose them for you. I took the baseball, went into the clubhouse after the game, and had him autograph the baseball." The Babe never started another game. After Si fanned him three times, Ruth knew he was through. And Si became the answer to a trivia question: "Who was the last pitcher to fan the Babe?"

Si had staying power, pitching from 1928 to 1947 for four NL teams, taking time out for World War II and a few trips to the minors. Si's younger cousin Lee Johnson told us that during the war, Si starred with Virgil Trucks and Schoolboy Rowe for the Great Lakes Naval Station team managed by Mickey Cochrane. Si was the Most Valuable Player, and Lee still treasures the Most-Valuable-Player wristwatch that Si gave him.

But Si Johnson's highlights are overshadowed by his legacy of defeat. He had 15 or more decisions nine times and posted an average won-lost record of 8–16 during those seasons. He had only 101 lifetime starts to show for 272 starts, over 2,000 innings, and nearly 500 appearances during his 17 big-league seasons. He lost 165 times, a dozen of them in a row in 1933. The Cincinnati teams he pitched for in the early 1930s were awful, and so were his Phillies of the early 1940s. He did sandwich in a few seasons with decent Cardinals' teams and ended his career with first-division Braves' teams, but most of the time he languished near the bottom of the league.

He loved his days with the St. Louis Cardinals, called the Gashouse Gang. "When you play with a bunch like that, a pretty good ball club, the season just flies by," he told us. "I didn't want the season to end. We were having so much fun. You know, you'd have tougher games, and the crowd was always with you. You didn't really know what was going to happen, and I enjoyed being there very much because you were always in the ball game and you always played to a big crowd. When I played with Cincinnati, sometimes we were lucky to have a hundred people in the stands."

Still, the fault wasn't only bad hitting, bad fielding, and poor support by the fans. Si's WAT of −9.6 indicates that the average pitcher on these tail enders would have won about ten more games than Si managed. He also had an ERA that was worse than the average pitcher in the NL, and his TPI of −11.6 was downright miserable, among the five worst of the century. His TPI indicates that he wasn't too adept at preventing runs with his pitching and fielding or at producing runs with his hitting. To Si, hitting was as easy as 1-2-3, as in a lifetime batting average of .123. The first pitcher he faced was Grover Cleveland Alexander, and he got a hit. Si told *Sports Collectors Digest:* "The next day the newspaper has something about me

Above: **Si Johnson spent most of his 17-year career pitching for various terrible teams in the National League. He won in double digits just three times, but lost a dozen or more in eight different seasons (photo courtesy of Si Johnson).**

being a good-hitting pitcher. I thought, yeah, they got that wrong. And those opposing pitchers went gunnin' for me after that. They made sure I failed at bat."

When Si was present at an important baseball event, he was often on the wrong side of history. On September 30, 1934, Dizzy Dean won his 30th game of the season and clinched the pennant for the Gashouse Gang by beating the Reds 9–0. Si obliged by starting and losing to old Diz, later his roommate with the Cardinals. ("Diz had his own rules you know, and I could say I roomed with his suitcase more than I roomed with Diz," Johnson told us.) While Dean was heading to the World Series and baseball immortality with his 30–7 record, Si Johnson was putting the finishing touches on a 7–22 mark and a Skunk Stearns trophy.

If Johnson had pitched for contenders, his lifetime mark probably would have been a little over .500, like Rube Walberg's. But he blended bad luck, bad teams, and just plain bad pitching into among the worst career stats of his era. Yet nothing can dampen his enthusiasm about baseball; it was his life and still flows in his veins. He recently told sportswriter Dave Newman, "I've never seen such a game as they play today, hitting gloves and sliding gloves, why they're a bunch of pansies." In a 1990 interview with *Sports Collector's Digest,* he sang the same tune: "As soon as a pitch moves 'em off the plate they're ready to charge the mound. . . . We had a dustoff sign right along with the regular pitch signs. . . . For me, it was just Lombardi snappin' his thumb off his forefinger, like you'd flip a coin. Ernie'd flick his thumb and the batter went down on my next pitch."

How would Si do in the majors now if he were 20-something instead of 80-something? "If I were pitching today, I'd win an awful lot of games," he told us. "Now all they do is tell them starting pitchers, 'You go five innings and then we got help for you.' They got middle relievers and then they got finishers and what have you. In my day, they expected you to start and finish. There was no middle relief or anything like that. You had to get hit pretty hard before they'd bring in a relief pitcher. But now, when they pitch five innings, they count your pitches. They never used to count pitches when we pitched. You pitched as long as you possibly could and as hard as you possibly could.

"I would love to pitch today. I don't blame the players for taking the money. I would probably get plenty."

And Si was always the competitor: "I would chew them out pretty good if they didn't hustle in back of me when I was pitching," he told us. "I didn't mind losing a tough ball game, but if I lost because they didn't hustle, why, then there was a little trouble."

We asked Si what it was like being on the short end of the final score so often in his career. "You feel like if it'd do any good, you'd go out and cry," he said. "I know my wife used to go to the ball games. I'd lose one to nothing or two to one. I'd go take my shower and she'd be sitting in the car—crying. I'd tell her there's no need to cry about it; that ain't going to do me any good. She took it harder than I did. You lost a tough ball game and you go home that night. I'll tell you the steaks don't taste very good."

MILT GASTON

We talked with soft-spoken, articulate Milt Gaston by telephone a week before his 95th birthday. Gaston's baseball days were the best years of his life; the man who debuted in 1924, the year that *Little Orphan Annie* first appeared, shared some of his memories with a touch of nostalgia. Although he was 28 when he joined Babe Ruth's Yankees in 1924, "I had to mind my p's and q's in those days because I was just a rookie," he told us. "And I didn't try to overstep my bounds. I liked the Babe. He was kind of rough, but he was one of the great ones, so you couldn't criticize him very well. But he was always nice as far as I was concerned. Joe Bush was very nice. In fact, they all treated me good. I had no complaints at all in my rookie year."

Gaston never played a day of minor-league ball—he played two games a week in the New Jersey sandlots when he was discovered—and was one of the few players of his day to go straight to the majors. He went from the Supreme Court in New York, where he was an attaché, to the Yankees.

Gaston, traded to the St. Louis Browns after going 5–3 with the Yankees, gave up 4 of the 60 home runs Ruth hit in 1927. No one gave up more, although Rube Walberg also contributed four to the cause. Like Si Johnson, Gaston was usually on the wrong side when history was in the making. In 1925, Ty Cobb, player-manager of the Tigers, was fed up with the Babe Ruth homerun hype. Before a May 5 game against the Browns in St. Louis, he announced to a group of writers: "Gentlemen, I would like you to pay particular attention today because for the first time in my career I will be deliberately going for home runs." He hit homers in both the first and second innings and went 6–6 on the day with a then-record 16 total bases. But it was his third home run of the day, hit off a Browns' reliever in the eighth inning, that made Cobb's boast apochryphal. And that hurler, naturally, was Milt Gaston.

"I didn't look up to Cobb," Gaston told us, "because he wasn't a very nice guy. But he was a great ball player and you couldn't take that away from him."

Milt was the AL's answer to the much-traveled and often-defeated Si Johnson, who toiled for four NL teams. Milt pitched for five AL teams, joining the Senators, Red Sox, and White Sox after wearing out his welcome in New York and St. Louis. "I was signed by a Yankee scout," he told us. "I had four or five different offers, but I lived across the river in New Jersey, and I wanted to be with a good ball club. And I regretted the

fact that I was traded the first year after. I was never with a good ball club after that." But more than 50 years ago, he told writer Henry P. Edwards, "No, I never got sore because I was swapped.... Anyway, I guess I had it coming to me every time I was traded."

He might have been traded once because he loved to throw the fork ball, but neither the batter nor the catcher (nor Gaston, for that matter) had any idea where Gaston's fork ball was headed. According to Edwards, rumor had it that Browns' president Phil Ball shipped Gaston to Washington "because he had to dodge so many fork balls that Milt threw into the grandstand." One catcher for St. Louis, Pinky Hargrave, recalled a game against the Yankees in which Gaston threw two straight fork balls with the bases loaded. The batter swung and missed twice; Hargrave reached and missed twice. The result: two runs for New York.

Gaston had a 20–17 record after his first two seasons, but then became oblivious to geography, piling losing season upon losing season in St. Louis, Washington, Boston, and Chicago. He had seasons like 10–18 (for the Browns), 2–13 with 12 straight losses (for the Red Sox), and 6–19 (for the White Sox), but there was usually someone who pitched just a little worse each year—except in 1932, when his 7–17 mark for Chicago earned him a Skunk Stearns trophy.

Gaston's one shot at immortality was broken up by his brother. While with the Browns in 1926, Milt was working on a no-hitter past the seventh inning against the Red Sox when his older brother Alex ripped a hit. "When we played on the sandlots around New Jersey, he never would hit

Above: **The American League's equivalent of Si Johnson, Milt Gaston pitched for the Yankees in 1924 and then hurled for four bad teams in the 1920s and 1930s. He lost 67 more games than he won—a record even if you go back to the 1870s (photo courtesy of Milt Gaston).**

the first ball," Milt told us. "It was almost a natural fact with him. So I remembered that from those days, and the first ball I threw him was a fastball, right down the middle. He hit it for a base hit and never let me forget it."

But in 1929, Alex Gaston gave Milt one of his fondest baseball memories, when Milt and Alex formed a brother battery with Boston, the second in AL history (Tommy and Homer Thompson for New York were the first in 1912). Unfortunately, things turned sour for Milt at that point. If his career had been passably bad through 1929 (61–83), a sore arm ended all hopes of mere mediocrity. His only 20-loss year in 1930 was followed by another dismal year, prompting the Red Sox to trade Gaston for Lefty Weiland. The trade was actually pretty even for the first two years—Gaston went 15–29, while Weiland was 14–30. In fact, Gaston squeaked by Weiland for the 1932 Skunk Stearns trophy. But Weiland, who broke into baseball with Si Johnson in the Mississippi Valley League in 1928, managed a few decent years for the Cardinals in the late 1930s. Milt just got worse.

"They didn't know I had a bad arm, but from 1930 on I wasn't much good. I got by on what I knew," Gaston told us, "because I didn't have much stuff then." A little more knowledge wouldn't have hurt; he averaged a 6–15 record his last four years until he was mercifully let go by the White Sox after the 1934 season.

Gaston's arm injury "was just one of those things," he said. "I think that if it happened in an era like this, where they've learned so much more about it, they might have been able to fix my arm today. They do this rotator cuff business that I read about, and they mend these guys up like new. But they didn't know much about it in those days." Baseball Hall of Fame pitcher Bob Lemon, mocking the run of arm injuries that afflict today's pitchers, has joked it's a good thing they hadn't discovered the rotator cuff in the olden days. Gaston was just a man ahead of his time.

We asked Gaston about the worst game he ever pitched. "You'd have to remember a lot of them, I guess. I think the worst game I ever pitched, and I got by with a shutout, was when I was with the Washington club, and Cleveland got 14 hits and no runs. I pitched a shutout, but I almost got my infielders killed!" That 9–0 win over the Indians in 1928 still shares the major-league record for the most hits by the losing team in a nine-inning shutout.

Gaston lost 164 games in his career, an average of 16 a year if you don't count his 5–3 rookie season. And the worst game he remembers pitching was a shutout!

Milt was a lifelong friend of his former Red Sox teammate Jack Russell; they both lived for years in Florida until Russell's fairly recent death. Russell was a terrible starter for Boston, an excellent reliever for the Senators in the mid–1930s (he was the first reliever named to the All-Star team

Though Jack Russell was the first relief pitcher to be named to the All-Star team, his poor record as a starter earlier in his career sealed his fate as one of the worst pitchers of his era (photo courtesy of George Brace).

in 1934), and a mediocre relief pitcher for the several Al and NL teams that passed him around near the end of his 15-year career. The final damage was an 85–141 mark, which ranked him fourth in the worst-pitcher-of-the-era sweepstakes. As a Red Sox starter from 1929 to 1931, Gaston averaged a 9–17 record; Russell was worse at 8–19.

Gaston and Russell did all right after they left baseball. Milt was a deputy sheriff in Tampa, Florida, for almost 17 years until he retired at the age of 76. Russell became the city commissioner of Clearwater, Florida, where he helped construct the Phillies' spring-training stadium, which is still known as Jack Russell Stadium.

"Jack Russell was just like me," Gaston told us. "He wasn't with a good ball club, so you couldn't show much record. But he had a good career." As with Si Johnson's record, though, bad ball clubs can't take all the blame. Russell had a lifetime WAT of −17.0. The average pitcher on the second-division teams he typically pitched for would have won 17 games more than Russell did—the average pitcher would have been 102–124, instead of Jack Russell's 85–141. The same was true for Gaston. He pitched for seventh or eighth-place teams for 6 of his 11 years, but his record was still 13 games worse than expected.

"When I was with the Yankees, they didn't have pitching coaches and so many coaches in those days," Gaston told us. "You got by on your own or what you could learn from the other pitchers." Maybe it wasn't too much. He retired with a 97–164 record, and the lowest winning percentage of the century for pitchers with 200 or more decisions. His 67 more losses than wins was never achieved by anyone else. No one did that in the 19th century, and no one except Si Johnson has come close since.

Single-Season Leaders: 1920–46
(Minimum of 15 Losses)

Order, Name, and Year*	Statistic
Losses minus Wins	
1. Ben Cantwell (1935)	21
2. Paul Derringer (1933)	20
3T. Roy Wilkinson (1921)	16
3T. George Smith (1921)	16
5T. Joe Oeschger (1922)	15
5T. Red Ruffing (1928)	15
5T. Dutch Henry (1930)	15
5T. Si Johnson (1934)	15
5T. George Caster (1940)	15
Winning Percentage	
1. Dutch Henry (1930)	.105
2. Curt Fullerton (1923)	.118
3. Ben Cantwell (1935)	.138
4. Lou Knerr (1946)	.158
5T. George Smith (1921)	.167
5T. Roy Wilkinson (1921)	.167
5T. Les Sweetland (1928)	.167
5T. Bob Savage (1946)	.167
Wins-Above-Team (WAT)	
1. Paul Derringer (1933)	−8.6
2T. Roy Wilkinson (1921)	−7.4
2T. Dolph Luque (1922)	−7.4
4. Dutch Henry (1930)	−7.2
5. Ben Cantwell (1935)	−7.1

Order, Name, and Year*	Statistic
Adjusted ERA	
1. Lefty Hoerst (1942)	64
2T. Les Sweetland (1928)	65
2T. Hal Gregg (1944)	65
2T. Roger Wolff (1944)	65
5T. Speed Martin (1920)	66
5T. Lou Knerr (1946)	66
Total Pitcher Index (TPI)	
1. Pat Caraway (1931)	−4.3
2T. George Caster (1940)	−4.0
2T. Hal Gregg (1944)	−4.0
4. Jack Knott (1936)	−3.9
5. Bobo Newsom (1942)	−3.3

*T = tie.

Career Leaders: 1920–46 (Minimum of 50 Losses)

Order and Name*	Statistic	
Losses minus Wins**		
1. Milt Gaston	67	(97–164)
2. Si Johnson	64	(101–165)
3. Jack Russell	56	(85–141)
4. Hugh Mulcahy	44	(45–89)
5. Rollie Naylor	41	(42–83)
Winning Percentage		
1. Ike Pearson	.206	
2. Al Gerheauser	.333	
3T. Rollie Naylor	.336	
3T. Hugh Mulcahy	.336	
3T. George Smith	.336	
Wins-Above-Team (WAT)		
1. Rube Walberg	−19.6	
2. Eddie Smith	−18.8	
3. Jack Russell	−17.0	
4. Sheriff Blake	−15.3	
5. Lloyd Brown	−13.7	

Order and Name*	Statistic
Adjusted ERA	
1. Les Sweetland	77
2. Ike Pearson	79
3. Don Black	80
4. Claude Willoughby	81
5T. Boom Boom Beck	86
5T. Alex Ferguson	86
Total Pitcher Index (TPI)	
1. Si Johnson	−11.6
2. Alex Ferguson	−10.7
3. Joe Oeschger	−10.5
4T. Buck Ross	−9.4
4T. Claude Willoughby	−9.4

*T = tie.
**W–L in parentheses.

5

1947–1968
The Jackie Robinson Era

◆ The 1941 season may have been baseball's finest, spiced by Joe Di-Maggio's 56-game hitting streak and Ted Williams' .406 batting average. When World War II broke out a few months after the season was over and players started to be drafted for the military, the face of baseball was changed beyond recognition. DiMaggio and Williams left after the 1942 season ended and didn't return until 1946; other stars followed suit. To many fans and writers, an era was changing before their eyes. And what better way to end an era than with the glory of 1941, with Williams insisting on playing both ends of a doubleheader on the last day of the season—and getting six hits—so he would hit a solid .400 instead of having his .3995 rounded up?

But 1942 did not begin a new age of baseball. The war years were an interruption, a decimation of talent, a chance for players who were too young, too old, or 4-F to show their stuff. It was not the beginning of a new era, but just an interlude. And what about 1946—the first postwar year—did that start the new era? Bob Feller came back from the military with his fastball blazing in glory. He fanned a then-record 348, was 26–15, and notched ten shutouts for the sixth-place Indians. Not to be outdone, Hal Newhouser proved that his wartime pitching heroics, which included back-to-back awards for Most Valuable Player, were no fluke. Prince Hal was 26–9, led the majors with a 1.94 ERA, and led the Tigers to second place. It would have been the best Cy Young race ever, but the award was still a decade away.

Yet the 1946 season didn't begin the new era either. All ambiguity ended when the 1947 season began, and Jackie Robinson played first base for the Brooklyn Dodgers against the Boston Braves. A new age had dawned, and neither baseball nor its records would ever be the same. Other eras began with changes of rules, a Babe Ruth–inspired barrage of home runs, or expansion. Even 1947 brought with it a juiced-up ball that increased home runs greatly and the emergence of television as a major force. But the Jackie Robinson Era was not about home runs or television; it corrected a social and human injustice that had been established by tacit agreement ever since Cap Anson refused to play on the same field with George Stovey, the great black International League pitcher, in an 1887 exhibition game.

By breaking the color barrier, Robinson changed baseball forever. He was the first black Most Valuable Player in 1949, and during the 1950s, eight of the Most Valuable Players in the NL were black. Although Cleveland's Larry Doby debuted a few months after Robinson in July 1947, the AL took its time before investing its stock in the black ballplayer. But by the 1960s, blacks from both leagues had rewritten the record books. Three of the top four career home run leaders are black. When Robinson broke into the majors, only Babe Ruth, Jimmie Foxx, and Mel Ott had more than 500 home runs. Since that time, 11 men—six blacks and five whites—surpassed Ott's 511 total. To take aim at Hank Aaron's 755, a player could average 35 homers for 21 years and still fall 20 short. And if Rickey Henderson of the Athletics stays healthy and motivated, he may put his all-time record for stolen bases just as far out of reach.

The influx of a new source of talent began with a trickle in the late 1940s, but stepped up its pace in the 1950s. It was a dangerous era for pitchers, especially for those with Skunk Stearns potential, because now they had to reckon with hitters like Robinson, Doby, Monte Irvin, and three-time Most Valuable Player Roy Campanella, who were no longer restricted to the Negro Leagues.

Some Skillful Skunks

The list of Skunk Stearns winners for the Jackie Robinson Era, from Preacher Roe in 1947 to Jim Bunning in 1968 (see the table of winners for 1947–68), is dotted with pitchers who flirted with greatness during their better days. Roe joined the Dodgers in large part because of baseball's great experiment with Jackie Robinson; he was traded by Pittsburgh with Billy Cox and future manager Gene Mauch after his skunk season in 1947 for disgruntled Dodger Dixie Walker and a pair of mediocre pitchers. All Roe did for Brooklyn during the next seven years was post a .715 winning percentage, including a 22–3 mark in 1951, partly because of a good spitter.

Jim Bunning, who was almost elected to Cooperstown and is now a Kentucky congressman, followed an alternate path. He won 20 once and 19 three times and pitched both a no-hitter and a perfect game before he tumbled in 1968. While most major-league pitchers were feasting during

Skunk Stearns Winners: 1947–68

Year	Winner	Team	Won	Lost	Percentage	ERA	Adjusted ERA	WAT	TPI
1947	Preacher Roe	Pittsburgh: NL	4	15	.211	5.25	80	-4.7	-1.8
1948	Art Houtteman	Detroit: AL	2	16	.111	4.66	94	-7.1	-0.2
1949	Howie Judson	Chicago: AL	1	14	.067	4.58	91	-6.3	-0.6
1950	Alex Kellner	Philadelphia: AL	8	20	.286	5.47	83	-2.4	-2.3
1951	Paul Minner	Chicago: NL	6	17	.261	3.79	108	-4.4	+1.6
1952	Art Houtteman	Detroit: AL	8	20	.286	4.36	87	-1.9	-1.6
	Virgil Trucks	Detroit: AL	5	19	.208	3.97	96	-4.7	-0.1
1953	Charlie Bishop	Philadelphia: AL	3	14	.176	5.66	76	-4.7	-2.5
1954	Don Larsen	Baltimore: AL	3	21	.125	4.37	82	-8.1	-0.9
1955	Camilo Pascual	Washington: AL	2	12	.143	6.14	62	-4.2	-2.9
1956	Camilo Pascual	Washington: AL	6	18	.250	5.87	74	-4.5	-3.1
1957	Chuck Stobbs	Washington: AL	8	20	.286	5.36	73	-3.2	-3.4
	Robin Roberts	Philadelphia: NL	10	22	.313	4.07	93	-6.8	-0.6
1958	Russ Kemmerer	Washington: AL	6	15	.285	4.61	83	-3.1	-2.1
1959	Bob Friend	Pittsburgh: NL	8	19	.296	4.03	96	-6.1	-0.2
1960	Frank Sullivan	Boston: AL	6	16	.273	5.10	79	-4.2	-1.9
1961	Frank Sullivan	Philadelphia: NL	3	16	.158	4.29	95	-4.8	-0.2
1962	Craig Anderson	New York: NL	3	17	.150	5.35	78	-4.2	-1.5
1963	Roger Craig	New York: NL	5	22	.185	3.78	92	-6.1	-0.6
1964	Galen Cisco	New York: NL	6	19	.240	3.62	99	-3.7	+0.1
1965	Jack Fisher	New York: NL	8	24	.250	3.94	90	-3.5	-0.9
1966	Dick Ellsworth	Chicago: NL	8	22	.267	3.98	92	-4.5	-0.6
1967	Jack Fisher	New York: NL	9	18	.333	4.70	72	-1.7	-3.2
1968	Jim Bunning	Pittsburgh: NL	4	14	.222	3.88	75	-5.1	-2.2

the year of the pitcher—the average ERA was less than 3.00 in each league—Bunning was awful and earned our Skunk Stearns trophy. He was 4–14 for a Pirates team that played better than .500 ball when the tall, sidearming right-hander stayed in the dugout. Maybe his major-league record of five 1–0 losses in 1967 took something out of him in 1968. Maybe not; Bunning still had 28 wins left in his arm to become the first pitcher since Cy Young to win 100 or more games or strike out 1,000 or more in each league.

Bunning was not the most famous 1947–68 Skunk Stearns winner to pitch a perfect game, and he wasn't even the best pitcher on the list. Those distinctions go to Don Larsen, whose World Series gem came just two years after his 3–21 skunk season, and to Baseball Hall of Famer Robin Roberts, respectively. Roberts had pinpoint control and gave up lots of home runs—a record 505 for his career and 46 in one season (a record broken by Bert Blyleven's 50 in 1986). The workhorse pitcher usually gave up solo shots when he won at least 20 games a year from 1950 to 1955, but the home runs became more damaging after shoulder problems took the zip out of his fastball in 1956. He managed a 19–18 record that season, then tumbled to 10–22 and a share of the 1957 Skunk Stearns trophy. Before his injury, he relied on a moving fastball and control, and that was about it. But to bounce back from the abyss, he developed a curve and became a finesse pitcher; he lasted until 1966 when he retired with 286 wins. But the great Roberts (160–102 his first eight seasons) was just a mediocre pitcher after his injury (126–143).

Roberts fell from a 19-win season to a Skunk Stearns Award, but others also had falls from glory. The Cubs' Dick Ellsworth was 22–10 with a 2.11 ERA in 1963, but three years later he virtually reversed his record to earn the Skunk Stearns Award. Alex Kellner was 20–12 in 1949, his first full season in the majors, then lost 20 the next year for the Athletics to win a Skunk Stearns trophy. Bob Friend of the Pirates also fell from the 20-win circle one year to a Skunk Stearns trophy the next. In 1958, Friend was 22–14 for the Pirates and finished just two votes short of Bob Turley in the Cy Young race. The next season, he was 8–19, and the Skunk Stearns Award was his.

Baseball history has been filled with pitchers whose up-and-down careers can only be described as schizophrenic. But no one deserves that label more than Virgil Trucks, co-winner of the 1952 Skunk Stearns trophy. Trucks won 20 in 1953, the year after his skunk season, but that's not so special; many pitchers have gone from bottom to top, and vice versa. Trucks' multiple pitching personality occurred during his Skunk Stearns season. He won five games for the last-place Tigers against 19 defeats, but his handful of victories included a two-hitter, a one-hitter, and a pair of no-hitters! He won his one-hitter and both no-hitters by 1–0 scores, but his two-hitter may have been the most exciting of all; it came six days after his first no-hitter, as Trucks almost duplicated Johnny Vander Meer's two consecutive no-hitters. He went 6⅔ innings before the Athletics got their first hit.

Trucks was used to tossing no-hitters, and even threw two in 1938 (and struck out over 400) in the Class C Alabama-Florida League, his first as a professional. Then he pitched no-hitters in the Texas and International Leagues, and completed his cycle of throwing one in every league he pitched when he no-hit the Senators in May of his Skunk Stearns season. Trucks' second no-hitter that year, against the Yankees in New York during the heat of August, didn't come easy. The *New York Times'* John Drebinger, as official scorer, first gave Phil Rizzuto a hit in the third inning when shortstop Johnny Pesky failed to handle his grounder. He changed his decision when Dan Daniel and a few other members of the writing fraternity challenged it. Drebinger yielded to pressure, but not before he spoke to Pesky, who admitted, "I just messed it up."

Trucks was on first base when the scoring change was announced, and the first-base umpire told Trucks to go get his no-hitter. "Look you ol' so and so, I'm not trying to pitch a no-hitter," Trucks told the ump, "I'm having enough problems just trying to win a game." He was right. The no-hitter brought Trucks' record to 5–15, but he then endured a winless September to wrap up his half of the Skunk Stearns Award. His bizarre 1952 season was something out of science fiction. Could there be a connection between his two no-hitters and the fact that UFOs were spotted twice above the White House that year?

Art Houtteman, who shared the 1952 Skunk Stearns Award with his teammate Trucks, was one of four pitchers from the 1947–68 era to win a pair of Skunk Stearns Awards, joining Camilo Pascual, Frank Sullivan, and Jack Fisher. Each of these double-dose hurlers finished first or second in one of our major awards. Houtteman's 2–16 season in 1948 was one of the worst of the era, while Fisher's career stats ranked him among the downtrodden of any era. Pascual's metamorphosis from two straight Skunk Stearns Awards to two straight 20-win seasons gave him our Joe Hardy Sell-Your-Soul Award; Sullivan, traveling a different road, fell from All-Star pitcher to double skunk, and earned our Asa Brainard Award.

Asa Brainard Humpty-Dumpty Award: Frank Sullivan

Frank Sullivan, the 6 foot 6½ inch lefty with the wry sense of humor, said in 1962: "I'm in the twilight of a mediocre career." Though his lifetime record of 97–100 would seem to put an exclamation point on his self-appraisal, Sullivan was wrong. He was never mediocre; he went from excellent to awful with barely a pause. His whole career was mirrored by his performance in the 1955 All-Star game. He relieved Whitey Ford in the eighth and pitched 3⅓ strong innings against the mighty NL lineup. That's the good part. Then the bubble burst when Stan Musial, leading off the bottom of the 12th, smashed a game-winning home run off Sullivan for a 6–5 comeback win; the NL had trailed 5–0 after six innings.

Sullivan was more successful in his major-league debut in July 1953, not long after serving in the Korean War. He was brought up by the Red Sox from the Eastern League, and his first test was as a relief pitcher against the Tigers with the bases loaded and no outs; he retired the side without a run scoring. Sid Hudson was winding down his career when Sullivan came up, but the rookie made an impression on the veteran. "The big lefty was a funny guy," Hudson told us. "He kept us all loose."

Sullivan was the ace of Boston's starting staff in 1954–55, and formed a potent lefty-righty duo with Tom Brewer for a few years after that. He averaged a 15–10 record from 1954 to 1958. In 1955, he tied for the league lead in wins (18–13) and led in innings pitched. He made the AL All-Star team for a second time in 1956, but wasn't given the chance to avenge Musial's home run; Sullivan stayed on the bench in 1956. In 1957, he was only 14–11, but he held batters to a .275 on base average, best in the league, and he allowed the fewest walks per game. He also topped the AL with a TPI of +3.8.

Sullivan stumbled in 1959 with a 9–11 record and then fell on his face in 1960 to win the Skunk Stearns trophy at 6–16 with a 5.10 ERA. The Red Sox had enough, and traded him that winter to the Phillies even up for 6 foot 8 inch ex–Celtic Gene Conley—the tallest pitcher in the AL for the tallest in the NL. Conley, ironically, beat Sullivan in the 1955 All-Star game, thanks to Musial's home run. Sullivan proved his versatility by winning his second trophy in as many years, as his won-lost record dwindled to 3–16. His victory total dropped in successive years from 13 to 9 to 6 to 3. His Humpty-Dumpty fall was complete. He was 4–4 with the Phils and Twins in 1962–63, and then he was gone, to become a golf pro in Kauii, Hawaii, with his former Red Sox roommate and catcher, Sammy White.

Sullivan's fall from top starter to skunk was sudden, irreversible, and dramatic, as shown in the following comparison of his record before and after his plummet:

Years	Won	Lost	Percentage	ERA	Adjusted ERA	WAT	TPI
1953–58	75	53	.586	3.19	134	+10.6	+13.4
1959–63	22	47	.319	4.45	93	−9.7	−2.3

Win or lose, though, nothing dampened Sullivan's sense of humor. Whether he was winning 15 games a year or competing for worst pitcher of the year, he had a ready quip. The 1961 Phillies had just ended their record 23-game losing streak and were returning home from a long road trip. The team was greeted by a crowd of several hundred at Philadelphia Airport. Sullivan (who lost three times during the streak), noting catcher Clay Dalrymple's hesitation about getting off the plane, said, "They're selling rocks at $1.50 a bushel; stay about five feet apart so they can't get us all with one burst." But the crowd (which swelled from a few hundred to a few thousand as the story got retold) treated the Phils—especially John Buzhardt, who beat the Braves' Carlton Willey 7–4 to end the streak—like returning heroes. Buzhardt, by the way, was runner-up to Sullivan for the Skunk Stearns trophy in both 1960 and 1961, when his two-year mark for the Phillies was 11–34 with a 4.18 ERA. (Sullivan was 9–32 with a 4.69 ERA.) Although Buzhardt later had a few winning seasons with the White Sox, he retired with the second-worst WAT of the 1947–68 era (–12.0).

Sullivan's penchant for losing with the Phils (he was 3–18 for them in 1½ seasons) didn't stop him from joking about his teammates. He said about a fellow Phillie: "We got a guy on our club who has such bad hands his glove is embarrassed."

But when it comes to embarrassment, no one can top the Asa Brainard Humpty-Dumpty runner-up for the era: Jim Bouton. Bouton embarrassed baseball, according to Bowie Kuhn, with his 1970 pitch-and-tell book *Ball Four* that exposed ball players as sex-obsessed "beaver shooters" who relied on "greenies" and alcohol to keep them going, and exposed just about everyone else associated with baseball—coaches, managers, general managers, and umpires—for something or other, be it stupidity, dishonesty, or bigotry.

He expanded on these themes in his later books, always with wit and a wonderful sense of timing (Bowie Kuhn would disagree) and proved to be enterprising. His flair for the creative (shredded bubble gum that could pass for tobacco, personalized baseball cards, and more) and his ability to generate funny quotes at will have made him successful and hard to avoid. (Not that his baseball contemporaries haven't tried. Many consider him the all-time skunk for breaking the clubhouse taboo.)

But Bouton was once a star for the great New York Yankees and even captured the fancy of the fans because his hat often flew off his head while he hurtled the ball and his entire body toward home plate. The man who would earn the nickname Bulldog debuted in the majors in 1962 with a seven-hit shutout of the Senators, was 21–7 the next year, and won two games against the world-champion Cardinals in the 1964 World Series, including a clutch win in game six. But Bouton's 18–13 record and postseason heroics in 1964 marked the abrupt end of his pitching success. Coinciding with the Yankees' own fall from grace, Bouton blew out his arm and lost his fastball. He was 4–15 with a 4.82 ERA for the Yankees in 1965 and 3–8 in 1966, when New York plunged into the cellar; his adjusted ERA of 71 in 1965 tied him for the third worst of the era.

After that, he floundered in the bull pen with the Yankees, Seattle Pilots, and Houston Astros; developed a knuckleball in the minors; and finally called it quits for a while after the 1970 season. He became a television sportscaster for a New York station and began his first sportscast by saying that people criticized his pitching and writing, but perhaps he had now found something he would be good at. He wasn't. He fumbled through the sports report and gave the scores of only a handful of baseball games. Among his profound insights were gems like "Who cares who wins the Phillies-Expos game?" He loved to play the game, but he wasn't much of a fan. He once said, "Statistics are about as interesting as first-base coaches." And he loves coaches, portraying them as part infant and part infantryman. "It's a boring job. But people who become coaches are not easily bored. You ever see a baby play with a rattle for two hours?" He added, "A lot of coaches would make good prison guards."

Bouton didn't quit trying to get back in the majors. He made an abortive attempt in 1975, but finally succeeded in 1978. He had spent that winter throwing at a wall every day ("I'm 11–0 against the wall," he said). Ted Turner, moving to the beat of his own drum (just like Bouton), let him bring his ever-so-slow knuckleball to the Braves. Five starts and a 1–3 record later, even Turner gave up. No one was more thankful than the opposing batters, who would have rather struck out against a utility infielder brought in to pitch in a lopsided game than to make an out against Bouton's wimpy tosses. "I don't want to see him again, and I don't want to face him again. Bouton [is] a joke," Bill Madlock told reporters. "If he's with [the Braves] next year, I wanna bring my boy out to hit against him."

Still, Bouton won a game for Atlanta, his first victory since 1970. The eight years between Bouton's wins outstripped Mike Norris' seven years (1983 to 1990) for Oakland, but fell far short of the major-league record. Cactus Johnson won two game for the Giants in 1923 (the year Lou Gehrig hit his first home run) and waited 15 years for his next win, in 1938 for the Browns (the year Gehrig hit his last home run). Bouton was 46–27 his first three seasons and 16–36 for the rest of his career, counting his last-ditch effort with Atlanta that pushed his final won-lost record from just above to just below .500. He was a true Humpty-Dumpty, who fell just short of the Asa Brainard Award. Not even Frank Sullivan, though, could outdo Bouton with quotable remarks. Showing a blend of honesty and self-insight, Bouton said in 1971, "Amphetamines improved my performance about five percent. Unfortunately, in my particular case that wasn't enough."

Joe Hardy Sell-Your-Soul Award: Camilo Pascual

History has been kind to Cuban right-hander Camilo Pascual. He is remembered as an excellent pitcher of the 1960s who had an awesome, explosive curveball. What many books overlook are his years of skunkhood with the Senators in the mid–1950s.

A 17-year-old Pascual was spotted in 1951 by Washington scout Joe Cambria. The teenager was pitching for a Cuban country club on Sundays, his only payment the use of the pool. Cambria was tipped off about "Little Potato" Pascual by none other than Camilo's older brother, Carlos "Big Potato" Pascual, whose entire major-league career was confined to two starts for the Senators in 1950.

Pascual debuted in 1954 with a 4–7 record and won his first Skunk Stearns Award in 1955 with a 2–12 record and a 6.14 ERA. We used our "dandruff" rule to give him the nod, despite having so few decisions, because he was head and shoulders above the next worst pitcher. He won his second straight trophy in 1956, when he won 6, lost 18, and had a 5.87 ERA. In fact, in his first five years with Washington he achieved a winning percentage as high as .400 only once. Then, like the fictional Washington Senator Joe Hardy, he became a sudden star. Did the native of Havana sell his soul to earn his niche? Compare his stats for his first and second five years in the major leagues and then decide.

Years	Team	Won	Lost	Percentage	ERA	Adj. ERA	WAT	TPI
1954–58	Washington	28	66	.298	4.66	89	−10.8	−5.7
1959–63	Washington-Minnesota	85	54	.612	2.99	134	+18.8	+16.2

Pascual's reversal of form was astonishing. His Washington teams of the mid–1950s played .380 ball, but Pascual couldn't crack .300. From 1959 to 1963, the Senators and Twins improved slightly, approaching the .400 mark, but Pascual was pitching at better than a .600 clip. He was a 20-game winner in both 1962 and 1963 and led the AL in strikeouts for three straight seasons. As the 1961 *Major League Baseball Handbook* noted, "Baseball men rate [Pascual] the best pitcher in baseball. . . . Has excellent speed and finest curve in the game."

Rational explanations for his change? For one thing, he developed a sidearm curve, to team up with his excellent fastball and control. For another, he was influenced by Joe Haynes, a former pitcher who served as executive vice president of the Senators. For a third, he was helped by

"Boom Boom" Beck, the Senators' pitching coach from 1957 to 1959. Pascual credited Haynes and Beck with converting him from a thrower to a pitcher. "They teach me to be smart," he said.

Beck got his nickname during a July 4, 1934, game when he heaved the ball toward the rightfield wall to protest Dodger manager Casey Stengel's decision to remove him from a game against the Phillies. The "boom boom" sound of the ball caroming off the tin wall in the old Baker Bowl awakened Hack Wilson from a daydream. The hung-over right fielder fielded the ball and made what Stengel called Wilson's best throw of the season. Boom Boom Beck was out of the majors after that season, but resurfaced five years later to begin a five-year stint with the Phils. His career mark was 38–69 (.355).

Si Johnson remembered his old Phillies' teammate. "Beck was a big sidearm pitcher, but he couldn't throw very hard," he told us. "He just had a big sidearm curve. He didn't have enough stuff." Did Beck teach the sidearm curve to Pascual and get him to a be a smarter pitcher? Maybe, but the devil theory may be a more likely explanation for the flip-flop.

Pascual had a bit of trouble pitching on opening day, even after he turned his career around. Because he was a perennial loser, no one was surprised when he pitched in relief and lost the 1957 opener to the Orioles, matching his opening-day loss to the Yankees in 1956. But in 1960, Pascual was stung by a 500-foot homer to Ted Williams in the first game of the year, and near the end of his 18-year career he repeated his feat of losing two consecutive opening-day games. With the expansion Washington Senators in the late 1960s, he lost both the 1968 and 1969 openers. Nonetheless, Sid Hudson, who was Pascual's pitching coach with the expansion Senators, had only praise for the right-handed curveball ace. "He was a very good competitor," Hudson told us. "He had good stuff."

And hitters feared facing Pascual for the first time. Before the 1963 opener, Indians' rookie Vic Davalillo was asked if he had ever seen Pascual. "Yes, many times," Davalillo replied, "but I never can hit him." "Where did you see him?" the reporter asked. "On the television," Davalillo said.

Pascual was a good hitter, but like his pitching, his hitting prowess suddenly turned around in 1959. Before that year, he hit .154 with no home runs. He suddenly turned into a .302 hitter in 1959 and ended his career with a .205 batting average and five home runs (two were grand slams). Even his brief tenure in the minor leagues followed the same Joe Hardy pattern. In 1951, he pitched for three teams in three leagues and had an overall ERA of 4.64. In 1952–53, he had a combined 18–12 mark with a 2.94 ERA.

Pascual's final major-league record was 174–170 with a 3.63 ERA. He ranged from terrible to great, and for several seasons with the Twins he

Camilo Pascual's curveball was one of the best ever, but he suffered through a legacy of losses before becoming one of the AL's dominant pitchers (photo courtesy of George Brace).

was just about the best pitcher in baseball. Even after his career was over, he had an eye for greatness. As a scout, he sent a young Cuban prospect to Medford hitting instructor Eddie Mathews in 1983, telling the Hall of Famer that he thought the kid could play. The kid's name? José Canseco.

The unlikely runner-up for the Joe Hardy Award is the great fireballer Sandy Koufax, the man whose explosive curve is sometimes compared to Pascual's. For the first six years of his career, the Dodger lefty was wild beyond belief. He compiled a 36–40 record (a .474 winning percentage) with a 4.10 ERA—not the stuff of greatness. For the final six years of his career, he was 129–47 (.733); his ERA of 2.20 included a record-setting five straight ERA crowns. Maybe it was sudden maturity. Maybe it was a tip from part-time Dodger catcher Norm Sherry. Maybe he sold his soul to the devil. But something changed Koufax from a thrower who couldn't hit a barn door to a pitcher with pinpoint control.

According to former minor-league pitcher Cecil Reynolds, Deacon Jones, Reynolds' manager in the 1972 Mexican-Pacific League, said he was a close friend of Koufax when they were both trying to get signed. "Jones talked about going with Koufax to the different clubs," Reynolds told us. "Jones said that Koufax was so wild that they would give him a basket full of baseballs and then roll the batting cage up around home plate. They'd take bets on how many he could throw inside the cage."

The story changed after Koufax found control. Then he became not only unbeatable, but often unhittable. It is interesting that his best four years (1963–1966) bear a remarkable resemblance to four consecutive years in another Hall of Famer's career—Mordecai "Three Finger" Brown:

	Sandy Koufax				Three Finger Brown		
Year	Won	Lost	Percentage	Year	Won	Lost	Percentage
1963	25	5	.833	1906	26	6	.813
1964	19	5	.792	1907	20	6	.769
1965	26	8	.765	1908	29	9	.763
1966	27	9	.750	1909	27	9	.750
Total	97	27	.782		102	30	.773

Perhaps the left-handed Koufax didn't sell his soul to acquire control; maybe he simply traded it for the soul of the right-handed Mordecai Brown!

Cherokee Fisher Rookie Award: Johnny Gray

None of the Skunk Stearns winners was a rookie and, in truth, no rookie had a year that was skunk-awful. We narrowed the Cherokee Fisher

Award to two pitchers who had identical 3–12 records in their first full seasons: Johnny Gray, of the 1954 Athletics, and Dick Weik, of the 1949 Senators. We gave the nod to Gray because of his 6.51 ERA (Weik checked in at 5.38). Gray, a burly right-hander from Florida, had experience losing in the minors, leading the Piedmont League in losses in 1951. He threw hard and led two minor leagues in strikeouts, but he averaged six walks per game in the minors—and nearly eight walks per game as an A's rookie. He returned to the minor leagues and had the best ERA in the American Association in 1956 (2.72 for Indianapolis), but every time he earned a promotion to the majors, he failed. He was 1–6 for the Athletics, Indians, and Phillies; the one win for Cleveland, his only major-league shutout, represented his one day in the sun. He left after the 1958 season with a 4–18 record and a 6.18 ERA.

Dick Weik is another pitcher whose highlight film would have been a short subject. His main claim to fame was being traded by the Senators to the Indians even-up for Mickey Vernon in 1950 in one of the most lop-sided deals in history. Weik, already 5–17 at the time of the trade, was even worse afterward, with a 3–11 mark for Cleveland and Detroit (he came to the Tigers in a trade that included two-time skunk Art Houtteman). Vernon, meanwhile, returned to the team that he starred for during the 1940s and won his second batting title in 1953. He played five solid years for Washington and was finishing out his 20-year career with the 1960 champion Pirates long after Weik had pitched himself out of the majors.

Sid Hudson, Weik's pitching coach at Washington, remembered the young Iowa hurler. "Well, he never really pitched much," Hudson told us. "He had a good arm, but he's another one of those who never really acquired any kind of control." Now that's a bit of an understatement. Johnny Gray was merely wild. Weik, nicknamed "Legs," was the Wild Man of Borneo.

Weik pitched 213⅔ innings in the major leagues and gave up more bases on balls (237) than hits (203)—for an average of ten walks per nine innings. He was tall and threw a blazing fastball, but he had no clue where the ball was going. Like Johnny Gray, Weik's minor-league pitching offered a glimpse of his major-league future: Weik walked 15 men in the first game he pitched, for Charlotte in the Tri-State League in 1946. As a rookie in 1949, he walked 13 in a six-inning game against the White Sox; four times he walked ten or more in games he started, and he didn't start all that many.

You've got to go back to 1887 to find Weik's equal in the majors. That season, when it took four strikes to get a man out and five balls to give him first base, the Giants rookie lefty Bill George never quite mastered the art of getting the ball over home plate. In a period of about a month, he walked 13, then 16, and then 13 again.

John Cassidy Root Canal Award: Hal Griggs

Johnny Gray (4–18) and Dick Weik (6–22) were great candidates for the John Cassidy Root Canal Award, but so were a lot of other pitchers—like Craig Anderson (7–23) and two 7–25 clones (Rip Coleman and Jim Duckworth). But they all fell just short of the numbers put on the board by Hal Griggs (6–26, .188, 5.50 ERA). Griggs, a thin right-hander from Georgia, had a short career from start to finish: He never played baseball in the Little League, in high school, or anywhere else. He was a bellhop in a Miami hotel when the owner of a minor-league team in DeLand, Florida, asked the 21-year-old to try out for the team. Griggs made the team and was promptly sold to Hickory in the Class D League for $100. He insisted that he never even held a baseball until his tryout. "Played a little football in grammar school, but that's all I knew about sports," he told reporters. "All I knew about baseball was that they played it with nine men on a team."

Griggs was not an instant hit at Hickory in 1950. He won three of his first four starts; then batters learned that all he had was a fastball. He lost 18 straight games and had to win his last four games of the year to salvage an 8–21 season (he led the league in walks, and his ERA was 5.86). He wasn't much better the next year (10–16), but he became so hooked on pitching that he got married in June 1952 at the pitcher's mound in Hickory, North Carolina. ("I couldn't hit, so there was no sense getting married at home plate," he said.) The ceremony at the pitcher's mound didn't jinx his marriage—and maybe it even helped his pitching—because suddenly he turned into a .500 minor-league pitcher as he climbed the ladder from

Above: **Hal Griggs, the winner of the John Cassidy Root Canal Award, went from being a bellhop to a minor-league pitcher without ever playing baseball (photo courtesy of George Brace).**

Class D to B to A. When he made it to Double-A ball in 1955, he actually became good. He was 15–9 for Chattanooga, including a seven-game winning streak early in the season. Griggs was a spring-training sensation for the Senators in 1955, and he almost made the big team. Thinking about his great start in Double-A ball that year, he mused, "Can you imagine what would have happened if I had that start in the big league? And I might have done it, too. I'd have been in tall cotton."

More likely, he'd have been in tall weeds. When Griggs got his chance with Washington in 1956, he was 1–6 with a 6.02 ERA. So down he went to Chattanooga, where he was 21–12 in 1957, and earned another promotion. But at the major-league level, he excelled in nothing but losing. He pitched in two games with the Senators in 1957 and then stayed with the team for the 1958 and 1959 seasons. Griggs had his moments. In one late-season game in 1957, Griggs got Ted Williams to ground out, halting Williams' major-league record of reaching base 16 straight times. And in 1959, he had one good week in July, beating Cleveland 3–1 and shutting out the Yankees 7–0 on two hits. Take away that one week, and Griggs was a cumulative 3–20 from 1957 to 1959. Griggs pitched in the minors in the early 1960s, and he pitched well. But he never got another crack at the majors, securing his niche as his era's John Cassidy Root Canal winner.

The Worst Single Season of the Era: Don Larsen

Don Larsen lost 18 games more than he won in 1954 and had a WAT of −8.1, the worst marks of his era, as shown in a table at the end of the chapter. His 3–21 record was the worst of the era, outdistancing these other inept pitcher-seasons (the top three among the century's worst):

Order, Pitcher, and Year	Won	Lost	Percentage	ERA	Adj. ERA	WAT	TPI
1. Don Larsen (1954)	3	21	.125	4.37	82	−8.1	−0.9
2. Art Houtteman (1948)	2	16	.111	4.66	94	−7.1	−0.2
3. Kent Peterson (1948)	2	15	.118	4.60	85	−6.2	−1.1
4. Roger Craig (1963)	5	22	.185	3.78	92	−6.1	−0.6
5. Craig Anderson (1962)	3	17	.150	5.35	78	−4.2	−1.5

When the St. Louis Browns moved to Baltimore in 1954, the scenery really didn't change that much. The 1953 Browns were 54–100, and the 1954 Baltimore Orioles were 54–100, although the new Orioles managed to escape the cellar. But Larsen's misfortunes were not just due to bad teammates. He was a .125 pitcher on a team that played nearly .400 ball without him. He won eight games fewer than the average pitcher would have won for the Orioles and compiled one of the five worst WATs of the century.

We all know Larsen for the perfect game he pitched against the Dodgers in the limelight of the 1956 World Series, for his no-windup delivery, and for his reputation as an all-night partier; his 3–21 travesty has been all but forgotten. Yet that abominable season helped put Larsen in a Yankee uniform because he had

the good luck to record two-thirds of his wins against New York. When the Yankees completed an 18-player trade with Baltimore after the 1954 season, mostly to put Bullet Bob Turley in pinstripes, they remembered Larsen's pair of wins and got him, too.

Larsen was shipped to the minors by Casey Stengel the next spring, but by the time the 1955 season was over, he had practically reversed his 1954 mark by going a combined 18–3: He won nine out of ten decisions at Denver and then posted a 9–2 record after his call-up to the Yankees. Only a shelling in game four of the World Series, which helped Brooklyn come back from a two-game deficit to win its first World Series, spoiled his campaign.

The next season, Larsen's glory year, almost ended before it began when a telephone pole got in the way of his car at 4:00 A.M. during spring training. But the Lenny Dykstra of the 1950s walked away unharmed. "He was probably mailing a letter," Stengel deadpanned. Stengel's ability to forgive, as well as his astuteness, helped Larsen shine in the World Series. Larsen was knocked out of five of his first seven games of the regular 1956 season; his fortunes didn't change until Stengel taught him the no-windup delivery he had learned from Bullet Joe Rogan, the Negro League ace.

When the year ended, Larsen was a decent 11–5; more impressive was the .204 that opponents hit against him—second in the majors only to the

Above: **Baseball fans remember Don Larsen as Mr. Perfect, but in 1954 his 3–21 record branded him with the worst season of his era (photo courtesy of George Brace).**

sensational Cleveland sopho-more Herb Score. The Dodgers weren't impressed. Larsen blew most of a 6–0 Yankee lead in game two of the 1956 World Series and didn't make it out of the second inning, for his second Fall Classic disaster in two tries. But Stengel didn't lose faith—perhaps because Ted Williams had insisted that Larsen's new delivery plus October shadows in Yankee Stadium spelled trouble for the Dodgers—and he handed the ball to Larsen for the crucial game five. Twenty-seven outs, 97 pitches, numerous wicked curveballs, and only one three-ball count later, Larsen was perfect, Williams was a prophet, and Stengel was a genius. Mr. Perfect was also a bit of a prophet; he told a cab driver on the way to the stadium that he had a feeling that he was going to pitch a no-hitter.

Larsen never approached the heights of the 1956 World Series, and he never came close to the 3–21 mark that branded him the single-season skunk of his era, though he did have 1–10 and 4–9 records later in his career. He was 7–12 as a Browns' rookie in 1953 and was the sad owner of a 10–33 record when the Yankees dealt for him. His record as a Yankee was good (45–24) but his career totals (81–91, 3.78 ERA) were mediocre. In the final balance, Larsen was probably a better hitter than a pitcher. He set a major-league record for pitchers with seven straight hits as a rookie, was often used as a pinch hitter, and had a lifetime average of .242. He hit 14 home runs, including four in 1958 when he batted .306.

ART HOUTTEMAN

Art Houtteman (pronounced *How*-ta-man, not *Who*-ta-man) pitched his first major-league game for Detroit in 1945 at the age of 17 and was a

Above: **The forgotten fourth starter on the Lemon-Garcia-Wynn Indians of 1954, Art Houtteman once won 19 games. But he also won two Skunk Stearns trophies and posted the second worst season of his era (photo courtesy of George Brace).**

nifty 7–2 the year he turned 20. His curve was sharp and his sinker deceptive, and the Tigers were primed for a big year. Instead, the 21-year-old posted a 2–16 record in 1948, to trail only Don Larsen in the worst single-season sweepstakes. Ironically, the pitcher Houtteman beat out for the 1948 Skunk Stearns Award (a 2–15 Kent Peterson of the Reds) finished with the third worst season of the era.

Houtteman, in his mid–60s and a steel executive in Michigan for about 30 years, was happy to share his baseball memories with us in a telephone conversation. He remembered his 1948 skunk season well.

"With 2–16, I was young," he told us. "That was '48, and I got bad breaks. I probably didn't handle it properly, mentally. I pitched well. When I was 2–12, I had the lowest ERA in the big leagues, with less than two. Then in the last six, seven weeks of the season, I got the hell kicked out of me, literally, and it ballooned. I pitched well, but I was pitching losing baseball. I couldn't get the guy out I had to get out. Chances are your attitude affects more things than the physical part."

In 1949, when he almost died in a car wreck during spring training, he proved that mental attitude can be more important than physical health: He came back to post a 15–10 record, despite a head injury, and was 19–12 the next year with a league-leading four shutouts. But the army was more impressed with his win total than his physical condition. "The 1950 season ended October first, I got married the seventh, and went into the service on Friday the thirteenth," he told us. "This is not complaining, but I had a double skull fracture in an automobile accident. I had permanent damage to the head, but I was 1A because I was a winning pitcher and the public doesn't look at it that way. They say, 'Hey, here he is; he can win 19 games, but he can't go in the service like all the rest of the boys.'"

Houtteman spent one year in the army and then suffered the painful loss of his baby in another car crash. When he returned to Detroit in 1952, it was as a 20-game loser; he won his second Skunk Stearns trophy, tying with teammate Virgil Trucks for the honor. "I didn't pitch bad," he told us. "I'll tell you, it's not easy to pitch a record like that because of the fact that to lose that many games, you have to get out there a lot. That meant that they didn't have anybody better to do it. It's just the ball club got old at the end of 1950 and 1951; it was poor, and it was just completely in bad shape. We couldn't score any runs. You had to darned near shut somebody out to beat them."

He almost joined Trucks in the 1952 no-hit club when he beat Cleveland 13–0, but gave up a single with two outs in the ninth. "What's funny about that," he told us, "is on that particular play, it was the only pitch I called that day. The catcher went down with something else, and I shook my head off, and he was all upset but we went with what I wanted and the guy got a single."

The worst game he ever pitched? "Well, one day I was warming up and really feeling confident; I just couldn't wait until I got out there. I was thinking mentally that I felt so good and I was throwing so hard that after they see it, they're going to want to quit. They hit the first pitch I threw against the fence in left field, and I couldn't believe I made a mistake. I threw another one and someone else hit that one real hard, so I started a bunch of garbage—junk and change-ups—and they just ripped the hell out of me. Every time I'd throw one harder, they'd just hit it a little farther. I had never in my life thought I had so much stuff. It was funny. They just turned me around and knocked me out of the ball game."

Houtteman was 2–6 for the Tigers in 1953, when the Tigers gave up on him and traded him to Cleveland in a four-for-four deal. He went 7–7 for the Indians that year and then was the fourth starter on the 1954 Cleveland team that won 111 games but was swept in the World Series by the Giants. But all any fan remembers is Bob Lemon, Early Wynn, and Mike Garcia. "I won fifteen, lost seven, and nobody knew I was on the ball club," he told us. And the World Series ended so quickly that he lost out on a start, appearing just once in relief. Herb Score's arrival on the Indians' scene the next year took Art out of the 1955 starting rotation, and by the age of 30 the 12-year veteran was washed up. In 1956 and 1957 he appeared in 30 games for Cleveland and Baltimore, mostly in relief, and was less effective than a batting-practice pitcher. He had an ERA of 7.85. With Baltimore for five games in 1957, batters hit .513 against Houtteman before he was let go.

His final stats (87–91, 4.14 ERA) were similar to Don Larsen's. And like Larsen, Houtteman was usually very good or bad, but rarely as mediocre as the bottom line may suggest. And through the good times and bad, "I had better success against the better hitters," he told us. "The lesser hitters hurt me."

ROGER CRAIG

Although many skunks have become pitching coaches and managers, few have excelled like Roger Craig. The current Giants' manager has been cited as a great pitching coach. He became Sparky Anderson's right-hand man during the early 1980s and helped lead the Tigers to the 1984 World Series, after paying his dues in San Diego and Houston. Anderson told reporters, "The man is a genius. I could drop dead tomorrow, but if we lose Roger Craig, we've got problems."

Though Sparky understated his own value to the Tigers, he was right about Craig, who left after the 1984 World Series to manage San Francisco. The late Clay Kirby had nothing but praise for his former Padres' pitching coach. "He knew how to motivate each person," Kirby told us. "There would be one guy you'd have to give a swift kick; another guy you could just talk to; another guy, you could give him a goal. He knew personalities and how to get the most out of each player."

Craig has also been a pioneer of the split-fingered fastball, teaching it to such stars as Jack Morris and Mike Scott. His Giants won the 1987 Western Division and the 1989 NL pennant (when the Grateful Dead sent Craig a congratulatory telegram during the play-offs, he thought it was from a funeral home). But just as Craig's name in now synonymous with winning baseball, it was once the epitome of losing baseball.

Craig started off fine, enjoying success with the Brooklyn Dodgers from day one when he and Don Bessent were brought up together from the minors in mid–July 1955. The rookies won a doubleheader to bail out a pitching staff that had been plagued by sore arms, preventing the team that began the season with ten straight wins (and was destined to win its first world's championship) from wilting in the heat of the summer. Craig, who started and won game five of the 1955 World Series and tied for the NL lead with four shutouts in 1959, has the distinction of being the last pitcher to take the mound for the Brooklyn Dodgers. He was heading for peaceful mediocrity in Los Angeles, after breaking his shoulder in 1960 and going 5–6 in 1961. But then the Amazing Mets paid $75,000 for him in the expansion draft, and pitching immortality was his.

Skunkdom was forecast even before Craig took the field. On April 9, he was among 16 Mets who were stuck in a hotel elevator for 20 minutes. And when Roger took the mound for the Mets on opening day, he again showed a sign of things to come. In the 11–4 bombing, the Cardinals scored the first run against the Mets when Craig dropped the ball during his wind-up, balking in future NL President Bill White from third base. Craig was chastised by manager Casey Stengel: "You're standing on two tons of dirt. Why don't you rub some of it on the ball?"

It was all downhill from there. Craig was 10–24 with a 4.51 ERA in 1962. "You can't win the game," he told reporters that year. "You go out there knowing that. So you try harder. Try too hard, it usually turns out. You're out there concentrating so hard that the first thing you do is make a mistake. The losing doesn't bother me. It's the not winning that hurts."

In 1963, Craig sank to even lower depths than in 1962. His 5–22 record, fully equipped with an 18-game losing streak, combined with a 3.78 ERA and a WAT of −6.1 to form the fourth-worst year of the era. The subzero WAT meant that an average pitcher on the Mets that season would have won six more games than Craig did. How humiliating to be so much worse than a team that lost 111 games and finished 48 games out of first! Of course, the Mets' offense didn't help Craig's cause any. The Mets were shut out eight times during his NL record-tying losing streak. After another loss, a reporter asked Craig if he believed in God. "Yes," he answered. "and he wouldn't be a bad guy to have in the lineup."

The streak finally ended on August 9, after Craig changed his uniform number to 13, when the Mets beat the Cubs 7–3. Craig took a 2–20 record into the game and pitched well, giving up three runs in nine innings. The game seemed to be heading for extra innings when Jim Hickman blasted a two-out grand slam to give Craig the victory. *Life* magazine ran a photo of Craig hugging his daughter after the streak was finally over, and today Craig has a blown up poster of the photo displayed in his den. In all, Craig was shut out nine times in 1963. Only Bugs Raymond (11 times in 1908) and Walter Johnson (ten times in 1909) have been shut out more this century.

Craig was traded to St. Louis after the 1963 season and won game four of the 1964 World Series with a sparkling relief performance, but was traded that winter to the Reds. He retired after stints with the Reds and Phillies with a 74–98 record. Most media-guide biographies of him tactfully skip over his years with the Mets, discussing his early years with the Dodgers and then moving on to his coaching and managerial career. But his 15–46 record in 1962–63 earns him a comfortable niche in our book.

In fact, Craig came close to winning two straight Skunk Stearns tro phies, but he was beaten out in the Mets' maiden year by teammate Craig Anderson. Whereas Roger suffered through five 1–0 defeats during his 10–24 season, Anderson just suffered with a 3–17 record and a 5.35 ERA that ranked as the fifth-worst season of the era. Anderson earned two of his three 1962 wins on the same day when he relieved in both ends of a 3–2, 8–7 sweep of the Milwaukee Braves, the first doubleheader-triumph for the Mets. When he went to sleep on May 12, he had a 3–1 record for 1962 and a career mark of 7–4. Things looked great for the young right-hander, but when his major-league career came to a halt in 1964, he was still stuck on seven wins—against 23 losses. He lost 16 straight in 1962 and was 0–3 during the next two seasons. He even lost the last game played at the Polo Grounds, when Chris Short and the Phils thumped the Mets 5–1 in September 1963. Stengel never took to Anderson's gentle, scholarly, non-aggressive manner. The college-educated hurler who refused to knock down a batter ended his career with 19 straight defeats, outdoing even Frank Bates's desperate swan song (14 straight losses) for the 1899 Spiders.

The Worst Pitchers of the Era: *Jay Hook and Jack Fisher*

Herm Wehmeier had the worst single-season TPI of his era, and his career TPI of −14.3 is the worst of the 20th century. Otherwise, the career stats of this journeyman who pitched mostly for the Reds from 1945 to 1958 were bad (92–108, 4.80 ERA), but not bad enough to qualify as one of the worst pitchers ever. In contrast, the other pitchers who dominated

Order and Pitcher*	Won	Lost	Percentage	ERA	Adj. ERA	WAT	TPI
1T. Jay Hook	29	62	.319	5.23	75	−6.0	−10.5
1T. Jack Fisher	86	139	.382	4.06	88	−14.6	−10.7
3. Phil Ortega	46	62	.426	4.43	75	−2.8	−11.7
4. Galen Cisco	25	56	.309	4.56	81	−5.5	−5.7
5. Sid Hudson	104	152	.406	4.28	95	−8.0	−0.9

T = tie.

our categories (see the table at end of the chapter) were truly terrible. Jack Fisher and Jay Hook were among the worst of the 20th century, while Phil Ortega and Galen Cisco made the century's "25 worst" list.

Although the New York Mets' Fisher and Hook didn't finish in a flat-footed tie in Chapter 7's ratings of the 20th-century pitchers, they were too close for us to pick one or the other as the worst of their era. So we called it a tie between the two men who gained most of their notoriety while pitching for Casey Stengel's Mets. The era's five worst:

JAY HOOK

Jay Hook was probably one of the most intelligent pitchers of the past 50 years and certainly one of the worst. He was an early bonus baby, signing with the Reds for $65,000 after earning a bachelor's degree in mechanical engineering from Northwestern. A member of the American Rocket Society, Hook wrote about the scientific aspects of the curveball

Above: **Jay Hook understood Bernoulli's principle, thanks to his training as an engineer, but he never could get the ball to hook (photo courtesy of George Brace).**

for *Sport, The New York Times,* and various magazines on hydrodynamics. Unfortunately, Hook was the epitome of unapplied knowledge.

"Just because you understand Bernoulli's Law doesn't mean you can apply it effectively," he told reporters. "Just because you know why a baseball curves doesn't mean you can throw one."

Hook started off with some solidly mediocre years for the Reds, although he showed signs of skunkhood with an 11–18 record in 1960 with a league-leading 31 home runs allowed. He had compiled a 17–28 record for Cincinnati through 1961, having suffered a bout of the mumps in 1961. "The mumps left me extremely weak, and I fell into bad habits trying to compensate for my loss of strength," Hook told reporters."I not only wasted a year, but actually regressed."

Like Roger Craig, the Mets chose him to join their unforgettable staff of skunks. Unlike Craig, he was one of the team's four $125,000 premium players. Little did they know...

Hook won New York's first game 9–1 over the Pirates on April 23 (after nine Mets losses), but his other wins were few. He was 8–19 in 1962, but was spared further indignities because of manager Casey Stengel's ego. "I'm not going to go down as the only manager in history to have three 20-game losers," Stengel said. Roger Craig and Al Jackson were already there, so Stengel sat Hook down after number 19.

Hook did have the distinction of dubbing Marv Throneberry "Marvelous Marv." As Hook told author Edward Kiersh, "I was sitting in the Mets clubhouse, and Throneberry came up to me, saying, 'Hey Hook, you went to engineering school, right? You can print good, right? I want you to put up a sign for me.' I really didn't know what to do at first, but I said sure. I finally printed out this 'Marvelous Marv' poster and hung it on top of his locker. The graphics were great. Wouldn't you know, he hit a home run that day, and after the game all the reporters saw the sign. From then on the name stuck."

Stengel wanted Hook (like Craig Anderson) to be more aggressive, but Hook didn't respond to Stengel's advice. "I got the smartest pitcher in the world," Stengel said, "until he goes to the mound." In fact, Stengel and Hook later became close friends.

"It didn't bother me if Casey got mad sometimes," Hook told Kiersh. "He'd like to scold me, and would always say, 'Hey, scientist, if you know so much about why it happens, why can't you do it better?'"

Hook followed his 1962 campaign with a 4–14 mark in 1963, while serving as the Mets' player representative. His 5.48 ERA was the worst on the staff. "I feel I have the ability to pitch," he told reporters during the season, "and it makes me mad when I fail as I do. I'm determined to work it out."

He didn't. After starting off the 1964 season 0–1 with a 9.31 ERA, he

One of the most versatile of all skunks, Jack Fisher gave up memorable home runs to Roger Maris and Ted Williams and lost 53 more games than he won during an underwhelming career (photo courtesy of George Brace).

retired at age 28. Using the master's degree in thermodynamics he earned while pitching, he took a job with Chrysler's product-planning department. He also took with him a 29–62 record, a 5.23 ERA—and one of the two worst careers of the Jackie Robinson Era.

"I know I wasn't much of a player," Hook told Kiersh. "Ask Aaron, I did a lot for him and his record."

JACK FISHER

Fat Jack Fisher, a two-time skunk who tied Roger Craig's 162-game record for most losses in a season (24), joins Hook as having the worst career of his era. But he would still be in this book without all his negative records, without ever joining the Mets. Fisher, more than any other pitcher this side of Tracy Stallard and Charlie Root, had a knack for giving up home runs. Not in great quantities, like Robin Roberts or Bert Blyleven, and not even ones that decided crucial games, like Ralph Branca or Ralph Terry. Fisher's specialty was historic home runs, two in two Septembers while he was pitching for his original team, the Baltimore Orioles.

In 1960, the second-year hurler was 21 and enjoying what would be his only winning season (12–11) in his 11-year major-league career. He was branded a sensation when he won six straight games that included consecutive shutouts of the White Sox, Yankees, and Indians. He broke Hoyt Wilhelm's Orioles' record for consecutive scoreless innings in the process, providing "evidence to support the contention that here is truly one of the game's future pitching craftsmen," wrote John Steadman in *The Sporting News*. Then on September 28 he faced Ted Williams at Fenway Park in the Splinter's final game and, ultimately, his final at bat. Fisher had pitched seven innings of shutout relief when he faced Williams in the bottom of the eighth inning.

"The first pitch was a fastball for a ball, and the next pitch he swung at for a strike," he recalled more than a quarter of a century later in an interview with Michael Madden. "Then I threw a fastball out over the plate." We'll let author John Updike ("Hub Fans Bid Kid Adieu" in the *New Yorker*) take over from there:

> Williams swung again and there it was. The ball climbed on a diagonal line into the vast volume of air over center field. From my angle, behind third base, the ball seemed less an object in flight than the tip of a towering, motionless construct, like the Eiffel Tower or the Tappan Zee Bridge. It was in the books while it was still in the sky.

A year later, almost to the day, Fisher was on the wrong end of Roger Maris' historic 60th home run, paving the way for Maris' immortal 61st blast against Stallard in the final game of the season. "Maris' was on a bad pitch. Ted hit a good pitch," Fisher told Madden. And as if Fisher felt lost without giving up memorable home runs, he also gave up one as a Met in late August 1965, when Willie Mays slugged a tape-measure shot, his 17th of the month, to break Ralph Kiner's NL record.

Fisher was 1–6 as an Orioles' rookie in 1959, but his sharp pitching in 1960 made A's scout Clyde Kluttz bemoan the fact that he'd lost Fisher to Baltimore. "I really wanted that boy for our organization," Kluttz said. "Even as an 18-year-old, he looked as if he knew what he was doing with every pitch." Fisher's hot streak seemed to make everyone forget about the skunk potential that was evident from day one. He was 0–5 at Knoxville in 1957, his first year in the minors, and lost eight straight minor-league games before earning his first win in 1958. In his first major-league exhibition start in 1959, he was pulled with no outs after giving up six straight hits to the Yankees. When he was brought up in midseason of that year, he took nearly three months to get his first win. Having no notion of the legacy of defeat that awaited him in his baseball future, Fisher, in 1960, looked back in despair at his minor-league past. "I can tell you that nothing has ever been tougher for me in my life than winning my first game," he said. "I was wondering if I was ever going to win. I had my doubts."

But in the wake of Fisher's hot streak in 1960, Steadman wrote, "He's the only 21-year-old . . . who pitched like he had a 41-year-old head." Little did the experts realize that the future "superstar" was about to start pitching as if he had a 41-year-old body. He walked 12 Angels in one game in 1961 en route to a 10–13 record, and compiled a 30–39 record in his four-year stint with the Orioles before they traded him to the Giants after the 1962 season.

San Francisco kept him for one year (6–10, 4.58 ERA) and promptly gave him his walking papers, peddling him to the Mets for just $30,000; he pitched the first game the Mets ever played in Shea Stadium in April 1964. The Mets lost to the Pirates, naturally, but Fat Jack escaped with no decision. That game began his four-year tenure with baseball's worst team, for which he carved out baseball's worst record: He won 38, lost 73, and copped two Skunk Stearns trophies. Yet he remained upbeat and didn't want to leave the Mets. Rumors that he'd be traded upset him. "I hope not," he told reporters. "I like it in New York. I like it with the Mets." But he was traded to the White Sox in 1968 and closed out his career with the Reds the next year, watching the Miracle Mets rise to the top. Fisher retired with 53 more losses than wins, the most by any pitcher who played most or all his career after World War II. And he left with stats that rank him among the worst of all time.

PHIL ORTEGA

Phil Ortega, a tall, thin Arizonan right-hander of Mexican and Yaqui Indian descent, had a lot in common with Jack Fisher. Both had to wait a while for their first major-league win (Ortega pitched in 32 games from

1960 to 1963, but didn't get his first win for the Dodgers until 1964), both pitched three shutouts in their first full season in the majors, and both of their teams grew impatient waiting for their potential to emerge.

The Dodgers traded Ortega to the Senators after the 1964 season in the Frank Howard-for-Claude Osteen deal. The blazing fastballer struck out seven consecutive Red Sox batters in 1966, but was erratic. When Ted Williams took over as manager of Washington in 1969, he told Ortega to throw curveballs for one-third of his pitches. Ortega told reporters in March 1969, "[Williams] wants 30 to 35 [curveballs] a game. I didn't throw that many in a month." He was sold to the Angels a month later, for whom he pitched five games in relief, and was gone from the major leagues for good.

Senators' pitching coach Sid Hudson remembered Ortega well. "Well, he was a tough one," he told us. "He didn't pitch very good for us, and he didn't take much advice. He thought he knew how to do it; he had his own ways. He didn't listen to hardly anyone. He wasn't too coachable."

GALEN CISCO

He was a very good fullback for the Ohio State team he cocaptained to a 1958 Rose Bowl victory over Oregon, and he is still an exceptional, highly respected pitching coach who is currently in charge of the Blue Jays' staff. But as a curveball pitcher, he was one of the worst of the 20th century. His winning percentage of .309, the worst of his era, is among the five worst of the century for pitchers with at least 50 losses, and his ERA of 4.56, which adjusts to 81, is also among the most undistinguished of any age.

He led the minor leagues twice in ERA, but in the majors he put together six straight losing seasons during the 1960s—including an 18–43 record with the Mets that featured a Skunk Stearns Award in 1964—before bowing out with a 1–1 record for the Royals in 1969. He came up with the Red Sox in 1961, but even the fact that he was related by marriage to BoSox executive assistant Milt Bolling didn't stop Boston from waiving Cisco to the Mets the following September.

How can a man who was so unsuccessful on the mound be so good at coaching other pitchers? We asked former Padres manager Greg Riddoch, who was on San Diego's coaching staff with Cisco in 1987, why so many bad pitchers have become good coaches. "Most people say the reason for that is that people who didn't achieve greatness as a player had to pay attention to detail," he told us. "They experimented a lot in order to be able to find out something that would allow them to compete with the better ability players. They paid more attention to detail, and mechanics, and those kind of things; that made them know more about mechanics than maybe a gifted player."

We hope that Riddoch's theory applies to poor hitters as well. Every fan knows about the "Mendoza Line" in the weekly lists of baseball batting averages. No one wants to fall below that line of incompetence, which was named for shortstop Mario Mendoza, who batted less than .200 five times and had a career mark of .215. Mendoza is now employed as the *hitting instructor* for the Angels' California League Class-A team in Palm Springs!

Cisco's one main claim to pitching fame was hurling the final nine innings of the 23-inning, seven hour, 23-minute marathon against the Giants on May 31, 1964. Two weeks earlier he had lost to Gaylord Perry in a 15-inning struggle, and Perry beat him again in the longest game (in elapsed time) in major-league history. The final score was 8–6, with Cisco giving up the go-ahead run on Del Crandall's ground-rule double with two out in the top of the 23rd. But neither Crandall's hit nor Cisco's solid nine innings was the real story of that game. Even Perry's ten shutout innings weren't the main story; rather, it was how he achieved them.

That game marked the first time Perry used the spitball, as the Hall of Famer recounted in his book, *Me and the Spitter*. Tired of being bottom man on the 11-man pitching totem pole, Perry took matters into his own hands that May evening. Entering the game in the 13th, he threw the spitter first to Chris Cannizzaro, who walked, and next to Cisco, who hit into a double play; Orlando Cepeda calmly rolled the ball back to the mound. Cisco became just a footnote in Perry's historical first spitball victory.

In June 1991, Cisco was proud of Blue Jays' reliever Mike Timlin, who was given a start and responded with six scoreless innings of one-hit ball.

Above: **Shown here as a Padres coach, Galen Cisco has excelled as a pitching coach, despite winning a Skunk Stearns Award and finishing his career with a .309 winning percentage (photo reprinted by permission of the *Times-Advocate*, Escondido, Calif.).**

In response to reporters, who asked him if Timlin was impressive, Cisco said: "Impressive? He was nearly impeccable, and there's a word I've always wanted to use." A look at Cisco's career stats indicates that, as a pitcher, he was quite the opposite of impeccable. The *Random House Dictionary* defines *peccable* as "liable to sin or error." Cisco was clearly a peccable pitcher, and that's a word that we've always wanted to use.

But the quiet ex–football star, who was in the same backfield as Howard "Hopalong" Cassidy at Ohio State, is impeccable as a person. "He was a great guy," Riddoch told us. "He had a great sense of humor, but you had to get to know him. He was very professional in the way he approached his job. He was somebody I'll always remember."

SID HUDSON

Like Galen Cisco, Sid Hudson excelled as a pitching coach for years, serving the Washington Senators on and off for 12 years from their debut in 1961, through their conversion to the Texas Rangers in 1972, and ending with the 1978 season. Now in his mid–70s, the transplanted Tennessee native still serves as the pitching coach for Baylor University in Waco, Texas. "I retired from Rangers' scouting in 1986," Hudson told us near the end of a long telephone chat. "The Baylor coach asked me to come out and work with his pitchers, and I've been doing that ever since. In fact, we just won a game today, 2–0. I'm just having a ball with all those young kids. I got some age on me, but I'm still pretty active."

Above: **A shoulder injury helped turn Sid Hudson, an overhand pitcher with a fine future, into a sidearmer with a combined 12–33 record in 1948–49. His stats were the fifth worst in his era and, ironically, he was pitching coach for two others who cracked our "five worst" lists: Phil Ortega and Pete Broberg (photo courtesy of Sid Hudson).**

As a youngster, Sid Hudson started off his career as if he'd be the new Bob Feller. Originally a first baseman-outfielder for Sanford in the Class D Florida State League in 1938, Hudson was sent in to pitch when the manager ran out of pitchers. He struck out six men in the two innings he worked and finished the season 11–7. The next year he was 24–4 for Sanford, leading the league in wins, percentage, and strikeouts, while posting a 1.80 ERA and completing every start. He made the jump to Washington in 1940, all the way from Class-D ball, increasing his salary from a meager $85 a month to a paltry $200 a month—and loving every minute. "It was a boyhood dream come true," he told us, "being a major-league pitcher and pitching against all those good hitters that I had been reading about."

Hudson got off to a 2–9 start for a Senators team that would finish the season in seventh place, and he remembered one of those early losses. "The worst game I ever pitched in my life was against Cleveland, the early part of the first year I was at Washington," he told us. "I walked the first three hitters to load the bases, and Hal Trosky, the first baseman, was the next hitter and he got a base hit. And I walked the next batter and I went away. We got beat about 23–4 or something."

Then Hudson caught fire. He took a no-hitter into the ninth against the Browns, and he remembers the June 21 game as it were yesterday. "Rip Radcliff hit a pop-fly double down the right-field line," he told us, "and I ended up winning the game 1–0." With Radcliff on third by a passed ball, the rookie calmly retired three in a row to preserve the shutout.

He ran off a six-game winning streak, and in August of that year he pitched a second one-hit shutout, against the A's. But the highlight of his rookie season was a pitching duel with an aging Red Sox hurler. "The biggest thrill I ever got was beating Lefty Grove 1–0 in 13 innings," Hudson told us. "Lefty Grove was my idol as a youngster growing up and I got to face him, so that was quite a thrill."

The tall, thin right-hander finished out the storybook season with a 17–16 record, and despite a 4.57 ERA, stardom was written all over him, unfortunately, in vanishing ink. Hudson pitched for 12 years with the Senators and Red Sox, and he never had another winning season. The Senators teams he played for during most of these years were bad, but Hudson was worse. He won a landmark game in 1947 (shutting out the Yankees 1–0 before 58,000 at Yankee Stadium on Babe Ruth Day), but had Skunk Stearns credentials in 1948, when he was 4–16 with a 5.88 ERA. His opposition that year came from Art Houtteman and Kent Peterson, who contributed two of the five worst seasons to the era, so he couldn't claim the trophy. But his stats rank him as the fifth-worst pitcher of his era. When he closed out his career in 1954 with his tenth losing season, he had lost 48 more games than he won (104–152). That number has been surpassed by only six pitchers this century, but just by one who began his career after 1930—Jack Fisher.

Hudson's record had already plunged to 10–17 by his third season, before he joined the military service, so it's hard to blame a wartime injury for his downfall. But when he returned to the AL in 1946, he had to cope with a bad shoulder. "I think I'd have won a lot more than I did, but I hurt my arm in the service, and I never was quite the same after that," he told us. "I came back and I couldn't throw as well as I could before, and it bothered me. I developed a bone spur on my shoulder during the war. The doctors told me I'd have to learn to throw from some other position or else I was through. I was a three-quarter arm pitcher; I dropped down to sidearm, threw every pitch from the side. I pitched that way for the last seven or eight years."

He blamed his worst seasons (1948–49, when he was 12–33) on the injury. "My shoulder was bothering me," he told us. "I was a little wild, starting off throwing everything to the side. They stuck by me, and I became a little better pitcher after that." Well, maybe he was more than a "little" wild. In 1948 he walked twice as many as he fanned and gave 12 free passes to the last-place Tigers on August 7.

Hudson was Ted Williams' teammate at Boston and his pitching coach at Washington, and he has fond memories of Ted. "One day in Boston we were playing the St. Louis Browns and I was pitching against Ned Garver," Hudson told us. Garver threw a lot of sliders, and the eighth inning rolls around and I'm behind 2–1 and it's my turn to hit with a man on first base. Williams didn't play this day, and he hit for me. He told me when he left the bench, 'Go on and get your shower, and I'll hit that little slider up in the right-field seats for you and win you a game.' And he did."

Hudson didn't mention it, but Williams claims that Hudson came the closest to beaning him in the majors. Ted told reporters, "I went to a 3–2 count on him in Washington, and he hit the bill of my cap and turned my cap right around."

"Yogi Berra hit me real good," Hudson told us. We'd go into Yankee Stadium and he'd say, 'Hey, Sid, how you doing, when you pitching?' He liked to hit at me. One day they sent him up to pinch-hit, and he hit a ball on his fist and it went trickling down the third-base line; it got by the third baseman and it went into left field for a double. It won the game. He got out to second base, and he said he'd been practicing that all spring."

We asked Hudson which current pitcher reminded him most of himself? "Oh, I don't know. I never tried to copy anybody, and," he laughed, "I don't think anybody tried to copy me."

Honorary Skunk: Warren Spahn

Warren Spahn won 363 games, more than any left-hander who ever lived, and he showed his flair for numerology by getting 363 lifetime hits.

He even slugged 35 home runs and has no right to be in a book on skunks. But if Sandy Koufax can be mentioned as runner-up for the Joe Hardy award, then Spahn can get an honorary skunk for his uncanny ability to give up home runs. Not just in bulk; the 434 he yielded is impressive, but Robin Roberts topped that with more than 500.

And it's not for giving up famous home runs, like the one he gave up to Willie Mays in 1951 to break the Say-Hey Kid's hitless streak at the start of his career or the one he yielded to Dale Long in 1956 during Long's eight-homers-in-eight-games streak (later tied by Don Mattingly) or the back-to-back homers he gave up to Ted Williams and Mickey Mantle in the 1956 All-Star game or the home run he gave up to Mays in the 16th inning to settle a marathon 1–0 contest in favor of Juan Marichal in 1963. Anyone can give up homers to those guys.

And it's not even for giving up a well-publicized home run to a 75-year-old Luke Appling in a 1982 old-timers game, although now we're getting warm. Spahn's honorary Skunk Stearns Award is for giving up home runs to the least likely suspects—other pitchers, including some who were awful hitters. Research by William Ruiz, published in the *SABR Bulletin*, revealed that Spahn gave up the following:

•Two homers in two years (1949 and 1950) to the "Hondo Hurricane," Clint Hartung, who was the "next Babe Ruth" only to Spahn.

•Two homers in the same game to Ben Wade (a .112 career hitter) in 1952.

•One of Koufax's two home runs, to beat Spahn 2–1 in 1962 (Koufax once struck out a record 12 straight times).

•Al Jackson's only home run of his career in 1964.

•Jim Bunning's first NL home run to decide a 1–0 contest in 1965.

Honorary Skunk: Pedro Ramos

Camilo Pascual's pitching partner-in-crime with Washington in the late 1950s was right-hander Pedro "Pistol Pete" Ramos, who did not win a˙Skunk Stearns Award, but gets an honorary one for leading the AL in losses for four years straight. Phil Niekro led the NL in defeats four times, but not in a row, and in one of those seasons he tied for the league lead in wins with his brother Joe. Pistol Pete, who was a cowboy television actor in Cuba, averaged a 12–19 record from 1958 to 1961 and paced the junior circuit with 18, 19, 18, and 20 losses. He lost 43 games more than he won in his major-league career (117–160), trailing only Fisher and Hudson among pitchers who started their careers since 1940.

Paul Richards once nearly caught Ramos wet-handed throwing a spitter. Although Ramos didn't deny the charges, he did object. "Me no throw spitter," he told Richards. When Richards asked what Ramos called it, Pedro smiled and said, "That's what we call a Cuban palm ball." While playing for Gil Hodges' Senators, Don Zimmer had a hard time hitting Ramos. "Pete had only two pitches," Zimmer told reporters, "the spitter and a sidearm slider. Everybody could tell when he was loading up a spitter. Gil would yell for me to step out of the box, so the spitter would dry. I said: 'Hell, I'd rather try to hit the spitter than that damned sidearm slider.'"

Zimmer aside, Ramos gave up many home runs—an astonishing one for every 7½ innings—while pitching much of the time in spacious Griffith Stadium. As John Thorn and John Holway wrote in *The Pitcher*, "When Pedro Ramos pitched, the old joke went, the ground crew dragged the warning track."

After baseball, Ramos was arrested several times in the late 1970s and early 1980s for concealing a weapon, drunk driving, and cocaine possession. When author Edward Kiersh interviewed Ramos in prison in the early 1980s, Ramos rambled disjointedly about conspiracies and being framed. However, a recent issue of *Baseball Cards* reported that Ramos, apparently back on his feet, is a vice president of a Miami firm.

Honorary Skunk: Carl Scheib

Carl Scheib, spotted during a high school game by a traveling salesman who knew Connie Mack, debuted for the Athletics on September 6, 1943, at 16 years, 8 months, and 5 days: the youngest pitcher in AL history. But he was in his early 20s when he earned his honorary Skunk Stearns Award. He was 3–10 (7.22 ERA) in 1950 and 1–12 (4.47 ERA) the next year—not enough decisions to capture a Skunk Stearns trophy. But if you combine his stats for those two consecutive seasons (4–22), Scheib lost 18 more games than he won—the same as Don Larsen's era-leading number. In fact, Scheib's two-year stats bear more than a passing resemblance to Larsen's during his worst season of the era (1954):

Year	Skunk	Team	Won	Lost	%	ERA	Adj. ERA	WAT	TPI
1950–51	Carl Scheib	Philadelphia: AL	4	22	.154	5.64	82	−7.5	−1.6
1954	Don Larsen	Baltimore: AL	3	21	.125	4.37	82	−8.1	−0.9

Though it took Scheib two years to accomplish what Larsen managed in one, we awarded an honorary Skunk Stearns trophy to the A's right-hander. After Scheib went 14–8 in 1948, Mack told reporters, "Scheib

could well be the pitcher of the year. That boy could win 20 games for us." Scheib didn't, and he was sometimes Mack's whipping boy. Mack let Scheib absorb a 13-run thrashing in one inning against the Red Sox and watched the White Sox rake Scheib for nine runs in the first inning, but he didn't even warm up a reliever. "Mr. Mack wanted to prove something to that boy, I don't know what," Jimmy Dykes once told Joe Falls.

Maybe it was to crush his morale. "It seems like, not just with our club but any club," Scheib told us, "you score two runs or three runs, and they score four. If you score one run, they score two." Scheib wanted a one-way ticket out of Philadelphia and an excuse to leave the mound. "I really would have liked to have been traded by my team," he told us. "And I would have liked to have played the outfield."

Scheib had one strong memory of his 1–12 season in 1951: "At the end of the year I got a raise." But that raise may have been for his hitting because he batted .396 with a .623 slugging average. And the former A's pitcher was not too influenced by his lifetime stats (45–65 with an inflated 4.88 ERA) when he told us how he'd do if he were playing now. "J'm sure I could do well today. The style of pitching today is completely different from our time." Have things changed *that* much?

Scheib was sold to the Cardinals in 1954, but the change of scenery didn't help. He pitched in three games, had an 11.57 ERA, and was returned to the A's in June. His major-league career was over at age 27; he pitched in the minors after that in places like Portland and San Antonio, but never made it back. There's not much more to say. As Scheib told us, "I was pretty dull."

Above: **As a 16-year-old in 1943, Carl Scheib was the youngest ever to pitch in the AL. As a young veteran in 1950–51, he had a combined record of 4–22 (photo courtesy of Carl Scheib).**

Single-Season Leaders: 1947–68
(Minimum of 15 Losses)

Order, Name, and Year*	Statistic

Losses minus Wins

1. Don Larsen (1954)	18
2. Roger Craig (1963)	17
3. Jack Fisher (1965)	16
4T. Art Houtteman (1948)	14
4T. Virgil Trucks (1952)	14
4T. Craig Anderson (1962)	14
4T. Roger Craig (1962)	14
4T. Dick Ellsworth (1966)	14

Winning Percentage

1. Art Houtteman (1948)	.111
2. Kent Peterson (1948)	.118
3. Don Larsen (1954)	.123
4. Craig Anderson (1962)	.150
5. Frank Sullivan (1961)	.158

Wins-Above-Team (WAT)

1. Don Larsen (1954)	−8.1
2. Art Houtteman (1948)	−7.1
3. Robin Roberts (1957)	−6.8
4. Joey Jay (1963)	−6.3
5. Kent Peterson (1948)	−6.2

Adjusted ERA

1. Rick Wise (1968)	66
2. Phil Ortega (1965)	68
3T. Jim Bouton (1965)	71
3T. Steve Hargan (1968)	71
5T. Alex Kellner (1954)	72
5T. Don Nottebart (1965)	72
5T. Jack Fisher (1967)	72

Total Pitcher Index (TPI)

1. Herm Wehmeier (1950)	−3.9
2. Sammy Ellis (1966)	−3.7
3. Chuck Stobbs (1957)	−3.4
4T. Harry Byrd (1953)	−3.2
4T. Jack Fisher (1967)	−3.2

T = tie.

Career Leaders: 1947–68 (Minimum of 50 Losses)

Order and Name*		Statistic	
Losses minus wins**			
1. Jack Fisher	53	(86–139)	
2. Sid Hudson	48	(104–152)	
3. Pedro Ramos	43	(117–160)	
4. Don Cardwell	36	(102–138)	
5. Ken Raffensberger	35	(119–154)	
Winning Percentage			
1. Galen Cisco		.309	
2. Jay Hook		.319	
3. Tracy Stallard		.345	
4. Duane Pillette		.365	
5. Tom Poholsky		.373	
Wins-Above-Team (WAT)			
1. Jack Fisher		−14.6	
2. John Buzhardt		−12.0	
3. Bo Belinsky		−11.4	
4. Mickey Harris		−10.6	
5. Art Houtteman		−9.6	
Adjusted ERA			
1T. Phil Ortega		75	
1T. Jay Hook		75	
3. Wade Blasingame		77	
4T. Galen Cisco		81	
4T. Fred Talbot		81	
Total Pitcher Index (TPI)			
1. Herm Wehmeier		−14.3	
2. Phil Ortega		−11.7	
3. Jack Fisher		−10.7	
4. Jay Hook		−10.5	
5. Lew Krausse		−8.0	

*T = tie.
**W–L in parentheses.

6

1969–1992
The Age of Expansion

◆ Some baseball eras are ushered in with drumrolls and drama, whereas others sneak in by a technicality, rule change, or majority vote. Babe Ruth and the Black Sox changed the face of baseball in 1919–20, and Jackie Robinson changed its color in 1947. Both sets of events moved baseball suddenly and dramatically into new dimensions: The live-ball era brought with it classic confrontations between pitchers and batters; the post–World War II era was accompanied by flaring tempers, threats of boycotts, and a classic confrontation between civil rights and wrongs.

But the era that began in 1969 was based on executive decisions and started with all the fanfare and excitement of a local city council meeting. Although expansion had begun earlier in the decade, when the majors went from 16 to 20 teams, the four additional teams that took the field for the 1969 season meant a realignment. The two leagues that had defined baseball since 1901 were each split in half, resulting in an increased dilution of talent, four "minipennant" races, four number one teams, and post-season playoffs to produce the World Series combatants. The Age of Expansion had dawned, by deliberate design, no different from the start of the new era in 1893, when the pitching distance was stretched to 60 feet 6 inches and the pitching box was replaced by a slab of rubber.

At least that was the grand plan. Who could have predicted that 1968 would take on its own unique personality and provide a dramatic punctuation point to mark the ending of the postwar era? It proved to be the Year of the Pitcher: Denny McLain, the AL's Most Valuable Player, was the majors' last 30-game winner; Bob Gibson, the NL's Most Valuable Player, had a 1.12 ERA that defied believability; and both leagues had average ERAs below 3.00 for the first time in 50 years and for the only time since World War I ended. Drastic steps were needed to bail out the hitter, and they were immediately taken: The pitcher's mound was lowered to ten inches, and the strike zone was shrunk more than a wool sweater in a dryer.

Skunk Stearns Winners: 1969–1992

Year	Winner	Team	Won	Lost	Percentage	ERA	Adj. ERA	WAT	TPI
1969	Clay Kirby	San Diego: NL	7	20	.259	3.80	93	-2.9	-1.0
1970	Grant Jackson	Philadelphia: NL	5	15	.250	5.29	75	-4.7	-2.2
1971	Denny McLain	Washington: AL	10	22	.313	4.28	77	-3.9	-2.4
1972	Bill Greif	San Diego: NL	5	16	.238	5.60	59	-4.2	-3.6
1973	Clay Kirby	San Diego: NL	8	18	.308	4.79	72	-2.4	-3.2
1974	Randy Jones	San Diego: NL	8	22	.267	4.45	80	-4.7	-1.9
	Ron Bryant	San Francisco: NL	3	15	.167	5.61	68	-5.8	-2.6
1975	Andy Hassler	California: AL	3	12	.200	5.94	60	-4.2	-3.2
1976	Mike Cuellar	Baltimore: AL	4	13	.235	4.96	66	-4.9	-1.9
1977	Jerry Koosman	New York: NL	8	20	.286	3.49	107	-4.3	0.0
1978	Jerry Koosman	New York: NL	3	15	.167	3.75	93	-5.5	-0.9
1979	Matt Keough	Oakland: AL	2	17	.105	5.04	80	-6.7	-1.6
1980	Mike Parrott	Seattle: AL	1	16	.059	7.28	57	-7.1	-2.7
1981	Juan Berenguer	Kansas City/Toronto: AL	2	13	.133	5.26	73	-4.6	-1.3
1982	Rick Honeycutt	Texas: AL	5	17	.227	5.27	73	-5.0	-2.2
1983	Dennis Martinez	Baltimore: AL	7	16	.304	5.53	71	-6.1	-2.0
1984	Mark Davis	San Francisco: NL	5	17	.227	5.36	65	-5.2	-3.7
1985	Jose DeLeon	Pittsburgh: NL	2	19	.095	4.70	76	-7.9	-2.3
1986	Rick Sutcliffe	Chicago: NL	5	14	.263	4.64	87	-4.0	-0.7
1987	Rick Honeycutt	Los Angeles: NL/Oakland: AL	3	16	.158	4.71	84	-6.2	-0.8
1988	Jay Tibbs	Baltimore: AL	4	15	.211	5.39	72	-3.7	-2.4
1989	Doyle Alexander	Detroit: AL	6	18	.250	4.44	86	-4.2	-1.3
1990	Jose DeLeon	St. Louis: NL	7	19	.269	4.43	88	-5.4	-1.4
1991	Kirk McCaskill	California: AL	10	19	.345	4.26	98	-5.1	-0.4
1992	Kyle Abbott*	Philadelphia: NL	1	14	.067	5.13	68	-6.4	—

*Abbott's Adjusted ERA was adjusted for league, but not for ballpark; his TPI was unavailable at press time.

The one-year domination of the pitcher was ended. But not even Nostradamus could have foretold the events of 1969 — the first year of the new era — when Neil Armstrong's brief walk on the moon had to take a backseat to the New York Mets' surreal rise from perpetual doormat to the decimators of the Cubs, Braves, and mighty Orioles on their journey to the World Championship. A new era, running on some hidden momentum and with a secret agenda, had begun with fanfare after all. The Mets, who provided us with five Skunk Stearns Award winners in the seven years of their existence, now laid claim to the 1969 Cy Young winner in the person of a 25-year-old, hard-throwing right-hander named Tom Seaver, whose win total matched his age.

At some point during the 1970s, the Age of Expansion really turned into the Age of the Relief Specialist, fossilizing the complete game and putting terms like "blown saves," "inherited runners," and "holds" into the sports pages. Certainly, relief pitching represents the essence of the new era, but for the world of skunks, the diluted talent that resulted from expansion is an even more compelling factor. And one of the four new teams, the San Diego Padres, took over the Mets' role as chief supplier of skunks by winning four trophies during their first six seasons and by providing a steady flow of candidates for virtually every Skunk Stearns Award during the 1970s and early 1980s (see the table of winners for this era).

The Padres' staff was manned by Bill Greif and Steve Arlin, perennial skunk candidates, who had the art of losing down to a science; by Randy Jones, who shared the 1974 Skunk Stearns Award, but later won a Cy Young Award; and by the late Clay Kirby, who won the Skunk Stearns trophy as a rookie in 1969 and showed that it was no fluke by winning another one in 1973. Although San Diego's stranglehold on the trophy ended abruptly in 1974, baseball was well into the 1980s before the team stopped offering a contender or two for the annual Skunk Stearns competition. The parade of pitchers whose records were top-heavy with losses included forgettable names like Dave Freisleben, Bob Owchinko, Dan Spillner, Steve Mura, and Bob Shirley. If it was hard being a bad Padre hurler back then, it may have been even more frustrating being a star pitcher on a bad staff. Relief ace Rollie Fingers, a Padre from 1977 to 1980 and a recent Hall of Famer, told us: "When I was with the Padres, we weren't doing very well. We were less than a .500 ball club, and you don't want to really remember those kind of teams that you played on. You want to remember the ones that you won with. That's why I can remember more games with the Oakland A's than with the San Diego Padres. We got along fine, but after games we went our separate ways.

"These guys were the Padres, and I can't remember them throwing really exceptional games. We were very low key. We didn't do too much winning. We didn't score too many runs," Fingers said.

But the Padres did provide strong candidates for every major award that we offer. As was true for Mets pitchers from the previous era, watch for the roll call of San Diego pitchers in this chapter. These pitchers won several awards and ranked high in a few others. And when the Padres didn't take the top prize, they were outwimped by hurlers from other expansion teams, especially the Blue Jays and Mariners (who joined the major leagues in 1977). The current era of Skunk Stearns Awards truly reflects the Age of Expansion, just as the next era is sure to be dominated by has-beens and never-was's from the Florida Marlins and Colorado Rockies.

A Quartet of Two-time Skunks

The first Padre to grab the limelight was Clay Kirby. The list of Skunk Stearns winners indicates that Kirby was the first of four pitchers from the Age of Expansion to take a double dip of skunk poison and come away with two trophies. Kirby was joined by Jerry Koosman, as well as by active hurlers Rick Honeycutt and José DeLeon.

At their best, right-handers Kirby and DeLeon and southpaws Koosman and Honeycutt would have anchored an outstanding, well-balanced starting rotation. Kirby won 15 games and had a .536 winning percentage in 1971 for a Padre team that had a .346 percentage when he wasn't on the mound. Koosman led the Miracle Mets of 1969 to the World Series championship with two wins, won 20 twice, and retired with 222 wins. José DeLeon led the NL in strikeouts in 1989; Rick Honeycutt led the AL in ERA in 1983. But at their worst, the quartet compiled some of the most embarrassing won-lost marks in history, spiced by DeLeon's 2–19 tragedy in 1985. Combine their two skunk seasons apiece, and you get a cumulative 43–144 record, which translates to a .230 winning percentage.

CLAY KIRBY

Kirby, a tall right-hander, debuted with San Diego in the Padres' 1969 maiden season, and his 7–20 record paced the last-place Padres to 110 losses. *The Sporting News* accused him of having an air of cockiness and quoted a 1970 spring-training observer as saying, "You'd think he just won 20 games in the big leagues instead of losing 20."

His former teammates agreed. In the *San Diego Union* article that told of Kirby's tragic death from a heart attack in October 1991, at age 43, Dave Campbell referred to him as "borderline cocky." Steve Arlin said, "No borderline to it. Clay was cocky, brash, arrogant and still very popular. He was a young kid who did not back down from anything or anybody.... And baseball was his life. He was born to pitch."

"I was able to pitch in the big leagues, and I was in the starting rotation," Kirby told us in a telephone interview less than a year before his

sudden death. "I never missed a start in 143 starts. That was from day one. That's pitching in a four-man rotation. Counting rain-outs, too. I never was put back a day for any reason."

Clay became the subject of a no-hit controversy in July 1970, when he kept the Mets hitless through eight innings and then was lifted for a pinch hitter by manager Preston Gomez. In the bottom of the eighth, trailing 1–0, Gomez had Cito Gaston hit for Kirby. The move backfired when the future Blue Jays manager struck out, and San Diego reliever Jack Baldschun promptly gave up two runs in the ninth. Instead of getting a shot at immortality, Kirby was saddled with his 12th loss against five wins (he ended up 10–16). The 10,000 fans booed Gomez's move, and one large fan jumped down from his box seat and faced the Padres dugout. "We were such a non-descript team," Nate Colbert told Joe Gergen, "that he didn't know who the manager was." Security guards took the fan away before he could find out.

Kirby, who relied mostly on a fastball and slider, thought he would have gotten the no-hitter. "I came off the eighth pretty high," he told us. "I struck out Tommy Agee, the last hitter, on three pitches. I felt pretty good, and the only hitter I had to face that I felt was going to be hard was Bud Harrelson. Then I had two right-handers, and that was it. I didn't feel like I had any problems with right-handers that day.

"The manager did what he was going to do. I would have liked to have completed it, but he said if it happened again, he'd do it again. Well, it happened again, and I happened to be there because it was the team we were playing against. So he stuck by his word, and you have to respect a man for that." All Gomez did that "next time," while managing Houston in

Above: **Clay Kirby, the man who ushered in the Age of Expansion with a Skunk Stearns trophy as a 7–20 rookie in 1969 didn't even live to see the end of the era. He died of a sudden heart attack in 1991, nine months after we interviewed him (photo courtesy of George Brace).**

1974, was deprive Don Wilson of a shot at his third career no-hitter for the Astros. "Respect" is probably not the word that came immediately to Wilson's mind when thinking about Gomez, but we'll never know. The former Houston star died from an apparent suicide just a few months later.

Kirby had more near no-hitters than skunk trophies. He had a perfect game going through eight innings against San Francisco in 1971, but like before, it was not to be. "Willie McCovey, the leadoff batter, broke up the perfect game, no hitter, and shutout with a home run," he told us. "It was the only hit of the game, the only thing that happened. He hit a one-and-two slider down by his knees, and it was very windblown. It was hit very high, but it didn't go very far. It basically hit the back of the fence, and then went down. It was a shame."

Kirby, who won that game 2–1, had flirted with another no-hitter five days earlier. Houston's Johnny Edwards doubled to break it up with one out in the eighth, and Kirby eventually lost the game in the ninth on an unearned run. The flip side of Kirby's three near no-no's: "I once went one-third of an inning and gave up six runs, all on singles," Kirby told us. "I walked a couple. When you don't get out of the first inning. . . . Luckily for me, it didn't happen very often."

Kirby did have three winning seasons, including a 15–13 gem in 1971 when the Padres lost 100 games. But sometimes his pitching made his managers sick, and at least once it made him sick—literally: "I was warming up to pitch a Sunday game against the Dodgers," he told us. "My back hurt real bad, but I was like, give me the ball and I'll throw it. I'm not going to come out of a game or not start a game because something hurts. I took some pain pills at that time, which were legal. Apparently they upset my stomach.

"I was on the mound, and just after warming up in the first inning, I called the third baseman and I said, 'I don't feel good.' He said, 'What's the matter?' and I said, 'I think I'm going to throw up.' So he put his arm around my shoulder, and I just kind of threw up. I turned around and finished the game. It wasn't much, but it was just enough to get the icky feeling out. I beat them 4–2."

After plummeting to 1–8 for the Expos in 1976, Kirby attempted a comeback with San Diego. He told reporters, "I think the Padres are getting a bargain." But "The Kid," as Kirby was called, was through. He believed that his downfall came from the downside of modern training techniques. "I tore both knees out, which ended my career," he told us. "In my opinion, I did it from running long distance, which was the new way of training, which I didn't care for. That was Dick Dent, the new trainer that came out of college with all the new theories of cardiovascular buildup. His theories are good and they're probably right, but they didn't fit my body."

Kirby's final ledger read 75 wins, 104 losses, and two Skunk Stearns Awards. If he were pitching today, he estimated he'd earn $900,000 to $1.5 million. Sounds about right, though Kirby conceded that today's salary structure is "fine from the player's point of view, but not in line with the rest of the world."

JERRY KOOSMAN

Jerry Koosman has the dubious distinction of being the best pitcher since Red Ruffing to win consecutive skunks. But unlike Ruffing, who had his skunk seasons as a young player and then posted Hall-of-Fame numbers, Koosman was a ten-year veteran coming off a triumphant 21-victory year when he began his two-year tour of skunkdom for the Mets. In fact, Koosman sandwiched his award-winning 8–20 and 3–15 records in between the only two 20-win seasons of his 19-year career.

In 1977, Koosman held opponents to a .232 batting average, the fifth-best mark in the NL. But he couldn't blame his 20 losses just on his teammates. He had a .286 winning percentage; without him, the Mets played at a .418 clip.

Dr. Cecil Reynolds is a former minor-league pitcher who spent two weeks with the Mets in their Miracle Year after signing with them as a seventh-round pick in 1969. He remembered Kooz fondly.

"Koosman was basically the team clown before Tug McGraw took that away from him," Reynolds told us. "He was real loose and relaxed and easygoing. In the clubhouse, he was always clowning around. He had that look about him, too. He was always goofing off."

Koosman looked like a clown at the plate. In 1968, he struck out 62 times in 91 at bats and then struggled through a 4-for-84 year in 1969; he finished his career with a .119 batting average for almost a thousand at bats. A trade to the Minnesota Twins after his second skunk year in 1978 saved him further indignities at the plate, courtesy of the AL's designated hitter.

Although Koosman prospered for Minnesota—his 20–13 mark in 1979 earned him the Comeback Player of the Year award—he didn't escape an occasional detour into the world of skunks. He challenged Juan Berenguer for the 1981 Skunk Stearns trophy with a 4–13 record for the Twins and White Sox. Berenguer and Koosman tied for the AL lead with 13 losses in that strike-shortened season. Koosman had given the Twins 36 wins in his first two seasons with them, but that didn't stop Twins' owner Calvin Griffith from complaining to reporters after a poor showing by Koosman: "It's a Goddamn shame when a fellow with the experience of Koosman is pitching so lousy. As old as he is, that was one of the dumbest pitching jobs I've ever seen."

After spending 84 days on the disabled list in 1985, Koosman (along with his 4.62 ERA) was released by the Phillies, ending his baseball career.

After the season ended, he organized the first Jerry Koosman World Series Elk Hunt. The five-day hunt was set to be held near Gunnison, Colorado, a place known for its elk. Koosman's party, which included five major leaguers, didn't see a single elk for the entire hunt. "There was no snow at all on the ground," Koosman told reporters, "And they could hear us coming a mile away. We had a lot of fun, but the elk won." Kooz lost 209 games in the majors, but his final defeat was to the Colorado elks.

RICK HONEYCUTT

Rick Honeycutt won the first of his two Skunk Stearns trophies for Texas in 1982, but he was aware that his pitching bag of tricks needed a boost while he was still on the Seattle staff. So he threw thumbtacks, Band-Aids, and sandpaper into the bag. But he was no more able to fool umpires than opposing hitters. After he was caught red-handed by umpire Bill Kunkel in a September 30, 1980, contest against the Royals, he left the game red faced—literally. As he walked off the field, Honeycutt wiped his hand against his forehead, leaving a bright red scratch. The well-traveled southpaw, currently a relief pitcher for Oakland, was fined $250 and suspended for ten days for cheating. He had hidden a thumbtack under a Band-Aid on his index finger, not to mention sandpaper in his glove.

"It was the third inning," Kunkel told reporters. "I wasn't looking for anything in particular, but Willie Wilson had complained about some of the pitches. I saw the Band-Aid on his finger and asked him what happened. When I grabbed his hand, I got stuck. I was shocked." Umpire Nestor Chylak said that catching Honeycutt cheating "was about as difficult as spotting a whale in a bathtub."

"I thought the thumbtack trick up all by myself," Honeycutt told reporters. "Pretty smart, huh? Look, I was desperate at that point in the season. I figured, 'What did I have to lose?' Well, as soon as I see Kunkel come out to the mound, I tried to get rid of the tack. But I had done too good a job taping it on. I felt like I was being pulled over for speeding."

Honeycutt had reason to be desperate. He had started 1980 with a 6–0 record, but wound up 10–17, losing 14 of his last 15 decisions. He was a true master of up-and-down pitching. He was included in an 11-man swap with Texas during the winter, where he promptly posted an excellent 11–6 mark in strike-shortened 1981, and led the major leagues by allowing the fewest walks per game. Then he hit bottom in 1982, winning his first Skunk Stearns trophy as a 5–17 hurler with a 5.27 ERA.

Honeycutt rebounded in 1983 when he split the season between the Rangers and the Dodgers, finishing 16–11. But once more he showed his tendency for Sybil-like multiple-personality pitching. He pitched often enough for Texas to lead the AL with a 2.42 ERA, but then he tumbled to a 5.77 ERA with Los Angeles. The next time Honeycutt split a season between the two leagues (in 1987), he proved to be consistent; he was terrible with the Dodgers (2–12), and he never lost a step when he joined Oakland (1–4). The result was his second Skunk Stearns trophy, making him the first pitcher since Roscoe Miller (in 1902) to win the award while pitching for teams in both leagues.

In 1987, he started out like a world beater for Los Angeles, blazing through April and half of May with a 2–1 record and a sub-2.00 ERA. He set career highs in strikeouts by fanning nine Cardinals on May 1 and whiffing ten Pirates on May 7; then he threw a four-hit shutout against the Cubs on May 12. He still looked sharp when he lost 5–3 against the Phillies the next week, when all five runs were unearned and he lowered his ERA to a league-leading 1.31. Then the roof caved in. He lost his next ten games, was traded to the Athletics, and continued to lose with regularity.

Honeycutt has cleaned up his act. He no longer needs thumbtacks and sandpaper, and he no longer loses a ton of games. Of course, he's not a starter anymore. Still, he was a valuable cog in the A's three pennant-winning teams in 1988, 1989, and 1990, and though he was slowed by injuries in 1991, he's still an integral part of Oakland's bullpen. His specialties are throwing sinkers that keep the ball on the ground, keeping base runners honest, and making left-handed hitters look like fools.

Mike Parrott, a Skunk Stearns winner in his own right, talked to us about his former Seattle teammate Honeycutt: "Back in the late seventies, early eighties, Honeycutt loved Steve Martin. Steve Martin always used to do a King Tut strut. He [Honeycutt] was always going around the clubhouse dancing like Steve Martin, always trying to be like Steve Martin.

"As far as pitching, he's still doing a good job for Oakland. He never threw real hard, a Tommy John kind of pitcher. I'll see Honeycutt on TV, and it looks like he really hasn't changed much at all. The only thing that's a little different is that he has better command, better location of pitches. He never throws the ball over the middle of the plate now; he's always nibbling inside, outside, trying to get the hitters to swing at a bad pitch. I'd say that being left-handed, and the way he pitches, he'll probably be able to pitch for three or four more years."

Parrott may be right. Honeycutt earned career-win number 100 with a victory over the Royals on opening day of 1992. Still, there's a bit of skunk left in him; he first had to blow a save in relief of Dave Stewart to qualify for his milestone victory.

JOSÉ DeLEON

From a scout's dream to a manager's nightmare: José DeLeon. As a youngster, DeLeon was considered a top prospect. After starting off with a 7–3 record and a 2.83 ERA, *Baseball's Digest*'s John Kuenster rated the

Dominican among the top ten young starters. And he had reason to—the flamethrowing forkballer flirted with no-hitters in his second and third major-league starts. But then DeLeon got a chance to pitch regularly.

He was bad in 1984 (a 7–13 record), but 1985 played host to the instant trough of DeLeon's career. He was 2–19 with a 4.70 ERA, with just one complete game to show for his 25 starts. DeLeon lost his first seven games before combining with Al Holland to shut out Atlanta on two hits. He then lost 1–0 on June 7 before winning his next start, fanning 11 Phillies to claim a 3–2 victory. But with respectability within shouting distance, he blew it. He lost his last 11 games, taking a month's detour in mid–July to go 4–0 in the minors. "It would get to his head," Tony Pena, DeLeon's catcher that season, told reporters. "He would say, 'I'm going to pitch a good game, but I'm going to lose because we don't score any runs.' He was pitching as well as he did the other years, but got too frustrated, too confused. He thought he wasn't any good."

DeLeon could accuse his teammates of nonsupport, and it's hard to argue. The Pirates were shut out for seven of his starts and scored two or fewer runs in 14 of his 19 losses. They averaged a little over two runs per game for him, while averaging about five runs for teammates Joaquin Andujar (21–12) and Kurt Kepshire (10–9). Kepshire is a good example of what might have been for DeLeon with a bit of offense in 1985, since both gave up about five runs per game. But with or without excuses, 2–19 is *bad*.

People still called DeLeon a major prospect, even after his first skunk season, but these compliments didn't ease his pain. "Some people tell me that only Dwight [Gooden] can throw better," DeLeon told reporters, "and I'm tired of hearing that and losing games." Syd Thrift found a better way of comforting DeLeon: He gave DeLeon a hefty salary raise from $27,500 to $160,000 after he lost 19 of 21 decisions. "He deserved it just for having the courage to go out there regularly," Thrift told reporters. For that kind of money, the Cowardly Lion would beg Thrift for a chance to pitch.

DeLeon was then traded to the White Sox for Bobby Bonilla, who became a star for the Pirates and a $6,000,000 man for the Mets. (We could field an All-Star team who were swapped for Skunk Stearns winners.) DeLeon was a respectable 15–17 for Chicago in 1986–87. Two of his four wins in 1986 came in a span of six days—against Cy Young winner Roger Clemens! The only thing that kept the 24–4 Clemens from a 26–2 season for the Red Sox was a two-time winner of the Skunk Stearns trophy. He was then traded back to the NL, where he enjoyed a 16–12, 3.05 ERA season for the Cardinals in 1989; he led the NL with 201 strikeouts. He credited the White Sox's urging him to rely more on his sinker for improvement. DeLeon told *Baseball Digest* in 1989, "Before then I didn't have much movement on my fastball. The sinker added velocity to my fastball as well as movement."

Pena, again DeLeon's catcher in 1989 with St. Louis, said, "Now I think he has a chance to be a great pitcher." But just when it looked like he was about to fulfill his star potential, DeLeon wound up fulfilling his skunk potential instead. In 1990, his 7–19 record was the worst in baseball; once again, some of the blame goes to his teammates. Though they averaged a bit more than three runs per start for DeLeon, the offense plummeted once spring gave way to summer. The Cardinals scored only 17 runs for him in his last 21 starts, shattering his confidence. Add to his self-doubt a loss in his fastball's velocity and the poor location of his two key pitches (fastball and fork ball), and you get a man who failed to lose 20 only because his manager benched him when he reached 19.

DeLeon might have been a Cy Young candidate in 1990 if left-handed batters had been banished from the NL. He held right-handed batters to a crisp .187 average, but he was plagued by lefties, who hit .286. Opposing managers got the hint and stacked their lineup cards with left-handed batters. It worked. Cardinals manager Joe Torre linked DeLeon's 1990 slump with the near-skunk slump of Steve Carlton, who lost 19 games in 1970. Carlton "was afraid to throw his fastball," Torre told reporters. "I think pitchers fall into that. When they start losing, they start to become defensive. Plus, with DeLeon, there was the confidence factor."

Although he failed to match Red Ruffing's three Skunk Stearns trophies, DeLeon never snapped out of his losing habit; he finished with a 5–9 record despite an excellent 2.71 ERA. His July 23, 9–1 win over the Astros was his first complete game since July 31, 1989. DeLeon won again five days later, but went zero for the last ten weeks of 1991. He didn't taste a victory until he beat the Cubs in April 1992. The Cardinals finally gave up on DeLeon after he had won only eight of his previous 61 starts. In September 1992, they released him, his 2–7 record and his 4½ earned runs per game; now the Phillies will try to deal with the frustration of watching him come close, only to come away empty.

DeLeon gets paid pretty well to lose. If he thought he was lucky to get $160,000 after his 2–19 season, he had the consolation prize of an annual salary of $1,666,667 in 1991—not bad for a pitcher with a career mark (through 1992) of 75–113, a winning percentage of .399, and a lifetime WAT that is one of the worst of all time.

The Asa Brainard Humpty-Dumpty Award: Denny McLain

The names of the quartet of two-time Skunk winners may dominate the list of Expansion Era Skunks, but the name that jumps off the list is that of a two-time Cy Young winner: Denny McLain, the last man to win 30 games and the recipient of our Asa Brainard Humpty-Dumpty Award.

After the 1969 season, Denny McLain looked like a pretty sure bet for Cooperstown. Only 25, he had two Cy Young awards behind him and boasted a 114–57 record. The publicity may have rubbed off even on McLain's father-in-law, Lou Boudreau. The former All-Star shortstop was on the Hall of Fame ballot for more than a decade without coming close until his son-in-law won 30 games. And after McLain (24–9) was co-winner of his second Cy Young award the next season, Boudreau, in his final year of eligibility, was elected to Cooperstown.

McLain threw a no-hitter in his first pro start in 1962 for Harlan (Kentucky) in the Appalachian League and made national headlines a half-dozen years later with his incredible 1968 campaign that produced a 31–6 record, a unanimous Cy Young victory, a Most Valuable Player award, and a trip to the World Series for the Tigers. His problem, however, was with his brain, not his arm; and the seeds were planted early. The White Sox, who signed McLain in 1962 after he posted a 38–7 record at a Chicago high school, were so fed up with his many fines and broken curfews that they failed to protect the young phenomenon in 1963.

In 1967, McLain told sportswriters, during a tight pennant race, why the Tigers wouldn't make it to the World Series. (They didn't.) He might have won 20 games that season, for the second year in a row, if a mysterious accident at home that damaged his toe hadn't cost him his last six starts. He grated on his teammates and on Detroit fans, and his antics drove manager Mayo Smith crazy. In a game against the Twins, McLain and teammate Norm Cash were openly rooting against each other so each would be named player of the game and earn $100 for appearing on the

Above: **Even Asa Brainard's plunge doesn't match Denny McLain's fall from a two-time Cy Young winner and cinch Hall of Famer to a Skunk Stearns trophy and a prison cell (photo courtesy of George Brace).**

postgame show. With Cash yelling for the Twins' Harmon Killebrew to hit a home run in the ninth inning, McLain pitched what some teammates called his best inning of the year. Denny returned to the locker after the postgame interview with the $100 bill glued to his forehead.

In 1969, the man with an addiction to Pepsi-Cola placed a dental appointment over starting the All-Star game. And the year before, after notching his 31st win, McLain was accused of lobbing an easy fastball to Mickey Mantle so the Mick could get a home run and break his tie with Jimmie Foxx. (Mantle did, and then hit one more to avoid the taint.) Baseball was plain fun to McLain, and he couldn't take anything too seriously.

But it wasn't until 1970 that McLain's downfall truly began. He was suspended for the first three months of the season for gambling and consorting with gamblers and declared bankruptcy. Later in the season, in August, he dumped ice water on two sportswriters, to earn a week-long suspension. After he was reinstated, Commissioner Bowie Kuhn had to suspend McLain again, this time for carrying a gun.

When he took time out to pitch in 1970, he didn't do too well: a 3–5 mark with a 4.65 ERA. In his first game, he surrendered three home runs. He was losing 5–3 when he left in the sixth, and only a Detroit rally deprived him of the loss. The man once known as "Mighty Mouth" and "Super Flake" was on the way down. He was traded to the expansion Washington Senators (later the Rangers) after the 1970 season and won a Skunk Stearns trophy in 1971. But that was about the only thing he was able to win, as he sank to a 10–22 record. Sid Hudson, who had one of the worst career records of the previous era, was McLain's pitching coach at Washington in 1971, and he remembered how the former ace pitched during his skunk season. "McLain was over the hump then," Hudson told us. "He was beyond help. He'd lost his fastball; he was a shell of his old self."

By 1972, Denny was through. He toiled in the minors for most of the year and was 4–7 for the Athletics and the Braves. A's manager Dick Williams told reporters, "From the way he's throwing, and the statistics show it, I don't think he could help anybody right now." McLain was confident he could still pitch. "They'll have to rip the uniform off me," he was quoted as saying. In fact, they did everything but.

The A's owner Charlie Finley offered McLain $25,000 to stop pitching, so he wouldn't have to pay him the rest of his $75,000 salary. When that ploy didn't work, Finley traded McLain to the Braves for the aging Orlando Cepeda. McLain toiled in the minors for the Braves before being brought up. One of his games was against Cecil Reynolds, the co–Most Valuable Player of the California League that year with a 12–3 record. Reynolds, now a well-known psychologist, remembered the shelling McLain endured. "We beat him pretty bad," Reynolds said. "We must have scored 15 runs off him. He was awful. He was real fat, and anybody who had a brain in their head would have looked at him and known that he didn't have any business being out there. He couldn't see himself. It was a slaughter; it wasn't even close. He was a little aloof. He acted like he was too good to be playing with us, although you wouldn't have known it to see him play."

McLain's problems didn't end when he left baseball. He was convicted of racketeering, conspiracy, extortion, and the possession and distribution of cocaine in the early 1980s. He spent more than two years in jail before he was granted a new trial and was subsequently released; he then wrote an autobiography with the apt name *Strikeout*. Today, he has a radio show, but a few years back—in a scene right out of the Twilight Zone—you would have found him playing the organ in a Michigan bar, with former heavyweight champ Leon Spinks serving as bartender.

But apart from the personal mess that has been McLain's life and the tragedy that still stalks him—his daughter Kristen was killed in a traffic accident near Detroit in March 1992—his major-league stats tell a dramatic story of what might have been for a man who pitched his last major-league game at age 28:

Years	Won	Lost	Percentage	ERA	Adjusted ERA	WAT	TPI
1963–69	114	57	.667	2.97	119	+23.8	+6.1
1970–72	17	34	.333	4.78	73	−6.0	−5.7

Other pitchers from McLain's era also tumbled badly: Mike Cuellar and Rick Sutcliffe went from Cy Young to Skunk Stearns trophies. LaMarr Hoyt led the AL with 19 wins for the White Sox in 1982, had a 24–10 Cy Young season in 1983, and had control that was nearly as pinpoint sharp as Cy Young himself. But he self-destructed like McLain, thanks to a persistent drug problem. Hoyt was 8–11 in 1986 and gone for good after that. He was invited to the ChiSox spring training camp in 1988, but was forced instead to begin his second prison term in February 1988.

Steve Blass' two key wins made the Pirates world's champions in 1971, and he was 19–8 the next season. Then, in 1973, he developed a mental block. Like the Mets' Mackey Sasser, who forgot how to throw the ball back to the pitcher, Blass couldn't fire his fastball and lost sight of home plate. He walked about one man per inning, often threw behind the batter, and lost 9 of 12 decisions. He had an ERA of 9.85, and his TPI of −5.1 was the lowest since Coldwater Jim Hughey's −5.3 for the 1899 Spiders. Blass never got over the block, though intriguingly he learned how to hit in 1973. He batted .417, to raise his career average to .172.

San Francisco's Ron Bryant declined as suddenly, rapidly, and

irreversibly as did Blass. Bryant had a diving-board accident, due to his alcohol problem, and toppled from 24–12 in 1973 to 3–15 and a Skunk Stearns trophy in 1974 (shared with Randy Jones). He pitched a handful of innings for the Cardinals the next season, and then was gone for good.

In other eras, Blass or Bryant—who both had their great falls at about the same time that Spiro Agnew and then Richard Nixon resigned from the White House—might have won the Asa Brainard Award hands down. Hoyt was a great candidate as well. But McLain was a man for all seasons. If he had pitched back in the 1870s, we probably would have named the Humpty-Dumpty Award after Denny instead of old Asa.

The Joe Hardy Sell-Your-Soul Award: Randy Jones and Mark Davis

Three Padres have won Cy Young Awards: Randy Jones in 1976, Gaylord Perry in 1978 (who also won for the Indians in 1972), and Mark Davis in 1989. Perry's path to his trophies and to Cooperstown was partly paved with K-Y Jelly and Vaseline, but the paths taken by Jones and Davis may have taken a detour through Hades. Both rose from the depths of a Skunk Stearns Award to Cy Young heaven, and both are co-recipients of our Joe Hardy Sell-Your-Soul Award. Although Dennis Martinez converted his Skunk Stearns trophy with Baltimore in 1983 into a perfect game with the Expos in 1991, he wasn't a candidate for the Joe Hardy Award. His turnabout was spectacular, but he had already known stardom before his Skunk Stearns trophy, and he was able to return to the top after conquering his own devil—alcohol.

Co-winners Jones and Davis seem to have leased their souls to the devil for two years instead of making a lifetime sale. They enjoyed two

Above: **Ron Bryant shared the 1974 Skunk Stearns trophy with Randy Jones and provided Denny McLain with a bit of competition for the Asa Brainard Humpty-Dumpty Award when he fell from 24–12 to 3–15 (photo courtesy of George Brace).**

seasons of glory before the magic disappeared as quickly as it came. Short-term deals are not uncommon.

As Oakland was winding down the 1991 season as an also-ran after three straight pennants, Moss Klein said in *The Sporting News*, "The [A's] pitching deteriorated so suddenly, it was as if some deal with the devil had expired, and he turned the invincible staff back into middle-aged men with nothing on their fastballs."

RANDY JONES

Jones seemed to fit in perfectly with the rest of the Padres staff when he tied for the 1974 Skunk Stearns Award with Ron Bryant by posting an 8–22 record with a 4.46 ERA. But whereas Bryant was on the downside of his career that year—down the chute and almost out the door—Jones' star was about to ascend rapidly.

After going undrafted out of high school, Jones went to Chapman College. He was signed in the fifth round by San Diego following gradua-tion, and he displayed his potential in his rookie season of 1973. He was 7–6 with a 3.16 ERA, including a 4–1, four-hit, no-walk victory over the Dodgers. But things came apart in 1974. He didn't let it faze him, however. After his fourth straight loss left him with a 3–10 record, he told reporters, "I've pitched better in these last four losses than I pitched in any four straight games all last year. If I pitch as well in my next four games, I'll probably be 7–10 by then." Not quite.

Jones was dubbed "the left-hander with the Karl Marx hairdo" by Padres announcer Jerry Coleman, one of the few who believes that the founder of socialism was one of the Marx Brothers. Jones nearly reversed his record the next season when he went 20–12 with a league-leading 2.24 ERA, to became the first Padres pitcher to win 20 games. He finished sec-ond to Tom Seaver for the Cy Young Award, but won the Comeback Player of the Year award—quite an accomplishment for someone who never was. And if baseball scribes weren't convinced that Jones was for real, he nearly duplicated his stats in 1976, going 22–14 with a 2.74 ERA. He wasn't denied the Cy Young Award that season, when he edged out another member of the Mets staff, Jerry Koosman, who proceeded to win two straight skunks.

Jones did it all in 1976. He led the majors with 25 complete games, tied with Jim Palmer for the major-league lead in wins, and paced the NL by holding opposing batters to a .267 on-base average. And that's just the beginning. He went 68 straight innings without giving up a walk, tying Matty for the NL record. He also was perfect with his glove, fielding 112 total chances without an error—the best ever for a pitcher.

His career turned around in a devilish way. His first two seasons, he was a combined 15–28 (a .349 winning percentage) with a 3.93 ERA. The next two saw a record of 42–26 (.618), accompanied by an ERA of 2.50. Jones suffered an arm injury after that, and he was never the same. His arm snapped and a nerve was severed; he told John Thorn and John Holway in *The Pitcher*, "My arm began to shrink. It just withered. There was no muscle, no bicep." The lease with the devil ran out, and Jones had six losing seasons in a row before calling it quits. In 1980–81, he was a combined 6–21, and he was gone after the next season, but people still talk about the man whose hairdo was described by Coleman as a "frisbee."

"He was a pretty good pitcher," his old teammate, Clay Kirby, told us. "He took his ability and turned it into some very good years."

Jones also made the best of opportunities for jokes. "I never met a [tobacco juice] spitter quite like Randy," Gary Lucas told *Baseball Confidential*. "When we played for San Diego, we wore white shoes and Randy thought nothing of coming up and decorating our shoes with tobacco juice. Once he went up to Rollie Fingers in the dugout and said, 'Rollie, I'm going to spit on your shoes.' Rollie said, 'No, that's boring.' So Randy spit right into Rollie's ear."

Jones retired with a 100–123 career mark, for a .448 winning percentage—the second lowest ever for a Cy Young winner. And who has the lowest? None other than Mark Davis, who had a .391 percentage (50–78) at the end of the 1992 season.

MARK DAVIS

Mark Davis, the winner of the 1984 Skunk Stearns Award and the 1989 Cy Young Award, joined Randy Jones in leasing his soul to the devil for two years. Davis was mired in a miserable career in 1988, when he came to the Padres in the Kevin Mitchell–Chris Brown deal. In 1984, he lost nine straight games during the summer and suffered through one of the worst seasons of the Expansion Era (5–17 with a 5.36 ERA). He had an especially hard time dealing with Chicago; the Cubs beat him in all four decisions, hammering him to the tune of a 9.00 ERA.

His subsequent years (5–12, 5–7) gave no indication of any discernible talent. When manager Larry Bowa was interviewed just after his Padres acquired Davis, he talked about how pleased he was at getting the Giant. It became evident to reporters that Bowa thought that the Padres had traded for Chili Davis, not Mark. Bowa's embarrassment upon learning he got the wrong Davis was matched only by his disappointment.

But while Davis was in San Diego, a strange thing happened. In the city that produced more skunks than lived in Bambi's forest, Davis' career did a 180-degree turn. In 1988, his record was only 5–10, but his ERA (2.01) and his save total (28) belonged to relief pitchers who won Rolaids awards, not those who sent their managers scrambling for a pack of Rolaids.

Predictably, it wasn't until Jack McKeon took the reins from Bowa that Davis and his wicked curveball began to prosper. He only got better. In 1989, he was the NL winner of the Cy Young Award, posting a 4–3 record with a 1.85 ERA and a league-leading 44 saves in 48 attempts. All this from a pitcher who went to the bull pen in 1984 by way of demotion. He became a star in San Diego, both as a pitcher and as a practical joker.

"He put some soap in the shower that is white, but when you put water on it, it turns black," former Padres' manager Greg Riddoch told us. "By the time I discovered that, my arms and chest and everything were completely covered with it. Here I am in the shower, and everybody's laughing at me. I looked down, and I got all this black stuff all over me."

Riddoch got revenge. "We [were] in Chicago, and we [were] dressing at Wrigley, and I decided to nail him. We wore these game underwear that go to your knee, so I watched him put them on every day, and he always put his right leg in first and then his left leg in. I sewed the bottom of the left leg on his game underwear shut," he said. "He put his right leg in first, and when he went to put his left leg in, he fell head first into his locker. That's a little of what we used to do to each other all the time.

"Mark told me he got Saberhagen in spring training [1991] with one of these exploding golf balls," Riddoch told us. "The guy hits it, and it explodes—it disintegrates. But he always had a locker full of gimmicks. It takes the edge off what we're doing. It's so serious, and it means so much that you need to keep it in perspective and play the game. But he's real serious when he gets on the mound. Most of the pranks were done in the clubhouse prior to going on the field."

Above: **Mark Davis, the Skunk Stearns winner of 1984, won the Cy Young award in 1989 to share the Joe Hardy Sell-Your-Soul Award with Randy Jones. Like Jones, he seemed to lease his soul for just two years (photo reprinted by permission of the *Times-Advocate*, Escondido, Calif.).**

And Riddoch added, "I remember him not only being our best relief pitcher [in 1989], but also what a quality human being he was, and what a caring type person he was. Not just from the baseball angle, but as a human being. He did a lot of wonderful things for me and for my family."

One reason Davis blossomed for the Padres is that he stopped throwing the split-fingered fastball, a pitch taught to him by former skunk Roger Craig. Another was that he loved being a reliever. "I like not knowing [if I am going to pitch]," he told reporters. "The hard thing for me as a starter were the four days between starts. I kept thinking about my last start over and over. If I was three games under .500, I wanted to win three games with one pitch. Everything was magnified."

Davis left San Diego in a free-agency mess, which meant leaving not only his friend Riddoch but noted pitching coach Pat Dobson. The day Davis signed his four-year, $13 million contract was the day that any contract with the devil ran out. He suffered through a 2–7 year in 1990, with his ERA ballooning to 5.11 and his save total shrinking to six. He gave up an incredible seven walks for every nine innings he pitched, yielded nine homers, and allowed 40 percent of all inherited runners to score.

After blowing four of six save opportunities, Davis was replaced by Jeff Montgomery as the Kansas City closer. "It wasn't the best of times, that's for sure," Davis told reporters. "I started out really well. Then I dropped a couple of decisions, and things just snowballed—for me and the team." When Dobson left San Diego to go to Kansas City for 1991, "experts" pegged Davis as the comeback player of the year. But Dobson didn't last the season, and Davis was to prove that if he did sign a contract with the devil, it wasn't as long as the one with the Royals. Injuries plagued the southpaw, as he was hurt twice while attempting to barehand comebackers.

His second stint on the disabled list was a result of a torn fingernail on his left index finger. And when he was finally able to pitch, he didn't find manager Hal McRae dancing with joy. "There's no place to start him and I don't want to upset the rhythm of our setup men and closers," McRae told reporters. "That could change if he performs well and does the job. But he will have to earn it." He didn't. He had his moments of competence—he did OK as a starter and even ended the Twins' Kevin Tapani's nine-game winning streak in September—but his 6–3 record masked his inconsistency and his repeated failures from the bull pen. He finished the year with an ERA of 4.45, and 1992 was even worse. He was a flop as a starter and was banished to the bull pen in early May after failing to make it into the third inning twice in a row. The Royals gave up on him in late July, sending Davis (1–3, 7.18 ERA) to the Braves for Juan Berenguer, the skunk of 1981.

As a fringe player with Atlanta, the former Cy Young winner was given the ultimate humiliation at the end of August: Davis was dropped from the roster for a couple of days to make sure that he wouldn't be eligible for postseason play.

Cherokee Fisher Rookie Award: Bill Greif

Bill Greif—that's *Grife*, not *Greef*, though he gave much grief to his teammates and managers—had one of the worst careers of the Expansion Era. And when he was 5–16 in 1972, he had one of his era's worst seasons. As we'll soon discover, Greif was the only pitcher in the Expansion Era to rank among the five worst in both the single-season and career competitions, though he wasn't quite the worst either time. But we have found an award that's all his—the Cherokee Fisher Rookie Award. Greif debuted in July 1971 for Houston and was 1–1 in seven games and 16 innings, but he pitched most of the year in Oklahoma City. His real rookie season was 1972, when he was 5–16 with a 5.60 ERA and an eight-game losing streak for the (who else?) San Diego Padres. Clay Kirby was 7–20 as a Padres rookie in 1969, Phil Huffman was 6–18 as a Toronto novice in 1979, and Kyle Abbott was 1–14 in his Phillies debut in 1992, but Greif takes home the prize, thanks to his adjusted ERA of 59. That value is the second worst of the Age of Expansion and the third worst of the 20th century for pitchers with at least 15 losses.

Greif showed potential for going far in the world of skunkdom in his first professional game, pitching for Covington, Houston's minor-league affiliate. "Our starting pitcher was wild, and I was nervous," he told reporters. "I went to the bullpen and threw the first pitch as hard as I could. The ball cleared two screens and sailed into the bleachers. It hit a woman on the wrist. The people in the bleachers were ready to lynch me."

But Greif's troubles that day were just starting. "When I got warmed up," he continued, "they called me into the game. I'll never forget my first pitch. When I threw it, I lost a contact lens and the batter got a hit. Now I'm on my hands and knees in front of the mound, looking for my lens. I finally found it and it was so dirty I had to go into the dugout and wash it off before I could put it back in. All this was taking time and the fans were all over me. They were yelling, 'Put that bum on a bus before he gets someone killed.'" Greif managed to pitch well that game, as he did in his 1972 debut for the Padres, a six-hit shutout of the Braves on April 16. He even pitched decently for the next month, evening out his record to 3–3 on May 6. That was the high point of his season. Several of his losses in 1972 came from terrible pitching; during one month-long stretch, he didn't survive the second inning three times. Some of his defeats came on terrible luck. On May 29, he took a 1–0 lead over the Braves into the ninth inning. The tall Texan gave up two singles to open the ninth. Mike Cor-

The most versatile losing pitcher of his era, Bill Greif had the third-worst season, was the third-worst pitcher overall, and won the Cherokee Fisher Rookie Award (photo courtesy of George Brace).

kins came in and provided no relief, hitting the next batter before giving up a game-winning single to Dusty Baker. Greif took the loss.

Greif lost his eighth straight game on June 26, blowing a 7–3 lead to drop his record to 3–11. After being sent to the bull pen, he came back to win two straight games, although his throwing error in his 5–4 triumph over the Phillies let in two runs to turn an easy victory into a nail biter.

He wrapped up his Cherokee Fisher year with two more early departures: a one-third inning, four-run shellacking and a 1⅓ inning, six-run blowout. But his most skunklike moment came on September 1 in a 14–3 crushing by the Cubs. After giving up back-to-back dingers to George

Hendrick and Carmen Fanzone, Greif brushed back Rick Monday. A brawl followed that left Greif with muscle spasms in his right elbow. He started (and lost, of course) only one other time that year.

The wild right-hander was branded a headhunter later in his career, and beefy sluggers, such as Greg Luzinski and Willie Crawford, charged the mound and tried to hurt him. Both Luzinski and Joe Ferguson predicted in the middle of the 1975 season that Greif would be badly hurt. Greif defended himself, saying, "I don't want to hurt anybody, but if they are going to brush back our hitters, then I have to brush back theirs."

Clay Kirby remembered Greif's fearlessness. "I will say one thing about [Greif]: He had no fear of knocking anyone down," he told us. "One year, we had a rule that if you got someone 0–2, then you'd brush them back. It was kind of an 'if-needed' type of rule. And every time he'd get two strikes on a hitter, he'd knock him down. That's what I remember. He was wild—hyper, in fact."

Greif finished his career in 1976 with San Diego and St. Louis, going a cumulative 2–8. The Cardinals traded him in the off-season to the Expos, but he was released without playing a game for them. After missing the entire 1977 season, he unsuccessfully tried out for the Mets.

Greif had a strange career. He never again reached the heights of his 1–1 record for Houston in 1971, putting together five straight losing seasons. As a regular Padres starter from 1972 to 1974, he averaged a 9–17 record in about 30 starts per year. He often looked awful, and he merited his niche as one of the worst pitchers of the century. But he had a good fastball and knuckle curve and knew how to pick his moments—when to turn up the juice. The sight of Cy Young winners pumped him up. In his rookie season, he beat Tom Seaver and fanned five straight Mets—and then ran off his eight straight losses. He was sharp against the Cardinals, but Bob Gibson edged him 3–2. The next year he pitched a two-hit 3–0 shutout against the Phils—and Steve Carlton, his third two-hitter of the year.

But his bottom line was a disaster—31 wins versus 67 losses, a .316 winning percentage, and a 4.41 ERA. And he was a lousy hitter, one of the worst ever: 12 hits in 166 at bats, a .072 average.

The John Cassidy Root Canal Award: Terry Felton

If Terry Felton took care of his teeth as well as he pitched, then it would take emergency dental surgery to repair the damage, let alone root canal. Felton established a major-league record by notching 16 consecutive losses at the start of his career, smashing Guy Morton's old mark of 13. But whereas Morton won his last decision for the Indians in 1914, Felton never did get a win. Not that he wasn't given chances. After throwing two scoreless innings

Many of the pitchers featured in this book had trouble winning in the majors, but only Terry Felton (0–16) *never* tasted victory (photo courtesy of George Brace).

in 1979, Felton showed a taste of what was to come when he posted a 0–3 mark with a 7.13 ERA in 1980. He lost all three games, including a 17–0 shelling by the California Angels, in a span of ten days.

The 6 foot 2 inch right-hander from Texarkana, Texas, was sent down to Toledo, Ohio, where he had a decent 7–8 record. Felton spent most of 1981 hurling for the Mudhens, ending with a 7–11 mark, although the Twins brought him up for one relief appearance, long enough for him to have an ERA of 40.50. But it was in 1982 that he would reach the epoch of incompetence and achieve true imperfection: Felton went 0–13. Although most of his 48 appearances were in relief, Felton was a multitalented pitcher; he could lose starting or relieving. He preferred starting, however: "At least the game starts off tied," he told reporters.

His 13 losses came in all shapes and sizes. In one of his rare starts, Felton held Seattle hitless into the sixth on August 15. But after two singles, he threw Manny Castillo's ground ball over the head of John Castillo, the Twins' first baseman. Two runs scored on his error, and he was losing 2–1 when he was relieved. The relief pitcher let the game get out of hand, and Felton was pinned with a 10–2 loss.

In another instance, the Twins' manager Billy Gardner put Felton in to relieve starter Brad Havens against the Royals in the fourth inning. The Twins were winning 7–4, so Felton was set: All he had to do was to hold KC for a few innings, and he could get his win. But he left in the sixth clinging to a 7–6 lead, with two runners on base. Ron Davis came in and promptly let the Royals score. The Royals went on to an 18–7 blowout, with Felton dropping to 0–12 for the season.

"When I first heard about the record, it was funny and I didn't really think I'd ever do it," Felton told reporters. "I thought I'd get a win before I'd even get close to the record. I think I've got a snake around my neck, biting me every time I'm out there."

Felton set the record not only for the most consecutive losses to start a career, but for the most losses in a career without a win, easily outdistancing Steve Gerkin's 0–12. During Felton's 0–13 season, he achieved a WAT stat of −6.4, indicating that he won between six and seven games fewer than expected, given the ability level of his teammates. No one in baseball history, except for Felton the trendsetter, has reached the −6.0 plateau with fewer than 15 decisions.

Felton tried anything to rid himself of the streak. Ron Davis rubbed garlic on Felton's shoulders and kept the cloves hanging on a rope in his locker to ward off evil spirits. "Sometimes I just don't put the ball in the right place," Felton understated. "Maybe I have to forget the rabbit foot and the garlic cloves and the horseshoes and just get meaner out there."

Felton never got the chance to discover if getting meaner would work. He was released after the 1982 season, taking with him a 0–16 lifetime mark and our John Cassidy Root Canal Award.

Mike Thompson, who was 1–15 from 1971 to 1975 for the Senators, Cardinals, and Braves, was runner-up to Felton. Thompson's sole victory came in his first season for Washington. The right-hander debuted at 1–6 and concluded at 0–6, sounding like he came out on the wrong end of a tennis match.

The Worst Single Season of the Expansion Era: Mike Parrott

The worst single seasons from 1969 to 1991 for the five categories that we've been using to determine the worst of the worst are listed in a table

at the end of the chapter. José De-Leon was the front-runner in two areas (Losses minus Wins, WAT) on the basis of his 2–19 record in 1985, while Mike Parrott took the honors by posting the worst adjusted ERA and winning percentage for his 1980 performance (1–16, 7.28 ERA). The worst TPI of the era (−4.1) was turned in by Matt Keough, but it was for his 1982 season, when he was 11–18 and not even a strong skunk contender, rather than for his abysmal 2–17 mark three seasons earlier. Actually, the Pirates' onetime star Steve Blass undercut Keough's TPI with a value of −5.1 in 1973, when he suddenly couldn't find home plate. Blass' mark was not only the worst of the era—it was the worst of the century. However, his 3–9 record left him well short of the 15 losses needed to qualify for our lists of worsts.

Overall, Parrott's 1980 season ranked among the five worst of the era in four of the five categories; DeLeon (1985) and Honeycutt (1987) ranked in three categories. Only Keough's name was listed for all five categories—three times for 1979 and twice for 1982. On the basis of the rankings presented in Chapter 7 for the entire 1901–91 span, these are the worst seasons of the Expansion Era (1992 had to be excluded because Palmer-Thorn stats were not available):

The Five Worst Seasons of the Expansion Era

Pitcher and Year	Won	Lost	Percentage	ERA	Adj. ERA	WAT	TPI
1. Mike Parrott (1980)	1	16	.059	7.28	57	−7.1	−2.7
2. José DeLeon (1985)	2	19	.095	4.70	76	−7.9	−2.3
3. Bill Greif (1972)	5	16	.238	5.60	59	−4.2	−3.6
4. Mark Davis (1984)	5	17	.227	5.36	65	−5.2	−3.7
5. Matt Keough (1979)	2	17	.105	5.04	80	−6.7	−1.6

Above: **A once-promising career was crushed by a line drive to the groin that helped Mike Parrott achieve one of the worst seasons (1–16, 7.28 ERA) of this century—or any other (photo courtesy of Mike Parrott).**

Entering spring training in 1980, Mike Parrott was considered the ace of the Mariners' staff. The Orioles' number one draft pick in 1973 was 14–12 with a 3.77 ERA for Seattle in 1979, setting a record for victories for the new expansion team. In a recent telephone conversation, Parrott—who lives in Colorado and is finishing a degree in business—talked freely about the good times and the bad. He recalled a road trip after the 1979 All-Star break, his one year in the sun.

"I pitched at Boston and I threw a five-hit shutout against the Red Sox," Parrott told us. "We went to Baltimore right after that, and we had never beaten Baltimore at Baltimore in the history of the Mariners at that time. I beat the Orioles 4–3 and got the win. From there, we went to the West Coast, and I threw a five-hit shutout against the Angels, who had a very good-hitting club back then. Probably those three games were as good as any I ever pitched."

He gave us a quick scouting report on his strengths and weaknesses: "I wasn't an overpowering pitcher, but I had a real good sinker. I guess I threw what you'd call a 'heavy ball,' a pitch that sinks hard, so they call it a heavy pitch. A lot of times you'll get ground balls. I had a pretty good slider that was really effective on the right-handed hitters. But I lacked a good off-speed pitch, a strict change. Probably, I did not hold runners on as well as I could have or should have."

Maybe Parrott wasn't overpowering, but he threw an occasional high, hard one. In late August 1978, he beaned Dwight Evans of the Boston Red Sox, knocking him unconscious and splitting his helmet. Seattle manager Darrell Johnson was impressed with Parrott's ability and touted the team's pitching as being the best in the club's three-year history; he had high hopes for 1980.

He was wrong.

Double-skunk Rick Honeycutt was 10–17; newly acquired Jim Beattie was 5–15; and, in just 94 innings, Mike Parrott was 1–16 with a 7.28 ERA. He put two men on base for each inning he pitched. The AL hit .348 against his tosses and had an on-base average of a cool .412. Beattie might have won a Skunk Stearns Award in other years, but no one could challenge Mike Parrott in 1980—no one on the Mariners' staff, no one in the major leagues, and only a handful in baseball history.

After recovering from a sore tendon in his right foot, Parrott got the call for the 1980 AL opener on April 9. He had a good start, pitching into the seventh inning and giving up three runs; despite sloppy relief, he got the 8–6 win. He lost his next three games, but two were by a 4–3 score, and no one would have guessed that he'd already won his only game of the year.

Then came THE game. Parrott had endured many injuries in his career—shoulder and elbow injuries, a bum knee suffered in a basketball game—but nothing compared to the line drive off the bat of the Twins' Roy Smalley that set off a chain of pain, bad luck, and bad pitching. Smalley led off the fifth with a smash one-hop grounder that caught Parrott in the groin.

"It was a straight change-up," Parrott told us, "which was definitely a big disadvantage when you're right-handed and you're pitching to left-handers. A lot of my pitches, including my fastballs, would sink down away from left-handed hitters. Left-handed hitters especially would take me up the middle a lot.

"Smalley's was one of those balls where we were playing outside—it was before they had the Metrodome in Minnesota—and the grass was wet. It was a day game, and the ball skipped off the wet grass. It was a one-hopper, and I couldn't get my glove down in time. It was hit that hard. In fact, it hit me so squarely that the ball went straight down between my legs. I reached down to throw him out at first, and I just crumpled on top of the ball. Before they could get the ball out, Smalley had a double. That's how dead away I was on top of the ball.

"What was worse was the fact that up until that point in my career, I never wore a protective cup. It was one of those things where you learn too late. I'm a pitching coach now for the Expos in the minors, and I use myself as an example to pitchers who don't wear cups now. Some, it changes their mind; some will have to learn the hard way just like I did."

Parrott spent six weeks on the disabled list, but was never the same.

"Things seemed to snowball. I even rushed it, coming back when I did, because initially they said I could be done for the year. They weren't real sure. So I came back in six weeks, and I was still pretty sore. I think I altered my delivery a little bit to compensate for my injury. I just started losing close games, games that I pitched well."

But for every 2–0 or 5–4 defeat, Parrott would get shelled. He simply couldn't win. On May 31, three runs scored on his own fielding error, the margin of difference in a 5–2 loss to Cleveland. On June 30, he retired the first six Texas batters. But in the third inning, the Rangers blasted him for six runs to claim an 11–5 win. Seattle pitching coach Wes Stock told reporters, "It's driving me crazy." A defeat that Parrott particularly remembered was a 5–2 loss to Detroit on July 20 that lowered his record to 1–11.

"I didn't get out of the first inning," he said. "It wasn't necessarily that I threw so bad; I remember that game because I had already lost a lot of games in a row and then I went out at home, hoping to end my losing streak, and didn't get out of the first inning."

That July contest was the last game Parrott would lose for Seattle until September. A trip to the minors during much of August deprived him of the chance to match the record 19-game losing streaks of Bob Groom and Jack Nabors three-quarters of a century earlier.

"A losing streak is one of those things where you really don't know why it keeps going on," Parrott told us. "I went to the bull pen as a short man after a while to work things out. . . . I picked up three saves, but I remember one game specifically that was my 15th loss in a row. In Kansas City, I pitched the last six innings of a 15-inning game. In the 15th, there was a guy on base, two outs, and George Brett fouled off about five or six pitches to make the count full. I made a mistake, tried to come inside on him, 3–2, and he hit a home run to right field. I had pitched 5⅔ innings of scoreless relief in extra innings up to that point, but it was just one of those things. There were a lot of games like that, but there were also a lot of games that I didn't get out of the first inning."

Parrott's streak ended in early 1981, when René Lachemann replaced Johnson as the manager of the Mariners.

"I ended the losing streak by beating the Brewers 8–1," Parrott said. "I don't know if Lachemann had anything to do with it, but there seemed to be more publicity, more emphasis on him taking over the club, than there was on my losing streak. The pressure was taken off me—and we scored eight runs. It was like getting a monkey off my back."

But the monkey never really left. After going 3–6 in strike-torn 1981, he was traded to the Brewers for Thad Bosley. Parrott's major-league career ended when he didn't make the Milwaukee club that would win the AL pennant. The final tally: 19 wins, 39 losses, a 4.87 ERA.

"I thought I got the club made when I was in spring training," Parrott said. "In fact, on the last day of spring training they were breaking the next day to go to Milwaukee. I was already looking for a place to live in Milwaukee and I was called in by the General Manager and told that I wasn't going to be making the club, and they weren't going to be sending me to Triple A; they were giving me my outright release. That was kind of a shock. That was the first time I'd ever been released."

Parrott signed with Kansas City and spent 1982–84 with Omaha, their Triple-A team. "I started all three of those years off thinking I could still pitch in the big leagues," he said. "It was one of those things where once you get released, it's really hard to get back into the big leagues for the second time."

Parrott made a name for himself the first time around. His 1–16 record and 7.28 ERA put his name at the top of the heap among terrible seasons. It was the worst of the Expansion Era and one of the worst ever.

That's quite an accomplishment for a pitcher who not only earned the right to start on opening day of his skunk season, but began the season in the win column. Only a little luck and a protective cup could have altered the course of history.

MATT KEOUGH

Hot dog or sushi? Matt Keough could pick both. The tall right-hander took his flamboyant, talkative personality to Japan for four years before returning in 1991 to try, unsuccessfully, to crack California's staff. His second attempt to make the Angels in 1992 nearly ended in tragedy, when he was struck by a foul ball while sitting in the dugout during a March 16 exhibition game against the Giants. Keough survived emergency brain surgery to relieve the pressure caused by a blood clot and made a spectacular enough recovery from his brush with death to throw out the first pitch at the Angels' opener in Anaheim just three weeks later. But that wasn't exactly the kind of pitching he had in mind as he doggedly tried to make it back to the majors.

Keough compared the blow to his head to drinking "16,000 bottles of Cuervo gold [tequila] in five minutes," and tired quickly of hearing everyone tell him how lucky he had been. "Luck," he told reporters, "is having the ball miss you by a foot."

Fifteen years before his Anaheim misadventures, Keough broke in with the Athletics and pitched for five managers, most notably Billy Martin, from 1977 to 1983. He is the only A's pitcher from the Billy Ball years to win a Skunk Stearns Award, thanks, in part, to Mike Parrott—whose 1–16 campaign overshadowed Brian Kingman's 8–20 disaster in 1980.

It's appropriate that Keough should have the skunk, however, because Keough was always the most critical of the late Billy Martin and of ex-A's owner Charlie O. Finley. "It's like you come to a controversy and a ball game breaks out," Keough said in 1982, referring to those games when Martin and the equally temperamental Earl Weaver would butt heads.

After going 8–15 in 1978 (but somehow making the All-Star team), Keough suffered through the fifth-worst season of his era, winning two games against 17 losses. His 5.04 ERA didn't help his cause, nor did his average of more than 11 hits surrendered per nine innings. Or maybe he didn't suffer through it, but merely slept through it. "Billy Martin would ask somebody on the bench what pitch was thrown, to see if you're paying attention," Keough reminisced in 1981. "I can remember in 1979 when you'd have trouble finding out from our bench who was up, what town we were in and what day it was."

Keough tied Joe Harris' 73-year-old major-league record by losing his first 14 decisions. In fact, when you add his last four decisions from 1978, he lost *18* straight games; Cliff Curtis, the skunk of 1910, holds the record with 23. Most of Keough's losses in 1979 weren't even close. He endured defeats by scores of 13–1, 11–2, and 10–1 and threw in a couple of 8–1 blowouts for good measure. The only tough-luck losers were the fans rooting for the A's on the days when he pitched. Only Finley's strict instructions to Martin kept Keough in the lineup, loss after loss. Keough didn't win his first game until September 5.

The infielder-turned-pitcher had a remarkable turnaround, going 16–13 with a 2.92 ERA in 1980 and capping the season with the Comeback Player of the Year award. (Where'd he come back from? His record during his first three seasons was 11–35.) In fact, he improved not only his pitching, but his attitude. Clint Hurdle, when asked to pick an All-Hot-Dog team for *Baseball Digest* in 1981, selected Keough as his pitcher. Why? "He would yell at hitters when he was 2–17 two years ago and didn't say a word when he won 16 games last year," Hurdle said. "I can't figure it out, but there's got to be a hot-dog in there somewhere."

By 1982, Keough was back to his usual self. He was 11–18, with a TPI of −4.1, one of the worst of all time. He was also getting back to his hot-dog days. "Playing for Billy Martin is like being married to him," Keough said in 1982. "Right now we're all sleeping on the couch."

Keough was thrilled when Finley sold the A's, telling reporters, "One day we woke up and the Wicked Witch of the North was dead and we were all children of Oz." Too bad Keough was pitching more like Auntie Em. But there's no need to insult him, since Keough did a fine job of insulting himself: "Charlie Finley gave me Catfish Hunter's old jersey," he told reporters. "By the time I got it all the wins had been used up."

After shuffling around with five teams, including three NL teams in 1985–86, Keough left the United States for Japan. "Everybody, especially when it's early in a career, should spend just one year playing in Japan," he told Mark Whicker. "I lived there when I was 11, when my father played there. I knew what to expect. It's just not America.

"You don't throw at people. You don't snap when you throw one right down the middle and they call it a ball and one of their pitchers gets a strike on the edge of the batter's box. Because if you *do* snap, it confirms, in their minds, that they're stronger. I refused to give them that satisfaction. In return, I got respect."

And wins. Keough, who imported the knuckleball to Japan, was 45–44 in his four years for the lowly Hanshin Tigers. He beat the hated Tokyo Giants six times in one year and was called "Giant Killer." He was also dubbed Matto Keough, which translates to "just a moment." After walking down the streets of Japan for just a moment, he told Whicker, "the camera and signboards would come out of nowhere. I was the Pied Piper.

"Baseball is far, far more important over there than it is here. Bigger than life."

Warren Cromartie and Vance Law returned to the AL in 1991 after playing in Japan to talk about the public humiliations given to players who did not perform. Law talked about his manager beating up a catcher who called the wrong pitch and of the pitcher who took more punishment from his own team than from the batters who knocked him out of the game: He had to spend the rest of the game kneeling on concrete. If there was one saving grace in Keough's terrible 2–17 season, it was that he did it for the A's instead of the Hanshin Tigers.

Keough didn't prosper back in the United States in 1991. He was rocked in the Angels' spring-training camp, including one shelling in which he gave up ten hits and five earned runs in three innings. "I'm still alive," he told *The Los Angeles Times*. "That's all I can say." After his near-fatal dugout beaning in 1992, that was saying plenty.

Because of father Marty's career, Keough has a photo of himself, at four years old, with Ted Williams. The Splendid Splinter wrote, "To Matty, you'll be a big leaguer like your father by 1975." Notice that Ted, who missed Keough's major-league debut by only two years, didn't say how good Matt would be.

The Worst Career of the Expansion Era: Jesse Jefferson

The five worst pitchers in each of our five categories are shown in a table at the end of the chapter. These lists are based on career stats and include only those who notched at least 50 lifetime losses. Jesse Jefferson, at 39–81, lost 42 more games than he won, the most for the Expansion Era. He is also the only pitcher to be ranked among the five worst in four categories. Fittingly, he spent his worst seasons with the expansion Blue Jays during their first four years of existence. The Padres' Bill Greif had the worst winning percentage of the era and made three of the "five-worst" lists. Pete Broberg was also included on three lists, and Mike Kekich had a prolific career: He had the worst adjusted ERA and TPI of the era. In fact, his adjusted ERA was the century's worst, and his TPI was third worst.

Mike Morgan, signed by the Cubs to a four-year $12.5 million pact after the 1991 season, finally emerged as one of the best pitchers in baseball in 1992. But through 1991, his WAT of −16.3 is the worst of the Expansion Era and one of the lowest in history. (It improved to the −12 range in 1992.) Morgan is known to bristle at reporters who remind him of his pathetic career record, but until 1991, when he had a 14–10 record for the Dodgers, he had never compiled a winning mark for any of the six major-league teams he had pitched for since 1978. And not until September 1991 did Morgan win as many as four straight games; his streak ended against the Giants on the next-to-last day of the season, clinching the division crown for Atlanta. Morgan was selected to the 1991 All-Star team as a replacement for injured teammate Ramon Martinez, but he'd already made a fool of himself when he responded to the initial snub by dismissing the game as "a joke."

Yes, Morgan pitched for poor teams throughout his career, and, yes, he pitched well in many games without earning wins (he was on the short end of Dennis Martinez's 2–0 perfect game). But—at the risk of arousing the hard-throwing Morgan's ire—his negative WAT means that his teams (even the rotten ones) consistently did much better when he was *not* on the mound. Still, he seems to have turned the corner in 1992 while pitching for a mediocre Cubs team. He put together a 7-game winning streak early in the season, had a 16–8 record (2.55 ERA), and ranked among the ERA leaders most of the year. Might he be a candidate for a future Joe Hardy award?

Morgan was not the only pitcher active in 1992 to rank among the era's worst. Trailing Morgan on the WAT list (through 1991) are two-time skunk José DeLeon (–12.9) and perennial loser Tim Leary (–12.5). Andy Hawkins, released by the A's during '91, is third on the TPI list (–10.4). In 1990, Hawkins pitched a no-hitter, yet managed to lose the game 4–0; in 1991, he became only the 11th pitcher this century to join the "–10" TPI club.

The five pitchers from the Expansion Era who ranked highest on the list of the worst pitchers of the 20th century are listed next, in order.

Worst Careers of the Expansion Era

Order and Pitcher	Won	Lost	Percentage	ERA	Adj. ERA	WAT	TPI
1. Jesse Jefferson	39	81	.325	4.81	83	–12.3	–8.8
2. Mike Kekich	39	51	.433	4.59	72	–5.7	–12.4
3. Bill Greif	31	67	.316	4.41	78	–9.3	–8.1
4. Pete Broberg	41	71	.366	4.56	78	–4.8	–10.5
5. Steve Arlin	34	67	.337	4.33	78	–7.3	–7.9

Jesse Jefferson never had a season bad enough to win a Skunk Stearns trophy, but his consistent and unrelentingly bad pitching gave him the career statistics to emerge as the worst pitcher of the Expansion Era. He was no real competition for Jerry Koosman in 1977–78, despite a combined record of 16–33 (Kooz was 11–35). In 1979–80, his combined 6–23 couldn't compete with the all-time-worst seasons turned in by Matt Keough and Mike Parrott (a joint 3–33). Jefferson is the analog of Juan Marichal and Dave Stewart, whose best seasons were always topped in the race for the Cy Young Award. Jefferson is the worst pitcher never to win a Skunk Stearns trophy.

Jefferson was selected in the fourth round of the draft by Baltimore. Unlike some other skunks, he wasn't even a good pitcher in the minors. He went 0–7 with an 8.21 ERA for Bluefield in the Appalachian League in 1969 (with 11 wild pitches in ten games), and a year later led the league

Jesse Jefferson never won a Skunk Stearns Award or even came close, but he's the worst since 1969 (photo courtesy of George Brace).

in losses with an 8–16 record. His wildness early in his career was astounding. He led three different leagues— Appalachian, California, and Texas— in walks; in 26 games for the Orioles and White Sox in 1975, he averaged more than eight walks per nine innings.

Jefferson won his big-league debut, defeating Boston 2–1 in ten innings, and it was all downhill from there. He had a decent 6–5 mark for the Orioles that year, but didn't even enjoy what proved to be his only successful year; he was too busy blaming his losses on other people. After an 8–3 loss to the Angels, he complained to reporters about the catching of his battery mate, Earl Williams: "I figured he was getting the signs from the bench. That's why I was going with my curve instead of my fastball, and I wasn't getting it over the plate. I'd rather have Elrod Hendricks or Andy Etchebarren catching. At least they know what they're doing back there."

Jefferson was traded in midseason 1975 to the White Sox for first baseman Tony Muser. He showed flashes of talent in his Chicago debut, when he held Minnesota hitless for five innings until he had to leave with an injured wrist from a line drive by Rod Carew. He got that win, but went 4–9 the rest of the year for the White Sox, including two different 10–1 losses to Vida Blue in July and a 13–2 loss to Vida in September. Blue won 22 games that year; the Oakland star didn't even send Jefferson a thank-you note.

Jefferson had already established himself as a prime candidate for inclusion in this book, but, to quote the shopkeeper waiting for his meat shipment, "The wurst is yet to come." After his 2–5 season for the ChiSox in 1976 (when opposing teams scored 51 runs in his five losses, he endured a 17–2 shellacking, and Paul Richards' most notable statement about him was that he "looked a mite goofy"), the Blue Jays selected him as their 24th pick in their expansion draft. He promptly went from being a seldom-used bad pitcher to an often-used terrible pitcher.

The Blue Jays 1977 Media Guide proclaimed that Jefferson was "considered awesome when control [is] sharp." By whom? And when is it sharp? He gave up nine walks in a June 18 contest against his former teammates, the Orioles. The tall right-hander who currently resides in his birthplace, the tiny town of Midlothian, Virginia, turned in four consecutive seasons with the Blue Jays when he lost eight or nine more games than he won for a Blue Jay composite of 22–56. On April 11, 1978, Jefferson demonstrated his versatility at pitching badly. Usually he lost because of bad control, but that day his former White Sox teammates used four homers to score most of the ten earned runs he gave up.

In 1980, while he was still with the Blue Jays, it looked like Jefferson had finally turned the corner. On July 27, he two-hit the Mariners 5–0; that improved his record to 4–6, which also included an 11-inning 1–0 whitewashing of Oakland. Toronto manager Bobby Mattick loudly proclaimed that Jefferson was his fourth starter. Pitching coach Al Widmar and Mattick worked with Jefferson, taking away his slow curve. "I never did like it," Mattick told reporters. "He never had the hard breaking stuff until now. Look at Steve Stone. How do you think he's won all those games? It's because hardly anyone can hit a good curve anymore." The key word was *good*. Jefferson lost his last seven games to plunge to his annual skunk-like record and was traded to Pittsburgh.

Although he won his only game in Pittsburgh, he was granted free agency and signed with California, where he went 2–4. He became a free agent again in 1982, when Baltimore signed him. But it was not to be. He was released a month later without ever pitching for his old team.

What does it mean to be a skunk of the highest magnitude? In the case of Jefferson and many other winners of the Skunk Stearns Award, it means getting no respect where you'd least expect it—such as in the value of baseball cards. In this era of outrageously priced baseball cards, those of some skunks are worth less than the paper they're printed on. According to Beckett's Baseball Card price guide, Jesse Jefferson's 1978 card in good condition is worth all of one penny!

MIKE KEKICH

Even if he didn't turn in the second-worst career in the Expansion Era, left-hander Mike Kekich would have to earn a place somewhere in our book for his famed wife swap with fellow Yankee southpaw Fritz Peterson. Though Peterson was one of the best control pitchers of all time (he allowed the fewest walks per game in the AL from 1968 to 1972), he is living proof that control on the mound doesn't translate to self-control. In the middle of the 1972 season (during one of Kekich's best years!), Kekich and Peterson, after lots of double dating, decided to swap wives, children, and even their family dogs. Kekich acquired Marilyn Peterson in exchange for his spouse, Susanne. Each pitcher had two children, and just in case the children were able to assemble some sanity out of this mess, the families split the children up, too. The oldest children stayed with their fathers, while the youngest went to their mothers. "There goes family day," general manager Lee MacPhail complained.

Despite the initial success of the family swap (they were even pondering a double wedding after their double divorce), Mike proved to be a loser in love as well as in baseball. Marilyn gave up on him just before the Yankees did. He was traded in the middle of the 1973 season to Cleveland.

Of course, the seeds for Mike's bizarre behavior were planted well before his wheeling-dealing days. The southpaw tried his hand at astrology, philosophy, skiing, scuba diving, living outdoors, fishing, hunting, and motorcycle riding. When he was honeymooning in Santa Barbara with Susanne in 1965, both were injured riding a motorcycle.

"Green but throws hard," *Baseball Digest* described him in mid-1965 (correct on both counts, although he never quite ripened); "Definite prospect." Others predicted he'd be the next Koufax. With the Dodgers in the mid- to late 1960s, Kekich showed signs of the blazing fastball that once struck out 11 consecutive batters in a 1964 game in the Florida State League. He even pitched a one-hit shutout against the Mets. Unfortunately, he won only one other game for the Dodgers while losing 11. So much for predictions.

After a few decent year with the Yankees, he was shuffled around to Cleveland and Texas before trying his hand in Mexico and Japan. He

The second-worst pitcher of his era, Mike Kekich was involved in one of the most bizarre trades in history, yet he never even changed teams during that transaction (photo courtesy of George Brace).

resurfaced with the expansion Mariners for one last year in 1977, going 5–4 (but with a 5.60 ERA).

"I'm not the first pitcher to take a little longer getting there than expected," he told reporters in mid–1972. "I feel like this is the year I will prove I am a major league pitcher."

Not exactly. A major-league swinger, maybe.

Kekich's 39–51 career record was among the best of the worst. Like Jesse Jefferson, he never even won a Skunk Stearns Award. But he allowed runs by the bucketload—more earned runs per game than just about anyone who took a regular turn on the mound for any team in either major league during the 20th century. Now that's quite a legacy.

PETE BROBERG

Pete Broberg ranked as the fourth-worst pitcher of his era and failed to win a Skunk Stearns trophy. It's just as well; he might have had it stolen from him. In 1972, while enduring his worst season (5–12), he and teammate Jim Panther were robbed while staying at the Essex House in New York.

Broberg was well traveled. He broke in with the expansion Senators in 1971, moved with the team to Texas in 1972, and then pitched for the Brewers, Cubs, and Athletics. At every stop during his eight-season career he had a losing season. In fact, he had eight losing seasons; the closest he came to .500 and respectability was the 14–16 mark (.467) he posted his first year in Milwaukee. Before the 1972 season, the wild right-hander surveyed the brand-new Arlington Stadium and told reporters, "I think I'm going to like this park. It probably should favor the right-handed pitcher."

Broberg started off the season 2–0, including a shutout, and *The Sporting News* proclaimed that he had conquered the sophomore jinx. "It's true I'm gaining confidence," he said.

But his pitching just got worse. The Dartmouth graduate climbed to 5–4 in mid–June, but didn't win another game all year. After losing six straight and being bombed for six runs in the second inning by the White Sox, he was sent to the bull pen in August. "When you've got a pitcher like Peter, there are a lot of things that can cause [his performance]," manager Ted Williams told reporters. "That's why we put him in the bull pen— to give him a chance to work some of these things out and not worry about starting."

The plan didn't work. He finished with a 5–12 record and a league-leading 13 hit batsmen and then combined for a 5–13 mark the next two seasons. His pitching coach at Washington and Texas, Sid Hudson (a former skunk contender), told us: "Broberg had a fine arm and all the natural ability in the world, but he never did fine-tune it all. I thought he was going to be a great one. He could throw hard, but he didn't learn to pitch until he'd lost his velocity." Hudson also told us that the Ivy Leaguer "wasn't the best student in the world —he didn't pick things up as easily as a lot of others." And the best game Hudson could remember Broberg pitching was a loss. "Broberg had the Angels shut out one night 1–0 in the ninth inning, and he got beat in the ninth," he told us.

The Rangers gave up and shipped Broberg to Milwaukee. But after his one good season, he overstayed his welcome. He won his first game, 5–4 against the Royals, before losing seven straight. He pitched well in spurts, including three straight 2–1 losses in May, but he allowed five earned runs a game, and the Brewers finally gave up, sending him to the NL.

"Bob Feller was the best pitcher I ever saw, and also the fastest,"

Hudson told us. Referring to Broberg, Hudson once said to reporters: "I thought we had another Bob Feller. But he's a hardhead."

STEVE ARLIN

Another 1970s Padres hurler, Steve Arlin, finished as the fifth worst of his era. He pitched too long to win our Root Canal Award, which is just as well: The San Diego dentist might have taken it the wrong way. Several dentists offered Arlin the chance to go into practice with them before his baseball career got under way, but the tall right-hander chose baseball—at least for a while. "If I pitch until I'm 34, I still can practice dentistry for 30 years," he told reporters. "If I didn't play baseball, I'm sure I would look back at age 40 and wonder about the blank spaces in my life. Baseball brings an added richness to my life." Unfortunately, most of the blank spaces were in his win column. Padres manager Preston Gomez said that Arlin possibly had the most talent on the staff, despite his 9–19 record in 1971. Arlin responded to these words of praise by going 10–21 in 1972. However, he sported an 8–10 record at the All-Star break, including three shutouts and a near no-hitter. He had a remarkable streak of allowing a mere 33 hits in 71 innings. When Arlin failed to make the All-Star team, his pitching coach, former skunk Roger Craig, told reporters, "I can't believe there are nine pitchers in the league better than Steve."

Arlin finished the season 2–11. The question then was whether there were nine pitchers in the league *worse* than Steve. He continued to pitch poorly and was traded to Cleveland in mid–1974. Indians' manager Ken Aspromonte told reporters, "Steve showed me a good fastball." Arlin also showed him a 2–5 record—his last in the major leagues.

The Ohio State graduate had baseball running through his veins; his grandfather, Harold Arlin, is credited with broadcasting the first baseball game on radio when he recounted the Phillies' battle with the Pirates at Forbes Field in 1921. Despite his history, Arlin missed his goal of pitching until he was 34; he was 29 when he exchanged being drilled on the mound for drilling in an office.

Clay Kirby remembered his former Padres' teammate, especially Arlin's brush with fame in 1972: "He was extremely smart, and probably had some of the best stuff on our staff," Kirby told us. "He almost threw a no-hitter one night, and it was kind of fun watching that. He had two outs in the ninth inning, and Denny Doyle bounced a high hopper over the third baseman's head. The manager [Don Zimmer] had just pulled him in to cover for a bunt. Otherwise he would have had it."

Zimmer took full blame for costing Arlin his rightful place in history. But thanks to Arlin's niche in our book, he finally fulfilled a goal that appeared in *The Sporting News*: "I want to be remembered in baseball. I want to make a name for myself."

Honorary Skunks

Some honorary Skunk Stearns Awards for a deserving few:

•*Storm Davis,* but not for his pitching in the majors or for his crybaby antics when Tony LaRussa bypassed him in his 1989 World Series rotation after the earthquake struck. We're giving an Honorary Skunk Stearns Award to Storm for his Little League performance in 1969 in Florida as a seven-year-old. Each year the biggest game was between Storm's Twins, coached by his dad George, and the hated Vikings. With the Twins taking a 16–0 lead into the last inning, George thought it was safe to bring Storm in from right field to make his pitching debut. With no one else to bring in to pitch, George let Storm pitch the whole inning. Storm blew the lead!

•*Wilbur Wood,* the White Sox's knuckleballer who started 40–50 games a year between 1971 and 1975. Wood started both games of a July 20, 1973, twi-night doubleheader against the Yankees. He was knocked out with one out in the first inning of the opener, giving up six of New York's eight runs. He lasted into the fifth of the nightcap, yielding all seven Yankee runs before getting knocked out of the box. He started the day at 18 12, but went to sleep with an 18–14 mark, thanks to 12–3 and 7–0 thrashings. Wood finished the season at 24–20.

•*Dock Ellis,* the Pirates sometime star hurler, who wore white hair curlers during batting practice until Bowie Kuhn banned it and who once began a game against the Reds by hitting the first three batters. Ellis pitched a 2–0 no-hitter against the Padres on June 12, 1970, and later admitted he used a foreign substance. Not vaseline or sandpaper, but LSD. He confessed that he was enjoying more than a pitcher's high at San Diego. Ellis was usually a headache to his bosses and caused a record *seven* managers to run for the aspirin bottle in 1977 when he played for the Yankees, Athletics, and Rangers.

•*Frank LaCorte* and *Tommy Boggs,* who each pitched from the mid-1970s to the mid-1980s and who had nearly identical records. Both were terrible. Boggs retired with a 20–44 career mark, and LaCorte retired with a record of 23–44. Boggs had a 3–20 mark in the 1970s before his one winning season in 1980. When he was asked what pitch he hit for a home run, he said, "I dunno. My eyes were closed." His Skunk twin LaCorte, who was known to vent his rage at his own incompetence by destroying clubhouse trash cans and setting fire to his uniform, posted a 5–26 record in the 1970s and then enjoyed his one winning season—also in 1980. Lightning hadn't struck twice with such authority since the Mets' lefty Al Jackson went 8–20 with a 4.40 ERA in 1962 and then repeated his underwhelming performance in 1965 (8–20, 4.34).

•*Don Sutton,* who won 324 major-league games, but was 0–13 against the Cubs.

•*Steve Ontiveros,* who tried but failed to make the Phillies in 1991 following major arm surgery. A symbol of the modern-day pitcher, Ontiveros has spent time on the disabled list every season since he reached the majors in 1984. According to Phil Collier, he has spent more months on the disabled list (21) than he has wins (18).

•*Tom Candiotti,* still with Cleveland in spring training, 1991, who asked a stranger looking over his shoulder if he wanted to get in on the players' NCAA basketball pool. The stranger was an FBI agent who was in town to warn the players about gambling.

•*Mike Schooler,* Seattle's onetime ace closer, who saved 63 games in 1989–90, but was injured for most of 1991. He earns an Honorary Skunk Stearns Award for his remarkable consistency in two straight games at the Kingdome on May 7–8, 1992. The Mariners had the Blue Jays down 7–1 after six innings, and the lead was still 7–4 in the ninth, when Schooler came in to put out the fire. Instead, Dave Winfield tagged Schooler for a two-out grand slam to give Toronto an 8–7 win. One day later, the Mariners led Detroit 6–0 after seven innings, and rookie manager Bill Plummer again called for his relief pitcher in the ninth to preserve a 6–2 lead. Schooler retired the side, but not before yielding five earned runs, capped by Lou Whitaker's two-out three-run homer. The final score: Tigers 7, Mariners 6. Schooler's ERA for those two games was 37.80. And lightning struck once more on September 6 when Schooler came in to preserve a lead the Mariners had forged in the top of the 12th inning. He gave up a grand slam to Carlos Martinez in the bottom of the inning to hand the Indians a 12–9 win. Schooler tied a major-league record by yielding four grand slams in 1992, and Plummer was given his pink slip when the season ended.

•*Matt Young,* who started 16 games for the Red Sox between May 20, 1991, and October 1992, and didn't win once. He was 0–10, and couldn't even capture a win when he pitched a complete game against the Indians on April 12 and held them hitless. He lost 2–1, thanks, in part, to seven walks; although his cap and glove were sent to Cooperstown, he didn't even get the consolation of pitching a no-hitter because of the 1991 rule by Fay Vincent that requires at least nine innings for a no-hitter to count (Young pitched eight, since Cleveland didn't have to bat in the ninth.) No matter. Young would have deserved an Honorary Skunk Stearns Award even if he had won the game and gotten credit for a no-hitter. Heading into the 1993 season, his career stats were among the worst for active pitchers with at least 100 decisions: He had the lowest winning percentage (.378), and his 4.35 ERA trailed only Bobby Witt (4.57). And, according to *Baseball America* magazine, Young made nine errors in one season, went almost two years without making a pickoff throw to first, and was ejected from two games in 1988 but appeared in none because of an arm injury.

Single-Season Leaders: 1969–91
(Minimum of 15 Losses)

Order, Name and Year*	Statistic

Losses minus Wins

1. José DeLeon (1985)	17
2T. Matt Keough (1979)	15
2T. Mike Parrott (1980)	15
4. Randy Jones (1974)	14
5T. Clay Kirby (1969)	13
5T. Ken Reynolds (1972)	13
5T. Rick Honeycutt (1987)	13

Winning Percentage

1. Mike Parrott (1980)	.059
2. José DeLeon (1985)	.095
3. Matt Keough (1979)	.105
4. Ken Reynolds (1972)	.118
5. Rick Honeycutt (1987)	.158

Wins-Above-Team (WAT)

1. José DeLeon (1985)	−7.9
2. Mike Parrott (1980)	−7.1
3. Brian Kingman (1980)	−6.8
4. Matt Keough (1979)	−6.7
5. Rich Honeycutt (1987)	−6.2

Adjusted ERA

1. Mike Parrott (1980)	57
2. Bill Greif (1972)	59
3. Gene Brabender (1970)	63
4. Mark Davis (1984)	65
5T. Ron Bryant (1974)	68
5T. Matt Keough (1982)	68
5T. Don Carman (1989)	68

Total Pitcher Index (TPI)

1. Matt Keough (1982)	−4.1
2. Mark Davis (1984)	−3.7
3. Bill Greif (1972)	−3.6
4. Jim Bibby (1974)	−3.3
5T. Gene Brabender (1970)	−3.2
5T. Clay Kirby (1973)	−3.2
5T. Joe Coleman (1975)	−3.2
5T. Don Carman (1989)	−3.2

*T = tie.

Career Leaders: 1969–1991 (Minimum of 50 Losses)

Order and Name*	Statistic
Losses minus Wins	
1. Jesse Jefferson	42
2. Skip Lockwood	40
3. Mike Morgan**	37
4. Bill Greif	36
5. Jim Beattie	35
Winning Percentage	
1. Bill Greif	.316
2. Jesse Jefferson	.325
3. Steve Arlin	.337
4. Dave Freisleben	.362
5. Pete Broberg	.366
Wins-Above-Team (WAT)	
1. Mike Morgan**	−16.3
2. José DeLeon**	−12.9
3. Andy Hassler	−12.8
4. Tim Leary**	−12.5
5. Jesse Jefferson	−12.3
Adjusted ERA	
1. Mike Kekich	72
2T. Steve Arlin	78
2T. Bill Greif	78
2T. Billy Champion	78
2T. Pete Broberg	78
Total Pitcher Index (TPI)	
1. Mike Kekich	−12.4
2. Pete Broberg	−10.5
3. Andy Hawkins	−10.4
4. Jesse Jefferson	−8.8
5T. Billy Champion	−8.2
5T. Pete Falcone	−8.2

* *T = tie.*
** *Active in 1992.*

7

The Worst Pitchers of the Twentieth Century

◆ OK, enough already. Forget this era-by-era stuff. Plain and simple, who had the worst season of the century? Who had the worst career? The major candidates are clear enough, but who had the worst season: Kaiser Wilhelm, 3–23 in 1905? Ben Cantwell, 4–25 in 1935? Don Larsen, 3–21 in 1954? Or Mike Parrott, 1–16 in 1980? And who was worse, Happy Jack Townsend, of the woeful Washington Senators of the 1900s, or Fat Jack Fisher and Jay Hook, of Casey Stengel's legendary Mets of the 1960s? And what about the 1970s bust, Jesse Jefferson?

The answers will come shortly; first, let's examine some lists.

The Worst Single Season, 1901–1991

We've assembled lists of the 25 worst single seasons of the 20th century in each of the five categories of interest to us (see the table at the end of this chapter): losses minus wins, winning percentage, adjusted ERA, WAT, and TPI. Kaiser Wilhelm (1905) had the worst WAT and ranked among the top 25 in every single category, while Mike Parrott (1980) tied for worst adjusted ERA and was listed in four categories. A number of other pitchers ranked in the top 25 in three areas, the most notable being Joe Harris (1906) and Jack Nabors (1916), each of whom cracked three "top tens."

Our system for ranking the worst seasons of the century is described in the Appendix. The runaway winner is Kaiser Wilhelm for his 1905 skunk season, followed by two pitchers from the same era: Jack Nabors and Joe Harris. The first truly modern pitcher to crack the list of worst seasons is fourth-place finisher Mike Parrott, for his 1–16 mark and 7.28 ERA for Seattle in 1980. Parrott had the worst season in the past 75 years, with two-time skunk José DeLeon not far behind for his 2–19 fiasco in 1985.

The 25 worst seasons, according to our point system, are listed here. (Because Palmer-Thorn stats were unavailable, 1992 isn't included.)

The 25 Worst Seasons of the 20th Century: 1901–91

Order, Pitcher, and Year*	Team	Won	Lost	Percentage	ERA	Adj. ERA	WAT	TPI	Total Points
1. Kaiser Wilhelm (1905)	Boston: NL	3	23	.115	4.54	68	-8.9	-3.7	118
2. Jack Nabors (1916)	Philadelphia: AL	1	20	.048	3.47	83	-8.5	-2.1	87
3. Joe Harris (1906)	Boston: AL	2	21	.087	3.52	78	-8.6	-1.6	78
4. Mike Parrott (1980)	Seattle: AL	1	16	.059	7.28	57	-7.1	-2.7	70
5. Rube Bressler (1915)	Philadelphia: AL	4	17	.190	5.20	57	-3.7	-4.1	58
6. Ben Cantwell (1935)	Boston: NL	4	25	.138	4.61	82	-7.1	-1.2	55
7. José DeLeon (1985)	Pittsburgh: NL	2	19	.095	4.70	76	-7.9	-2.3	52
8. Don Larsen (1954)	Baltimore: AL	3	21	.125	4.37	82	-8.1	-0.9	50
9. Paul Derringer (1933)	Cincinnati/St. Louis: NL	7	27	.206	3.30	103	-8.6	+0.3	49
10. Jack Townsend (1904)	Washington: AL	5	26	.161	3.58	74	-6.3	-3.5	41
11. Fred Glade (1905)	St. Louis: AL	6	25	.194	2.81	91	-7.8	-1.1	39
12. Pat Caraway (1931)	Chicago: AL	10	24	.294	6.22	68	-4.0	-4.3	36
13. Dutch Henry (1930)	Chicago: AL	2	17	.105	4.88	95	-7.2	0.0	34
14. Bill Greif (1972)	San Diego: NL	5	16	.238	5.60	59	-4.2	-3.6	32
15. Art Houtteman (1948)	Deroit: AL	2	16	.111	4.66	94	-7.1	-0.2	30
16. Mark Davis (1984)	San Francisco: NL	5	17	.227	5.36	65	-5.2	-3.7	28
17. Tom Sheehan (1916)	Philadelphia: AL	1	16	.059	3.69	78	-6.5	-1.5	26
18. Cliff Curtis (1910)	Boston: NL	6	24	.200	3.55	94	-7.0	-0.3	25
19T. Tom Fisher (1904)	Boston: NL	6	16	.273	4.25	65	-2.9	-3.6	24
19T. Walt Dickson (1912)	Boston: NL	3	19	.136	3.86	93	-6.9	-0.4	24
21. Matt Keough (1979)	Oakland: AL	2	17	.105	5.04	80	-6.7	-1.6	23
22T. Roy Wilkinson (1921)	Chicago: AL	4	20	.167	5.13	83	-7.4	-1.6	22
22T. George Caster (1940)	Philadelphia: AL	4	19	.174	6.56	68	-6.2	-4.0	22
22T. Jimmy Ring (1928)	Philadelphia: NL	4	17	.190	6.40	67	-3.7	-3.8	22
25. Lou Knerr (1946)	Philadelphia: AL	3	16	.158	5.40	66	-5.0	-2.9	16

*T = tie.

On the basis of the rankings of the worst seasons of the century, the worst seasons by decades are as follows:

Decade	Pitcher	Won	Lost
1900s	Kaiser Wilhelm (1905)	3	23
1910s	Jack Nabors (1916)	1	20
1920s	Roy Wilkinson (1921)	4	20
1930s	Ben Cantwell (1935)	4	25
1940s	Art Houtteman (1948)	2	16
1950s	Don Larsen (1954)	3	21
1960s	Roger Craig (1963)	5	22
1970s	Bill Greif (1972)	5	16
1980s	Mike Parrott (1980)	1	16

Of all the decade leaders, only Roger Craig of the 1963 Mets failed to crack the list of 25 worst seasons of the century; he takes the prize for the 1960s by a half over teammate Craig Anderson, 3–17 for the 1962 Mets. Two Chicago White Sox teammates also engaged in a competition of sorts in the early 1930s. Dutch Henry (2–17) put together the 13th worst season in 1930, but Pat Caraway did him one better in 1931, when his 10–24 mark (paired with the worst TPI of the century) grabbed the 12th slot.

And is there any question that Kaiser Wilhelm had the worst single season when he was 3–23 in 1905? On the basis of our point system, he ran away with the title, leaving Jack Nabors (1–20 in 1916) in the dust with a decisive 118 to 87 triumph. No doubts, right? Not exactly. Of the 25 pitchers on the worst-seasons list, *Total Baseball* and *Baseball Encyclopedia* agree on the won-lost records of 23 — all except two members of the Boston Braves' pitching staff from the early 1900s: Tom Fisher and Kaiser Wilhelm. The difference in Fisher's record (6–16 versus 6–15) doesn't affect his ranking, but the extra win that the *Baseball Encyclopedia* gives to Wilhelm, bringing his 1905 record to 4–23, shakes things up a bit.

If we had used the *Baseball Encyclopedia* data as the official stats, then Wilhelm's ranking would drop from first to fifth in the WAT sweepstakes, and his ranking would also be less extreme in losses minus wins and winning percentage. Wilhelm would remain the only pitcher to rank among the top 25 in each category, but the net results of the shifts would be a virtual three-way tie for worst season by Wilhelm, Nabors, and Harris. In fact, Nabors would rank first, Wilhelm second, and Harris third. So Nabors might have had the worst season of the 20th century, depending on which source is used. Regardless, Nabors and Tom Sheehan are undoubtedly the only roommates on the 25-worst list.

Kaiser Wilhelm had a year to forget in 1905 whether he was 4–23 or 3–23. He was banished to the Southern League for two years, where he led Birmingham to the 1906 pennant. He gave an exhibition of pitching during 1906 and 1907 that had fans linking his name with major-league legends. Cy Young pitched the first perfect game of the 20th century in May 1904 for the Boston Red Sox, beating the Philadelphia Athletics 3–0. In July 1906, Wilhelm pitched the second perfect game in organized baseball, shutting down Montgomery 7–0 for Birmingham. Only two balls were hit out of the infield. A Montgomery writer referred to his local team as "Babes in the hands of a giant," while a writer for the *Birmingham News* proclaimed Wilhelm, who also pitched 61 consecutive scoreless innings, as "the idol of local fans," who has been "viewed with askance by jealous writers around the circuit." Perhaps those rival writers reminded Birmingham fans of Wilhelm's 1905 disaster in Boston.

Wilhelm earned a promotion back to the majors in 1908, this time with the Brooklyn Superbas, and he had one more brush with glory. The Giants' Red Ames pitched 9⅓ innings of no-hit ball against Brooklyn on opening day of the 1909 season at the Polo Grounds in what was to become one of the first great games in the Dodgers-Giants rivalry. Wilhelm matched Ames nearly pitch for pitch, not yielding his first hit until there was one out in the eighth. Ames gave up seven hits in the extra innings and was blasted for three runs in the 13th, while Wilhelm calmly pitched a three-hit shutout. If not for the man who had the worst single season of the century, Red Ames, not Bob Feller, would have been the first pitcher in history to pitch a no-hitter on opening day. (Ames was hurt as much as Babe Ruth by Fay Vincent's 1991 committee that dropped the asterisk from Roger Maris' home-run record. Ames lost credit for a no-hitter in the game against the Kaiser, as well as for a five-inning gem against the Cardinals in 1903, the first abbreviated no-hitter of the century.)

Wilhelm soon returned to his senses, remembering that he was in the majors, not the minors. He lost 13 of his remaining 15 decisions in 1909 and dropped seven of ten decisions the next season, also for Brooklyn. But it was with the Boston Braves that he gained lasting fame for his unparalleled 1905 escapades. In fact, five of the 25 worst seasons of the century were by Braves' hurlers. Only the Athletics, with six, topped that dubious record (five from Philadelphia, one from Oakland). The other franchises with more than one honoree in the top 25 list are the White Sox (three) and the Browns/Orioles (two).

The Teams of the Skunk Stearns Award Winners

The Braves' and Athletics' domination of the "worst single season" list prompted us to investigate which teams produced the most winners of the Skunk Stearns Award from 1901 to 1992. Counting co-winners and Kyle Abbott's 1992 award, we awarded 98 annual trophies. Several winners pitched for two teams during their unforgettable season; we gave credit to both teams only when the pitcher had more than five decisions with each team. That happened only once, in 1902, when Skunk Stearns winner Roscoe Miller was 6–12 in the AL for Detroit and 1–8 for the NL's New York Giants.

Through the 1992 season, the AL and NL were tied 49–49 in the skunk competition for trophies (with Miller counting for both leagues); the Federal League took home one trophy, by Mysterious Walker in 1914. Now that's what we call parity between the AL and NL! The franchise-by-franchise breakdown of Skunk Stearns winners follows:

Franchises with the Most
Skunk Stearns Winners: 1901–1992*

Franchise	League	Number of Skunks
Philadelphia Phillies	NL	12
Philadelphia (9)/Kansas City (0)/Oakland (1) Athletics	AL	10
Washington Senators (9)/Minnesota Twins (0)	AL	9
Boston (7)/Milwaukee (0)/Atlanta (0) Braves	NL	7
New York Mets	NL	7
Boston Red Sox	AL	6
Chicago White Sox	AL	6
St. Louis Browns (2)/Baltimore Orioles (4)	AL	6
Detroit Tigers	AL	5
Pittsburgh Pirates	NL	5
Chicago Cubs	NL	4
San Diego Padres	NL	4
St. Louis Cardinals	NL	3
New York (1)/San Francisco (2) Giants	NL	3
Washington Senators (1)/Texas Rangers (1)	AL	2
Cincinnati Reds	NL	2
Brooklyn (1)/Los Angeles (1) Dodgers	NL	2
California Angels	AL	2
Cleveland Indians	AL	1
Seattle Mariners	AL	1
Toronto Blue Jays	AL	1
Pittsburgh Federals	FL	1

The New York Yankees, Kansas City Royals, Milwaukee Brewers, Montreal Expos, and Houston Astros had no Skunk Stearns winners.

The Phillies edged the Athletics 12–10 for the number one ranking, followed by the original Washington Senators, Braves, and New York Mets.

The Braves haven't won an award since Ben Cantwell's 4–25 mark in 1935, while the Mets, in existence only since 1962, matched the Braves' total of seven in record time. José DeLeon, in 1990, was the first Cardinal to win since Jess Haines in 1924. Regardless of the league, Philadelphia takes home the prize for spawning 21 skunks, followed by Boston (13), Washington, D.C. (10), Chicago (10), New York/Brooklyn (9), and Pittsburgh (6).

By era, the teams with the most Skunk Stearns winners are as follows:
- 1901–19 — Boston Braves: five
- 1920–46 — Philadelphia Phillies: eight
- 1947–68 — New York Mets: five
- 1969–92 — San Diego Padres: four.

The Senators (1955–58) and Mets (1962–65) had four Skunk Stearns winners in a row, while the White Sox (1930–32) and Padres (1972–74) had three straight.

The list of winners by franchise reveals that the Yankees are the only old-time franchise never to have received a Skunk Stearns trophy. But they are not unblemished and even provided three candidates for the 1991 trophy: Jeff Johnson (6–11, 5.95 ERA), Wade Taylor (7–12, 6.27 ERA), and Tim Leary (4–10, 6.49 ERA). Also, Russ Ford won the dead-ball era's Asa Brainard Humpty-Dumpty Award, and Mike Kekich, holder of the worst lifetime adjusted ERA of the century, did most of his damage wearing Yankee pinstripes. The Reds and Dodgers won only two skunks, and Cleveland, a team that the current generation knows for its consistently poor pitching, won just one trophy—the first of the century, given to Pete Dowling. Dowling, an erratic lefty, pitched two one-hitters and briefly held the AL strikeout record with 11 during his skunk season. He spent time in an asylum and died in 1905 after being hit by a train.

Winners of Multiple Skunk Awards

The following pitchers achieved the unhappy distinction of winning more than one Skunk Stearns Award:

Skunk	Years
Red Ruffing	1925, 1928, 1929
Jim Hughey	1898, 1899
Joe Oeschger	1918, 1922
Art Houtteman	1948, 1952
Camilo Pascual	1955, 1956
Frank Sullivan	1960, 1961

Jack Fisher	1965, 1967
Clay Kirby	1969, 1973
Jerry Koosman	1977, 1978
Rick Honeycutt	1982, 1987
José DeLeon	1985, 1990

The Worst Careers of Pitchers in the 20th Century

The Skunk Stearns Award honors pitchers for a season here and a season there, but which pitchers were the worst over time? Who put numbers on the board year after year to lay claim to the title of worst pitcher of the century? The table at the end of the chapter shows the 25 worst lifetime stats in each of our five categories for pitchers having at least 50 losses. Three hurlers showed remarkable consistency by making all five lists: the 1970s Jesse Jefferson, Kaiser Wilhelm (who proved to be more than a one-year wonder), and old-timer Bill Bailey. Three others flashed their skunk credentials by finishing among the top ten in three categories—Happy Jack Townsend, Jay Hook, and Jack Fisher.

Milt Gaston lost 67 more games than he won during the 1920s and 1930s—the most ever, even stretching back to the 1870s. And although no one has ever achieved a WAT of −20.0 by winning 20 fewer games than the average pitcher on his team would have won, Gaston's contemporary, Rube Walberg, came close with −19.6. And one other all-time champion came from the dead-ball era: Ike Pearson, with his .206 winning percentage. Other number one hurlers include modern-day Mike Kekich, whose adjusted ERA of 72 has gone unchallenged, and Herm Wehmeier of the 1940s and 1950s, whose TPI is −14.3.

Hats off to each champion, although Walberg's winning record (155–141) disqualified him from any "worst-ever" consideration. Wehmeier, a three-time NL leader in walks, certainly had skunk credentials, but he failed to crack any top 25 besides the TPI, so he, too, was eliminated. To be considered for the list of worst 20th-century pitchers, a man had to be consistently bad—an all-around dud when it came to losing games and allowing runs by the bucket. The most notable pitcher to be disqualified was Eddie Smith, best known for giving up a single to Joe DiMaggio during a 13–1 White Sox win in 1941; that mild beginning proved to be the first of the Yankee Clipper's 56 straight games. Smith (73–113) deserves to be remembered as well for his lifetime WAT of −18.8, second-worst in history. He didn't make our "25 worst" list because his TPI of +6.2 was much too good (Catfish Hunter made the Hall of Fame with a slightly lower TPI).

To determine the worst pitchers of the century, we followed the same point system and rules as we did for deciding upon the pitcher with the

The 25 Worst Pitchers of the 20th Century: 1901–1991

Order, Pitcher, and Years*	Won	Lost	Percentage	ERA	Adj. ERA	WAT	TPI	Total
1. Happy Jack Townsend (1901–06)	35	82	.299	3.59	85	–18.3	–8.5	95
2. Jesse Jefferson (1973–81)	39	81	.325	4.81	83	–12.3	–8.8	72
3. Jay Hook (1957–64)	29	62	.319	5.23	75	–6.0	–10.5	71
4. Jack Fisher (1959–69)	86	139	.382	4.06	88	–14.6	–10.7	69
5. Dolly Gray (1909–11)	15	51	.227	3.52	75	–13.3	–5.0	67
6. Kaiser Wilhelm (1903–21)	56	105	.348	3.44	83	–13.8	–8.1	59
7. Mike Kekich (1965–77)	39	51	.433	4.59	72	–5.7	–12.4	58
8. Bill Bailey (1907–22)	38	76	.333	3.57	80	–12.7	–8.1	54
9T. Si Johnson (1928–47)	101	165	.380	4.09	92	–9.6	–11.6	50
9T. Ike Pearson (1939–48)	13	50	.206	4.83	79	–11.1	–6.1	50
11. Milt Gaston (1924–34)	97	164	.372	4.55	97	–13.3	–2.7	49
12T. Phil Ortega (1960–69)	46	62	.426	4.43	75	–2.8	–11.7	47
12T. Harry McIntire (1905–13)	71	117	.378	3.22	83	–14.6	–8.3	47
14. Jack Russell (1926–40)	85	141	.376	4.46	97	–17.0	+0.8	44
15. Bill Greif (1974–76)	31	67	.316	4.41	78	–9.3	–8.1	41
16. Buster Brown (1905–13)	51	103	.331	3.20	96	–7.4	+0.4	38
17. Pete Broberg (1971–78)	41	71	.366	4.56	78	–4.8	–10.5	34
18. Gus Dorner (1902–09)	36	69	.343	3.37	78	–8.2	–8.2	33
19. Galen Cisco (1961–69)	25	56	.309	4.56	81	–5.5	–5.7	30
20. Hugh Mulcahy (1935–47)	45	89	.336	4.49	89	–2.0	–4.9	28
21. Steve Arlin (1969–74)	34	67	.337	4.33	78	–7.3	–7.9	27
22T. Mal Eason (1900–06)	36	72	.333	3.39	85	–12.7	–6.3	25
22T. Billy Champion (1969–76)	34	50	.405	4.69	78	–2.8	–8.2	25
24. Rollie Naylor (1917–24)	42	83	.336	3.93	102	–5.6	+0.4	24
25. George Smith (1916–23)	41	81	.336	3.89	94	–11.4	–5.3	23

*T = tie.

worst single season (see the Appendix). Heading the list is landslide winner Happy Jack Townsend, who toiled mostly for the Washington Senators in the new AL at the start of the century. Jesse Jefferson pulled up in second place, showing that you don't have to be a real old-timer to be among the worst of all time.

Two 1960s pitchers—Jay Hook and Jack Fisher—finished third and fourth, respectively, and Dolly Gray parlayed his brief (1909–11) but potent stay in the majors into the fifth-worst career of the century.

The 25 worst pitchers of the century, all with at least 50 losses, are listed in order on the following page. Point totals are based on the system in the Appendix.

The worst seasons endured by the five "champions" are shown in the following table:

Happy Jack Townsend		Jesse Jefferson		Jay Hook		Jack Fisher		Dolly Gray	
Year	W–L	Year	W L	Year	W–L	Year	W–L	Year	W–L
1902	9–16	1975	5–11	1960	11–18	1959	1–6	1909	5–19
1903	2–11	1977	9–17	1962	8–19	1963	6–10	1910	8–19
1904	5–26*	1978	7–16	1963	4–14	1964	10–17	1911	2–13*
1905	7–16	1979	2–10			1965	8–24*		
1906	3–7	1980	5–13			1967	9–18*		
						1968	8–13		

* *Skunk Stearns Award.*

The point totals for Jefferson, Hook, Fisher, and Gray are almost too close to call, although the quartet finished well ahead of Kaiser Wilhelm in sixth place. Hook's worst seasons don't stack up to the numbers put on the board by the other high finishers, but remember that his main forte was allowing runs. His career ERA of 5.23, which adjusts to 75, is one for the books. And Dolly Gray didn't exactly live up to the advance billing he was given by the Senators when they plucked him from the Pacific Coast League in 1908 for about $4,000. The Senators hailed him as the Rube Waddell and Christy Mathewson of the PCL, only to discover they'd bought the next Happy Jack Townsend.

Si Johnson and Ike Pearson were the highest-ranking pitchers of their era (1920–46), but they barely cracked the top ten on the "worst-of-the-century" list. Milt Gaston trailed Johnson and Pearson by a scant point, so all three had about equal claims to the title of worst pitcher of the long-ball era. Johnson and Gaston had few peers in their ability to pile up losing season after losing season; their worst efforts are shown below.

Si Johnson		Milt Gaston	
Year	W–L	Year	W–L
1931	11–19	1926	10–18
1933	7–18	1927	13–17
1934	7–22*	1928	6–12
1935	5–11	1929	12–19
1940	5–14	1930	13–20
1941	5–12	1931	2–13
1942	8–19	1932	7–17*
		1933	8–12
		1934	6–19

* *Skunk Stearns Award.*

Jack Fisher is the only pitcher on the 25-worst list to win two Skunk Stearns Awards, while nine others captured one. A majority of the worst pitchers, however, achieved their niche by a gradual accumulation of negative stats. The most striking example is Jesse Jefferson, who emerged as the century's second worst, yet never wore the Skunk Stearns laurels for even one season. Jefferson had the knack of avoiding notoriety. The inverse of Rodney Dangerfield, Jefferson just "could get no disrespect." Though he was 2–10 for the hapless 1979 Toronto Blue Jays, George Robinson and Charles Salzberg somehow avoided mentioning Jefferson's name in their book on baseball's worst teams. In their chapter on the 1979 Jays, the authors discussed the exploits of no fewer than ten Toronto pitchers with nary a peep about Jefferson.

So we'll give him his just due. *Jesse Jefferson was the worst pitcher of his era and perhaps the second-worst pitcher of the 20th century!*

Which brings us to the worst. Happy Jack Townsend, a fastball pitcher with a lifetime of control problems, started his career like a man possessed. As a Phillies' rookie in 1901, he was 9–6, but—get this—he led the majors by holding his opponents to a .223 batting average. Christy Mathewson was a distant second at .230, followed by Cy Young's .232. Townsend jumped to the Senators in 1902, doubling his salary to $2,400, and the rest of his career was a downhill roller coaster. The Pennsylvania Supreme Court ordered him to return to the Phillies in April 1902, but he insisted on pitching for Washington—not exactly a bonus for the Senators.

Jack may have been happy, but he wasn't too bright. He developed arm pain in 1903 and decided to follow the advice given in anonymous letters by a person who proclaimed himself "A Surgeon." By July, one of his hands became seriously abscessed. The Washington media had a field day with Townsend, referring to him as the "nonpitching pitcher" and making him the butt of their jokes. The newspapers added insults to his injuries, claiming that he never missed a meal and that he seemed happier taking tickets than his turn on the mound. They even suggested that he pick up the megaphone and earn his keep by announcing the lineups.

Catcher Mal Kitteridge, an excellent fielder and handler of pitchers, thought that Happy Jack could have been outstanding if he wasn't so stubborn and just threw what his catchers called for. But Townsend was stubborn, wild, injury prone, and probably the worst pitcher of the century.

Except for his first season with the Phillies and his finale with the Cleveland Naps, Townsend was Washington's misfortune. Since Dolly Gray pitched his entire three-year career for the Senators, Washington has some negative claims to fame. Two Mets also cracked the top five, although both Hook and Fisher divided their time with other teams.

Which teams produced the most pitchers on the "25-worst" list? That's not an easy question because so many of the bottom-of-the-barrel hurlers were nomads. But if we focus on the one or two teams with the most legitimate claims on a hurler, then the Phillies had five—Si Johnson, Ike Pearson, Hugh "Losing Pitcher" Mulcahy, Billy Champion, and George Smith. The Dodgers also had five if you merge the Brooklyn contingent (Kaiser Wilhelm, Harry McIntire, and Mal Eason) with Los Angeles' Mike Kekich and Phil Ortega.

Some Final Words

A century's worth of skunks reveals a slight bias toward pitchers from the early 1900s, but the lists of worst single seasons and worst careers are spiced with hurlers from every decade, right up to the present. Andy Hawkins, released by the Athletics in 1991, ended the season with a lifetime TPI of −10.4; only ten pitchers in this century did worse. Before Mike Morgan caught fire in 1992 to finally become a star, the most likely "20" for him was not 20 wins, but a lifetime WAT of −20. Now it looks like some future skunk will have to take unwitting aim at Rube Walberg's record of −19.6.

And don't forget about two-time Skunk Stearns winner José DeLeon, whose complete-game drought stretched from August 1989 to July 1991, and whose wins are few and far between. The right-hander fell short of his third Skunk Stearns Award in 1991 and 1992, when he had too few decisions to compete. But Red Ruffing's skunk record won't be secure until the Phillies let DeLeon go and no one else hands him the ball. The onetime strikeout champ still looks sharp on occasion; he's simply forgotten how to win. DeLeon's WAT of −12.9 at the end of 1991, like Tim Leary's −12.5, is among the worst ever. Not far behind are a group of pitchers, also active in 1992, whose WATs are in the −10 to −11 range: Mark Davis, Walt Terrell and Matt Young.

Ex-Yank Tim Leary and Boston's Matt Young, roommates at UCLA in 1979, combined for a 17–37 record in 1990. Even though they challenged DeLeon for the skunk trophy, they were given similar three-year contracts worth a combined $12.35 million. When the 1991 season was over, Leary (58–85) and Young (54–85) also had similar lifetime marks. Leary's last 1991 win came in June, and Young's came in May (which helped earn the BoSox lefty an honorary skunk); combined, they were 7–17 with a 5.93 ERA. They both earned their huge contracts by sitting on the bench in September (they pitched a total of 4⅓ innings the last month) and saw their managers fired within days of the season's end. In 1992, Leary was 8–10 with a 5.36 ERA for the Yankees and Mariners, and Young dropped all four of his decisions with the Red Sox (ERA=4.58). It sounds like their UCLA economics professor was a better teacher than were their baseball coaches.

There are always scouts and fans who talk about the Ramon Martinezes and Jack McDowells and who pick the next Nolan Ryan or the next Warren Spahn. But who is picking the next Happy Jack Townsend, the next Jesse Jefferson? Will it be Jim ("He's No Catfish") Hunter, whose 1991 rookie season for Milwaukee featured an 0–5 record and 7.26 ERA? How about Detroit's Kevin Ritz, who went 6–18 from 1989 to 1992 with a 5.85 ERA? Can we ignore the Yankees' lefty-right rookie duo of Jeff Johnson and Wade Taylor, who combined for a 13–23 record and a 6.10 ERA in 1991? Or the Phillies' Kyle Abbott and the Mets' Anthony Young who entered the 1993 season with career marks of 2–16 and 4–19, respectively.

And then there's Rod Nichols, who once tried to flush his glove down the toilet while in the minors. Nichols began his career with four straight losing seasons for the Indians, highlighted by 13 consecutive losses; he had a lifetime mark of 11–30 when the 1992 season ended with a 4.39 ERA. Despite a 2–11 mark in 1991, he had a 3.54 ERA and was quite sharp on occasions (he hurled a three-hit shutout against the White Sox in late August, ignoring several interruptions from swarms of flying insects). In 1992, Nichols was usually ineffective. If he sticks around for a while, then his potential for leapfrogging the Bill Greifs, Ike Pearsons, and Jay Hooks is unlimited. As long as baseball continues to speed toward the 21st century, especially with expansion on the brain, one thing is clear: For every bear or lion who toes the rubber, there's going to be a litter of skunks.

Single-Season Leaders: 1901–1991, Losses Minus Wins (Minimum of 15 Losses)

Order, Name, and Year*	Losses minus Wins	W–L
1T. Happy Jack Townsend (1904)	21	5–26
1T. Ben Cantwell (1935)	21	4–25
3T. Kaiser Wilhelm (1905)	20	3–23
3T. Paul Derringer (1933)	20	7–27
5T. Fred Glade (1905)	19	6–25
5T. Joe Harris (1906)	19	2–21
5T. Bob Groom (1909)	19	7–26
5T. Jack Nabors (1916)	19	1–20
9T. Gus Dorner (1906)	18	8–26
9T. George Ferguson (1909)	18	5–23
9T. Cliff Curtis (1910)	18	6–24
9T. Don Larsen (1954)	18	3–21
13T. Beany Jacobson (1904)	17	6–23
13T. Harry McIntire (1905)	17	8–25
13T. Vic Willis (1905)	17	12–29
13T. George Bell (1910)	17	10–27
13T. Roger Craig (1963)	17	5–22
13T. José DeLeon (1985)	17	2–19
19T. Mal Eason (1905)	16	5–21
19T. Jim Pastorius (1908)	16	4–20
19T. Walt Dickson (1912)	16	3–19
19T. Roy Wilkinson (1921)	16	4–20
19T. George Smith (1921)	16	4–20
19T. Jack Fisher (1965)	16	8–24
25T. Long Tom Hughes (1904)	15	9–24
25T. Bill Bailey (1910)	15	3–18
25T. Tom Sheehan (1916)	15	1–16
25T. Harry Harper (1919)	15	6–21
25T. Joe Oeschger (1922)	15	6–21
25T. Red Ruffing (1928)	15	10–25
25T. Dutch Henry (1930)	15	2–17
25T. Si Johnson (1934)	15	7–22
25T. George Caster (1940)	15	4–19
25T. Matt Keough (1979)	15	2–17
25T. Mike Parrott (1980)	15	1–16

Single Season Leaders, 1901–1991, Winning Percentage; ERA (Minimum of 15 Losses)

Order, Name, and Year*	Winning Percentage	Order, Name, and Year*	Adjusted ERA	Actual ERA
1. Jack Nabors (1916)	.048	1T. Rube Bressler (1915)	57	5.20
2T. Tom Sheehan (1916)	.059	1T. Mike Parrott (1980)	57	7.28
2T. Mike Parrott (1980)	.059	3. Bill Greif (1972)	59	5.60
4. Joe Harris (1906)	.087	4T. Oscar Jones (1905)	62	4.66
5. José DeLeon (1985)	.095	4T. Elmer Myers (1917)	62	4.42
6T. Dutch Henry (1930)	.105	6. Gene Brabender (1970)	63	6.02
6T. Matt Keough (1979)	.105	7T. Dan Griner (1913)	64	5.08
8. Art Houtteman (1948)	.111	7T. Lefty Hoerst (1942)	64	5.20
9. Kaiser Wilhelm (1905)	.115	9T. Tom Fisher (1904)	65	4.25
10T. Curt Fullerton (1923)	.118	9T. George Bell (1908)	65	3.59
10T. Kent Peterson (1948)	.118	9T. Les Sweetland (1928)	65	6.58
10T. Ken Reynolds (1972)	.118	9T. Hal Gregg (1944)	65	5.46
13. Don Larsen (1954)	.125	9T. Roger Wolff (1944)	65	4.99
14. Walt Dickson (1912)	.136	9T. Mark Davis (1984)	65	5.36
15. Ben Cantwell (1935)	.138	15T. Willie Sudhoff (1904)	66	3.76
16. Bill Bailey (1910)	.143	15T. Speed Martin (1920)	66	4.83
17. Craig Anderson (1962)	.150	15T. Lou Knerr (1946)	66	5.40
18T. Burleigh Grimes (1917)	.158	15T. Rick Wise (1968)	66	4.55
18T. Lou Knerr (1946)	.158	19T. Mal Eason (1905)	67	4.30
18T. Frank Sullivan (1961)	.158	19T. George Winter (1906)	67	4.12
18T. Rick Honeycutt (1987)	.158	19T. Bob Harmon (1910)	67	4.46
22. Jack Townsend (1904)	.161	19T. Jimmy Ring (1928)	67	6.40
23T. Jim Pastorius (1908)	.167	23T. Kaiser Wilhelm (1905)	68	4.54
23T. George Smith (1921)	.167	23T. Case Patten (1907)	68	3.56
23T. Roy Wilkinson (1921)	.167	23T. Gus Dorner (1908)	68	3.54
23T. Les Sweetland (1928)	.167	23T. Hub Pruett (1927)	68	6.05
23T. Bob Savage (1946)	.167	23T. Pat Caraway (1931)	68	6.22
23T. Hal Brown (1964)	.167	23T. George Caster (1940)	68	6.56
23T. Ron Bryant (1974)	.167	23T. Phil Ortega (1965)	68	5.11
23T. Jerry Koosman (1978)	.167	23T. Ron Bryant (1974)	68	5.61
		23T. Matt Keough (1982)	68	5.72
		23T. Don Carman (1989)	68	5.24

Single Season Leaders, 1901–1991, Wins-Above-Team; Index (Minimum of 15 Losses)

Order, Name, and Year*	WAT	Order, Name, and Year*	TPI
1. Kaiser Wilhelm (1905)	−8.9	1. Pat Caraway (1931)	−4.3
2T. Joe Harris (1906)	−8.6	2T. Rube Bressler (1915)	−4.1
2T. Paul Derringer (1933)	−8.6	2T. Matt Keough (1982)	−4.1
4. Jack Nabors (1916)	−8.5	4T. Irv Young (1907)	−4.0
5. Don Larsen (1954)	−8.1	4T. George Caster (1940)	−4.0
6. José DeLeon (1985)	−7.9	4T. Hal Gregg (1944)	−4.0
7. Fred Glade (1905)	−7.8	7T. Jack Knott (1936)	−3.9
8. George Bell (1910)	−7.6	7T. Herm Wehmeier (1950)	−3.9
9T. Roy Wilkinson (1921)	−7.4	9T. Case Patten (1907)	−3.8
9T. Dolph Luque (1922)	−7.4	9T. Jimmy Ring (1928)	−3.8
11T. George Winter (1908)	−7.2	11T. Kaiser Wilhelm (1905)	−3.7
11T. Dutch Henry (1930)	−7.2	11T. Vive Lindaman (1907)	−3.7
13T. Ben Cantwell (1935)	−7.1	11T. Dan Griner (1913)	−3.7
13T. Art Houtteman (1948)	−7.1	11T. Mark Davis (1984)	−3.7
13T. Mike Parrott (1980)	−7.1	11T. Sammy Ellis (1966)	−3.7
16. Long Tom Hughes (1904)	−7.0	16T. Tom Fisher (1904)	−3.6
16T. Cliff Curtis (1910)	−7.0	16T. Oscar Jones (1905)	−3.6
18T. Walt Dickson (1912)	−6.9	16T. Bill Greif (1972)	−3.6
18T. Rube Marquard (1914)	−6.9	19T. Bill Phillips (1901)	−3.5
20T. Robin Roberts (1957)	−6.8	19T. Kaiser Wilhelm (1904)	−3.5
20T. Brian Kingman (1980)	−6.8	19T. Jack Townsend (1904)	−3.5
22T. Frank Allen (1913)	−6.7	19T. Bob Harmon (1910)	−3.5
22T. Matt Keough (1979)	−6.7	19T. Elmer Myers (1917)	−3.5
24T. Patsy Flaherty (1903)	−6.6	24. Chuck Stobbs (1957)	−3.4
24T. Jim Pastorius (1908)	−6.6	25T. Bobo Newsom (1942)	−3.3
24T. Harry Harper (1919)	−6.6	25T. Jim Bibby (1974)	−3.3
24T. Larry French (1938)	−6.6		

* T = tie.

Career Leaders: 1901–1991,
Losses Minus Wins
(Minimum of 50 Losses)

Order, Name, and Years*	Losses minus Wins	W–L
1. Milt Gaston (1924–34)	67	97–164
2. Si Johnson (1928–47)	64	101–165
3. Jack Russell (1926–40)	56	85–141
4. Jack Fisher (1959–69)	53	86–139
5. Buster Brown (1905–13)	52	51–103
6. Kaiser Wilhelm (1903–21)	49	56–105
7. Sid Hudson(1940–54)	48	104–152
8. Happy Jack Townsend (1901–06)	47	35–82
9. Harry McIntire (1905–13)	46	71–117
10T. Long Tom Hughes (1900–13)	44	131–175
10T. Hugh Mulcahy (1935–47)	44	45–89
12. Pedro Ramos (1955–70)	43	117–160
13. Jesse Jefferson (1973–81)	42	39–81
14. Rollie Naylor (1917–24)	41	42–83
15T. Ned Garvin (1896–1904)	40	57–97
15T. Eddie Smith (1936–47)	40	73–113
15T. Slim Harriss (1920–28)	40	95–135
15T. George Smith (1916–23)	40	41–81
15T. Skip Lockwood (1969–80)	40	57–97
20. Buck Ross (1935–45)	39	56–95
21T. Socks Seibold (1916–33)	38	48–86
21T. Bill Bailey (1907–22)	38	38–76
23T. Chick Fraser (1896–1909)	37	175–212
23T. Ike Pearson (1939–48)	37	13–50
23T. Mike Morgan (1978–91)	37	67–104

Career Leaders, 1901–1991, Winning Percentage; ERA (Minimum of 50 Losses)

Order, Name, and Years*	Winning Percentage
1. Ike Pearson (1939–48)	.206
2. Dolly Gray (1909–11)	.227
3. Jack Townsend (1901–06)	.299
4. Galen Cisco (1961–69)	.309
5. Cliff Curtis (1909–13)	.315
6. Bill Greif (1971–76)	.316
7. Jay Hook (1957–64)	.319
8. Jesse Jefferson (1973–81)	.325
9. Buster Brown (1905–13)	.331
10T. Bill Bailey (1907–22)	.333
10T. Mal Eason (1900–06)	.333
10T. Al Gerheauser (1943–48)	.333
13T. Hugh Mulcahy (1935–47)	.336
13T. Rollie Naylor (1917–24)	.336
13T. George Smith (1916–23)	.336
16. Steve Arlin (1969–74)	.337
17. Walt Dickson (1910–15)	.342
18. Gus Dorner (1902–09)	.343
19. Tracy Stallard (1960–66)	.345
20. Kaiser Wilhelm (1903–21)	.348
21. George Bell (1907–11)	.352
22. Boom Boom Beck (1924–45)	.355
23. Tommy O. Hughes (1941–48)	.356
24. Lum Harris (1941–47)	.357
25T. Chappie McFarland (1902–06)	.358
25T. Socks Seibold (1916–33)	.358

Order, Name, and Years*	Adjusted ERA	Actual ERA
1. Mike Kekich (1965–77)	72	4.59
2T. Phil Ortega (1960–69)	75	4.43
2T. Jay Hook (1957–64)	75	5.23
2T. Dolly Gray (1909–11)	75	3.52
5T. Les Sweetland (1927–31)	77	6.10
5T. Wade Blasingame (1963–72)	77	4.52
7T. Steve Arlin (1969–74)	78	4.33
7T. Jim Pastorius (1906–09)	78	3.12
7T. Billy Champion (1969–76)	78	4.69
7T. Gus Dorner (1902–09)	78	3.37
7T. Bill Greif (1971–76)	78	4.41
7T. Pete Broberg (1971–78)	78	4.56
13T. Ike Pearson (1939–48)	79	4.83
13T. John D'Acquisto (1973–82)	79	4.56
15T. Bill Bailey (1907–22)	80	3.57
15T. Don Black (1943–48)	80	4.35
17T. Galen Cisco (1961–69)	81	4.56
17T. Elmer Myers (1915–22)	81	4.06
17T. Claude Willoughby (1925–31)	81	5.84
17T. Fred Talbot (1963–70)	81	4.12
21. Rardy Lerch (1975–86)	82	4.53
22T. Kaiser Wilhelm (1903–21)	83	3.44
22T. Harry McIntire (1905–13)	83	3.44
22T. Jesse Jefferson (1973–81)	83	4.81
22T. Dave Freisleben (1974–79)	83	4.30
22T. Jerry Johnson (1968–77)	83	4.31

Career Leaders, 1901–1991, Wins-Above-Team; Index (Minimum of 50 Losses)

Order, Name, and Years*	WAT	Order, Name, and Years*	TPI
1. Rube Walberg (1923–37)	-19.6	1. Herm Wehmeier (1945–58)	-14.3
2. Eddie Smith (1936–47)	-18.8	2. Case Patten (1901–08)	-12.7
3. Jack Townsend (1901–06)	-18.3	3. Mike Kekich (1965–77)	-12.4
4. Ned Garvin (1896–1904)	-17.6	4. Phil Ortega (1960–69)	-11.7
5. Jack Russell (1926–40)	-17.0	5. Si Johnson (1928–47)	-11.6
6. Mike Morgan (1978–91)	-16.3	6T. Alex Ferguson (1918–29)	-10.7
7. Sheriff Blake (1920–37)	-15.3	6T. Jack Fisher (1959–69)	-10.7
8T. Jack Fisher (1959–69)	-14.6	8T. Jay Hook (1957–64)	-10.5
8T. Harry McIntire (1905–13)	-14.6	8T. Pete Broberg (1971–78)	-10.5
10. Kaiser Wilhelm (1903–21)	-13.8	8T. Joe Oeschger (1914–25)	-10.5
11. Lloyd Brown (1925–40)	-13.7	11. Andy Hawkins (1982–91)	-10.4
12T. Dolly Gray (1909–11)	-13.3	12T. Claude Willoughby (1925–31)	-9.4
12T. Milt Gaston (1924–34)	-13.3	12T. Buck Ross (1936–45)	-9.4
14. José DeLeon (1983–91)	-12.9	14. Jesse Jefferson (1973–81)	-8.8
15. Andy Hassler (1971–85)	-12.8	15. Happy Jack Townsend (1901–06)	-8.5
16T. Mal Eason (1900–06)	-12.7	16. Harry McIntire (1905–13)	-8.3
16T. Bill Bailey (1907–22)	-12.7	17T. Gus Dorner (1902–09)	-8.2
18. Tim Leary (1981–91)	-12.5	17T. Billy Champion (1969–76)	-8.2
19. Jesse Jefferson (1973–81)	-12.3	17T. Pete Falcone (1975–84)	-8.2
20. Skip Lockwood (1969–80)	-12.1	20T. Bill Bailey (1907–22)	-8.1
21. John Buzhardt (1958–68)	-12.0	20T. Kaiser Wilhelm (1903–21)	-8.1
22. Eric Rasmussen (1975–83)	-11.8	20T. John D'Acquisto (1973–82)	-8.1
23. Jim Beattie (1978–86)	-11.6	20T. Bill Greif (1971–76)	-8.1
24T. George Smith (1916–23)	-11.4	24T. Chick Fraser (1896–1909)	-8.0
24T. Bo Belinsky (1962–70)	-11.4	24T. Hub Perdue (1911–15)	-8.0
		24T. Lew Krausse (1961–74)	-8.0

* T = tie.

Epilogue

The Saga of Anthony Young

◆ The first printing of this book came out just in time for the start of the 1993 season—just in time to witness one of the most memorable, sustained Skunk performances of the ages by right-hander Anthony Young, then 27 and still with the New York Mets. Young's heroics occurred before a trade for shortstop Jose Viscaino late in March 1994 turned him into a Cubbie; before an elbow injury knocked him out of the box during July of the juiced-ball, strike-infested, Selig-cancelled 1994 season; and before Young had Tommy John surgery in mid-August to repair his right elbow, making his future as cloudy as that of major league baseball.

But these rumblings and uncertainties cannot diminish the ex-Met's awesome accomplishments on the mound. The 6-foot-2 Texan, a former safety at the University of Houston, notched one loss for each year of age in a streak that started in early May of 1992 and didn't end until late July of 1993. When the right-hander closed out 1992 with 14 straight losses, we were impressed with his consistency: He lost the first 7 as a starter and the last 7 in relief. With that kind of balance we saw a great future for him; in Chapter 7 (page 200) we listed Young among a handful of contenders for the thrones occupied by Happy Jack Townsend and Jesse Jefferson.

Had we known Young would start off 1993 at 0–13, helpless to halt his losing streak until it stretched out to 27, we might have named our Skunk trophy after him instead of good old Bill Stearns. As *Los Angeles Times* columnist Allan Malamud suggested after the streak reached 25, "Maybe two Young awards should be presented in each league—the Cy for the best pitcher and the Anthony for the worst."

But we were a bit late to immortalize Anthony as the inverse of Cy. Instead, we have to be content to offer Anthony Young the Skunk Stearns Award for 1993. His final stats were 1–16, a winning percentage of .059, and a WAT of −7.2, world-class numbers. Sure, we know he has a live arm (or at least he did prior to his TJ elbow surgery), and no way is he the worst pitcher around. But he has mastered the essence of what our Skunk trophies are all about: pitching just well enough to stay in and lose, whether it's 2–1 or a 12–2 blowout, and doing it consistently. His winning percentage in 1993 ties for second worst *ever* for a pitcher with at least 15 losses, and his WAT cracks the all-time dirty dozen (see pages 202 and 203 for lists of worsts that go through the 1991 season). Young's negative WAT means that he won *seven* games fewer that was predicted for him, based on his team's won-lost record when other Mets hurlers toed the rubber. And the 1993 Mets had a worse record (59–103) than the expansion Marlins and Rockies.

The Mets lost more games than even the self-destructing Padres, who tried to ignore the Harris jinx (see pages 59–63) by sporting two Harrises (Greg and Gene) for more than half a season in 1993. Greg proved that the Harris jinx was alive and well in 1993 after San Diego traded him to Colorado in early August. He gave a two-month imitation of the original Harris, the Red Sox's Joe, by posting a 1–8 record, fully equipped with a 6.50 ERA, for the Rockies. And the Harris jinx thrived in 1994. Greg showed that his 1993 flop was no fluke, as he compiled a 3–12 record for Colorado (with a 6.65 ERA and a WAT of −4.4) to capture the 1994 Skunk Stearns Award. He just edged another of our favorites, the Cubs' Mike Morgan (see pages 177–178), whose 2–10 record in 1994 gave him a lifetime mark of 95–137.

Harris' 4–20 record for the Rockies in 1993–94, punctuated by a season-closing eight straight losses, is reminiscent of Joe Harris' career mark of 3–30. Colorado was expected to release Greg and his $1.9 million contract during the (perhaps endless) off-season. The other Greg Harris knew what it was like to be released. He was let go twice within 15 days in 1994, first by the Red Sox in late June (8.28 ERA) and then by the Yankees in mid-July (shortly after blowing a game to the A's by grooving a go-ahead homer to Geronimo Berroa). And the Padres' Gene Harris, a solid closer in 1993, was banished to Detroit in May after butting heads with manager Jim Riggleman earlier in the season. Gene was a bust with both the Padres (8.03 ERA and the Tigers (7.15 ERA), and his save total plunged from 23 in 1993 to 1 in 1994. No reliever this side of Mitch Williams, who never recovered from the trauma of being the Blue Jays' true MVP in the 1993 World Series, slid so far in one year. Wild Thing fell from 43 saves for the Phils in 1993 to 6 for Houston in 1994 before he and his 7.65 ERA self-destructed and were given a one-way ticket out of baseball.

Fortunately, Mitch Williams didn't pitch in the American League in 1994; otherwise the league's ERA of 4.80 might have been elevated enough to set a new futility record. As it was, the AL posted the third worst ERA of the twentieth century, trailing only the AL's 5.04 in 1936 and the NL's 4.97 in the legendary 1930 season.

But we're getting away from the feature Skunk story of the 1990s, a story that took Anthony Young into more family rooms via television media (and bathrooms via print media) than all of the Cy Young contenders combined. Anthony Young became "A.Y.," the media darling. Rescued from the obscurity he would have faced had he squeaked out a single victory in April or May of 1993, he became the focus of feature articles in *The New York Times*, *The Sporting News*, *Sports Illustrated*, and a slew of other newspapers and magazines. In early August, about a week after getting the monkey off his back with a relief win over the Marlins, a candid and cheerful Young appeared on *The Tonight Show*.

Lose 27 straight games in the early 1990s and you get Jay Leno. Lose 23 straight in 1910 and 1911, as the Boston Braves' Cliff Curtis did, and you find oblivion. A.Y.'s steady climb toward Curtis' record, a mark that once seemed as unreachable as DeMag's 56 straight, sent sportswriters scurrying through the archives. The Boston newspapers of 1910–11 didn't once mention the Curtis streak, not while he was setting it and not when he finally broke it. The lead story after he notched his first win after months of futility was about a fire that devastated Coney Island. Even the account of the Braves' win said nothing about the end of Curtis' dry spell.

In 1993, however, Curtis was granted more coverage than he had had in a lifetime of inept pitching (28–61 over a five-year span). Before the season began, this book had honored Curtis with the 1910 Skunk trophy, thanks to the 6–24 record he compiled while getting his losing streak off to a jump start. That season even cracked our "25 worst" list (see page 190), and the oldtime right-hander's winning percentage of .315 is among the worst ever (page 205). But almost no one heard of Curtis until A.Y. came along. Then stories appeared about the ghost whose shadow Young was reluctantly chasing. The media's timing wasn't great for Curtis, who died of a heart attack in 1943 after fighting a grass fire, but Curtis' grandchildren enjoyed their Andy Warhol 15 minutes of fame.

Young's streak started innocently enough. After compiling a 2–5 record for the Mets as a rookie during the last two months of the 1991 season, he began 1992 with two quick wins. He was one win away from a career .500 mark when he dropped a decision to the Reds in early May and chalked up two more losses in the next week and a half. Then the defeats started to snowball, although an injury to John Franco gave him a chance to shine for a while as the Mets' closer.

"He'd hit a wall every start," one Mets official told reporters. "After being demoted to the bullpen, he saved 12 straight games. All throughout, he battled an injured knee."

Young also impressed Jeff Torborg, then the Mets' manager: "He never refused the ball. Not once. I mean, if you manage long enough, you see players who are hyperventilating late in the game. They don't want the ball. A.Y. never complained."

If Young lost any sleep over his parade of losses, it didn't show. He was upbeat as he entered the 1993 season with a 4–19 record. "I was happy with saving 12 straight games," he told reporters before the season started. "I never worry about losing. I'm not that kind of guy." Self-insight is evidently not one of Young's strong points. Frustrated after loss number 18, he took a kick at a roll of toilet paper, missed, and struck the toilet, nearly breaking his toe!

Young started off the 1993 season in the bullpen. He dropped his first 5 decisions to stretch his losing streak to 19 games, tying Craig Anderson's club record set in 1962–73. Young was put into the starting rotation and pitched 6 scoreless innings in his first start (without getting the win, of course) to encourage manager Dallas Green to stick with him. Despite the streak, the Mets fielded offers from the Phillies and Reds about Young's availability.

Anderson, Skunk Stearns winner from the Class of '62, offered words of support to Young as the New York hurler tied his club record: "You have to be a good pitcher to lose 19 straight."

If Anderson's words are true, then Anderson was a good pitcher and Young would soon prove himself to be a great pitcher. He was put into the rotation in June and promptly lost 3 starts to put himself within one game of Cliff Curtis's record. It was about that time that the media picked up on Young's plight in earnest, and he managed to handle the Big Apple limelight with a maturity that he hasn't been able to match on the mound.

A few interesting happenings during the chase:

- Before losing number 22, Young started to cry on the mound and had a hard time stopping. A.Y. said he had an allergic reaction to a drying substance used on the wet field after a rain-delay, which made his eyes tear. Now that's the kind of ingenuity that John Coleman could have used back in 1883 when he dropped 48 games.

- While eating dinner with former teammate Gregg Jeffries prior to starting the game against the Cards that proved to be the record setter, people had the audacity to ask Young if he wanted the record to be in the books. His response showed class. "No, I don't want the record," he told them. "I don't think it would be nice to end up that way." We wonder how Charles Barkely would have handled these inquisitive fans.
- A medium called the Mets' offices and offered to try to contact the spirit of Cliff Curtis for some words of advice. Young declined. Other fans sent A.Y. rabbit-feet, coins, plastic trolls with orange hair, a Buddha statuette, and a miniature horseshoe. They didn't work.
- On June 12, the day before Anthony Young lost number 21, Matt Young won his first game in over two years. Matt, the left-handed Young (whose Skunk exploits were highlighted on page 186), was quietly creeping up on Curtis' mark when he snapped a 14-game skid with a 10–9 relief win over the Rangers. In reply to a question that A.Y. heard many times— did he fear he'd never win again—A.Y said, "I wouldn't be out here if I didn't have the confidence to win a game." Mr. Confidence posted a 1–6 record for Cleveland in 1993 and was gone in 1994. He last won a start in May 1991, coming away empty 24 straight times. Put the two Youngs together and you've assembled an ambidextrous Skunk who can't win in either league. The not-quite-Cy Youngs combined for a 4–40 record in 1992–93.
- One fan who said he was a surgeon wrote to Young with words of encouragement just before A.Y. matched Curtis' 23 straight losses: The doctor claimed to have lost 22 straight patients, but the 23rd operation ended being up being a winner. We'd like the doc's name in case we ever write a book about the worst physicians of all time.

A.Y. tied the record on June 22, 1993, in a start against Montreal, the last team Young had been able to beat. A 6–3 defeat —with three runs unearned due to four Mets errors—put Young's name in the record books alongside that of Cliff Curtis. He started on only three days' rest, but unfortunately, as Joe Sexton of the *New York Times* News Service reported it, "The rest of the Mets looked as if they were playing on six months' rest." Young was able to keep his sense of humor, though; facing reporters after the game, he wore a T-shirt saying, IF I HAD ANY LUCK, IT WOULD BE ALL BAD. He told them: "I'm a little rattled. I expected to end the losing streak, but a couple of bad plays behind me cost 3 unearned runs. No one wants to be 0–23. Am I that bad? It's hard, but I'm a fighter and I'm not going to give up. I'll hang in there. I'm embarrassed because I know I'm a better pitcher than that."

It's a difficult thing for him to go through," Mets manager Dallas Green told reporters. "That's why we've had stiff hands out there. Everyone's trying to do a little too much." Including Green himself, who was ejected during the fifth inning of the record-tying game for kicking dirt on umpire Charlie Williams and arguing a little too much.

The Mets scored two runs against the Cards in the first inning on June 27, Young's next start, and it looked as though he'd share—but not break—Curtis' infamous mark. But he gave up 3 runs in the fourth and 2 in the sixth, and St. Louis came away with a 5–3 victory. If you think Young was the only nervous pitcher in the historic game, think again. Imagine what it's like to be the first one in a millennium to lose to Anthony Young. Opposing pitcher and winner Joe Magrane told reporters afterward: "It was a pressure-packed situation. Pitching against Young was like being on top of Mount Vesuvius waiting for the volcano to blow."

After the game, A.Y. felt relief. "I thought I would go out there and win today," he told reporters. "In a sense I'm glad this is over with. I broke the record for losses. Now, maybe the media will leave me alone. Now maybe I can just go out there, relax, and win my next game." But none of that happened, because Young, like Henry Aaron, was fated to not only break an unassailable record but to put it out of reach for anyone else.

A.Y.'s next start was scheduled for Cliff Curtis' 110th birthday, July 3, but he ended up pitching a day earlier. It didn't help. He lost to the Giants, 3–1, for his 25th consecutive loss in a game that was called after five innings due to rain. Like another perennial loser, Charlie Brown, Young never lost heart. "I believe I have found every which way to lose," he told reporters. "The rain stopped it. I can't do anything about it. I felt if we could have played the whole game, we would have scored a few runs and won the game."

On July 7 against San Diego he notched number 26 despite pitching more like C.Y. (Cy Young) than A.Y. He retired 23 straight Padres at one point, yet lost 2–0 to Andy Benes when he gave up a two-run eighth inning homer to Archi Cianfrocco. "I pitched the best I have in two years," Young told reporters. "All I got for it was another loss."

Young's teammate Jeff Kent had a theory as to why Young's streak continued despite decent pitching. "When A.Y. pitches, we want to win so badly that we put pressure on ourselves to do too much, especially at bat," he told reporters. "That is messing us up and leaving A.Y. with no chance." Mets hurler Jeff Innis added emphasis to Kent's point. "Did you see the plays we made after he left [in the record-tying loss]?" Innis asked.

However, New York manager Green didn't want people to assign all of the blame away from Young. "He's got a good arm," he told reporters. "If you are evaluating arms and just sitting up there as a scout, you've got to say that the guy's got an arm. But I think it's important to scout head and heart, and that's what I'm doing right now. I understand the youth and I understand making some mistakes, but again, it's accepting responsibility for those mistakes and pitching through it and learning from each one."

A.Y. was demoted to the bullpen, where he pitched like a Skunk even when he wasn't adding to his streak. On July 10, he was put in to hold on to a rare Mets lead, 6–0 against Los Angeles. He promptly gave up hits to the only four batters he faced, and the Mets had to hang on for a 7–6 triumph. "I was committed to A.Y. until the All-Star break," manager Dallas Green told reporters. "That was trying to help out Anthony. Now it's time to worry about the team. We had a six-run lead, and I thought he might do the job out of the bullpen."

Green does know about losing. He was a member of the Phillies team that lost 23 straight games. "That was very difficult to handle, but I was young and got over it," he told reporters. "Anthony's young and he'll get over it. That's why I'll keep running out there, and hopefully he'll get through it quickly so he can get back to being a normal human being again."

Young was blunt: "I was terrible today," he told reporters. "I was lucky they got me out of there. If Dallas says I'm a relief pitcher, then I'm a relief pitcher." And not a very good one. He collected his 27th straight loss, dropping to 0–13 on July 24 against the Dodgers, when he walked Dave Hansen with the bases loaded in the bottom of the tenth to give Los Angeles a 5–4 victory.

The streak finally ended on July 28, but A.Y. did his best to make it number 28. He was brought in to face the Marlins in the top of the ninth in a 3–3 game, and he promptly gave up the go-ahead run (unearned, naturally). The Marlins brought in their ace, Bryan Harvey, who would convert 45 out of 48 save opportunities in 1993. Who could have predicted that one of those three blown saves was about to unfold?

In the bottom of the ninth, Ryan Thompson singled in the tying run, and Eddie Murray doubled in Thompson to give the Mets—and

Anthony Young—a 5–4 victory. It was the first time Young's name had been in the w column since he had beaten Montreal more than 15 months earlier! (A game-by-game account of the 27 straight losses that made that year and a quarter so memorable for Young appears in the chart on page 216.)

"It's wonderful," Young told reporters as he drank champagne and was given bouquets of roses. "I feel great. I haven't had a monkey on my back. It's been a whole zoo. I have talent and the Mets know it. I'm going to win a lot more. The Mets had offers for me and they're going to keep me. I never doubted it. This is almost like winning the World Series."

Young does have talent. He was the 1990 Texas League pitcher of the year with a 15–3 record and 1.65 ERA. He began that year with 21 straight scoreless innings and ended with nine straight wins (to tie the Mets' minor league record). But the Mets did not interpret his single win as a sign that he had turned the corner. On August 17— eight days after Young appeared on *The Tonight Show*—the Mets sent him down to the minor leagues.

"We all thought the only way to save Anthony was to get him in a pitching situation now where he is comfortable working on the pitches he needs to be successful," Green told reporters. "My evaluation is he won't have a job in the big leagues if he continues pitching the way he has."

Young was brought up from the minors for the remainder of the 1993 season and saw his record drop to 1–16 before his season ended on September 16 with surgery to repair a torn ulnar collateral ligament in his left thumb. He suffered the injury on September 5 against the Cubs while diving for a ball. Young also underwent surgery on his right elbow on September 28, 1993, almost a year before his Tommy John surgery on that same elbow.

How good can A.Y. be? "Everybody is looking for pitching out there," Gerry Hunsicker, the Mets' vice president for baseball operations told reporters. "You see what other clubs are sending out to the mound. It ain't great and it's sometimes ridiculous. Anthony Young has a great arm and two good pitches. He's a guy with good stuff who hasn't become a good pitcher."

No, he hasn't. During the 27-game losing streak, his ERA was 6.32, which breaks down to a 5.25 mark in the 14 starts that he lost and a whopping 11.81 ERA in relief. The Mets' opponents outscored them 139–71 in the 27 games, and Young gave up 60 percent of those runs. In 1994, as a Cubs hurler, Young improved to a 4–6 record, entering the stratosphere of a .400 winning percentage. Nonetheless, A.Y.'s lifetime record through 1994 was an uncomfortable 9–41, producing a winning percentage of .180. His career WAT stands at −14.9, about 15 games worse than the records of his Mets or Cubs teams that finished either last or next to last during each of his four seasons. A.Y.'s only solace is that his Cubs teammate in 1994, Mike Morgan, has so consistently performed worse than the teams he's pitched for that his cumulative post-1994 WAT is the third-worst ever. His near-Skunk performance in 1994 lowered it to −18.6. Morgan is just one mediocre season away from becoming the first pitcher to crack the −20 circle. After the 1991 season, Morgan just missed making the list of the 25 worst pitchers. Three years later, his stats push him comfortably into the hallowed group, just ahead of Pete Broberg as the 17th worst pitcher of the twentieth century (see page 196).

Will A.Y. join Morgan among the elite? It depends on his ability to bounce back from surgery. If Young never returns to the majors, his career stats compare to those of Jack Wadsworth (6–38, −12.1 WAT), whose lifetime mark matches exactly the record of the all-female Colorado Silver Bullets, managed by Phil Niekro, in their 1994 maiden season. Wadsworth, the Skunk of 1894, was one of the worst pitchers who ever pitched in the majors in any century (see page 70). Sure, A.Y. is no Jack Wadsworth. In Wadsworth's dreams, he never pitched a game as good as Young's 2–0 loss to the Padres' Benes or had an ERA below 4.00. (Young's career ERA at the end of the 1994 season was 3.85.)

But if A.Y. does return to the majors, a great likelihood in view of his self-confidence and work habits and the sorry lot of pitchers who occupy the number nine and ten slots in most rotations, then watch out. Once he notches his 50th loss and becomes eligible for our grand competition, he might fit in nicely with the 25 worst hurlers of the century. His WAT is approaching the worst of all time, and his winning percentage of .180 is lower than Ike Pearson's chart-leading value of .206 (see page 205). And if Young's ERA starts to rise as his WAT continues to descend, then no one—not even Happy Jack Townsend—is safe from attack.

But if Young recovers fully from his difficult ligament surgery and lives up to the potential that so many continue to believe in, we're ready for that too. We've got a Joe Hardy Sell-Your-Soul trophy for the next era tucked away in a safe-deposit box, already engraved with the initials A.Y.

Ex-Mets hurler Anthony Young, not to be confused with Cy, who closed out the 1992 season with 14 straight losses and—for an encore—managed to lose the first 13 of 1993. Young's streak of 27 straight may be present as formidable a challenge to future Skunks as DiMaggio's 56 straight has presented to Silver Sluggers. (photo courtesy of Wide World Photos, Inc.)

A Game-by-Game Account of Anthony Young's 27-Game Streak

Loss #	Date	Opponent	Score	Winning Pitcher	Young's Stats	
	1992				**Innings**	**R/ER**
1.	5/6	Cincinnati	5-3*	Greg Swindell	6.0	5/5
2.	5/11	San Diego	4-2*	Andy Benes	6.0	4/4
3.	5/17	Los Angeles	6-3*	Ramon Martinez	5.2	5/5
4.	6/8	Montreal	6-0*	Ken Hill	6.0	3/3
5.	6/15	Montreal	4-1*	Mark Gardiner	7.0	2/2
6.	6/20	St. Louis	6-1*	Bob Tewksbury	4.2	2/2
7.	6/25	Chicago	9-2*	Greg Maddux	2.0	9/3
8.	6/30	Chicago	3-1	Greg Maddux	2.0	1/1
9.	7/4	Houston	3-1	Al Osuna	2.0	2/2
10.	9/3	Cincinnati	4-3	Rob Dibble	0.2	2/2
11.	9/5	Cincinnati	6-5	Norm Charlton	0.2	2/2
12.	9/13	Expos	7-5	Mel Rojas	0.1	3/3
13.	9/17	St Louis	3-2	Mike Perez	1.0	1/1
14.	9/29	Philadelphia	5-3	Bob Ayrault	0.0	3/1
	1993					
15.	4/9	Houston	7-3	Doug Jones	2.0	4/4
16.	4/25	San Diego	9-8	Tim Scott	2.0	1/0
17.	4/30	San Diego	7-6	Rich Rodriguez	1.0	1/1
18.	5/16	Montreal	4-3	Jeff Fassero	1.1	1/1
19.	5/28	Cincinnati	5-2	John Smiley	0.1	3/2
20.	6/8	Chicago	5-1*	Mike Morgan	6.0	4/3
21.	6/13	Philadelphia	5-3*	Ben Rivera	6.0	3/3
22.	6/18	Pittsburgh	5-2*	Paul Wagner	7.0	5/5
23.	6/22	Montreal	6-3*	Mel Rojas	6.0	6/3
24.	6/27	St. Louis	5-3*	Joe Magrane	7.0	5/5
25.	7/2	San Francisco	3-1*	Dave Burba	5.0	3/3
26.	7/7	San Diego	2-0*	Andy Benes	8.0	2/2
27.	7/24	Los Angeles	5-4	Jim Gott	2.2	1/1
				TOTAL	98.1	83/69
					ERA = 6.32	

*Losses as starting pitcher

APPENDIX:
STATISTICAL TERMS AND
PROCEDURES USED IN THIS BOOK

Explanations of Some Palmer-Thorn Statistics

We've used three statistics throughout this book to help compare pitchers from one generation to the next, stats that take into account the fluctuating standards of excellence (or, in our case, incompetence) that have characterized each era of major-league baseball. These stats were developed by Pete Palmer and John Thorn, authors of *The Hidden Book of Baseball* and the two editions of *Total Baseball*.

These innovative procedures allow direct comparisons of players from different eras, leagues, and home ballparks. Brief explanations of these three stats—adjusted ERA, wins-above-team (WAT), and total pitcher index (TPI)—are presented here for the interested reader.

ADJUSTED ERA (EARNED RUN AVERAGE,
ADJUSTED FOR LEAGUE AND BALLPARK)

The adjusted ERA converts the familiar earned run average to a new system, one in which a value of 100 reflects the performance of the average pitcher in each league during every season of major-league baseball. Average ERAs have fluctuated widely from year to year and even from league to league: In 1985, NL pitchers averaged 3.59 and AL pitchers, 4.15; in 1936, NL hurlers allowed four earned runs a game, while AL pitchers yielded five. Palmer and Thorn adjusted each pitcher's ERA to account for these shifts by dividing the league's average ERA in a given year by the pitcher's ERA and then multiplying by 100 to get rid of decimals. The adjusted ERA was further modified by Thorn and Palmer to take into account the "park factor" (a stat that evaluates the impact of a pitcher playing mostly in the close confines of a ballpark like Wrigley Field or in the relative safety of the spacious Astrodome).

An adjusted ERA of 100 is average for any pitcher in any league in any season; values above 100 are reserved for the best pitchers in the league, while values below 100—sometimes in the abominable 60–70 range—belong to the heroes of this book. The best lifetime adjusted ERAs, all in the 145 to 150 range, belong to one pitcher from each of the four 20th-century eras: Walter Johnson, Lefty Grove, Hoyt Wilhelm, and Roger Clemens. The worst adjusted ERA of the century for pitchers with at least 50 losses was Mike Kekich's 72; Kekich was trailed by a trio of pitchers whose ERAs adjusted to 75—Dolly Gray, Jay Hook, and Phil Ortega. All but old-timer Gray pitched during the 1960s. If you go back to the 1870s, the lowest lifetime adjusted ERA was 51, belonging to none other than Bill Stearns—the National Association pitcher for whom we named the Skunk Stearns Award.

WINS-ABOVE-TEAM (WAT)

This Palmer-Thorn stat compares the number of games a pitcher won to the number the *average* pitcher would have won for the same team. The formulas for computing WAT compare the pitcher's winning percentage with his team's winning percentage when other pitchers were on the mound. There are two different formulas, depending on whether the pitcher's percentage is better or worse than his team's; both formulas, however, come up with the *difference* between the number of games the pitcher won and the number of games the average pitcher would have won, given the teams overall hitting and fielding ability.

Since the WATs for Skunk Stearns candidates are routinely below zero, we're really looking at "wins-below-team." The WAT was particularly important to include among our criteria because it kept us honest; it prevented us from being seduced only by a pitcher's poor won-lost record or ballooned ERA. It helped us distinguish between pitchers who were merely victims of shoddy support from their teammates (their WATs were only mildly negative, or maybe even positive) and those with all-time skunk credentials: Those hurlers who lost more games than expected, even when they pitched for rotten teams.

Thorn and Palmer included the WAT statistic in the first edition of *Total Baseball*, but discarded it for the second edition because of some cautions associated with it. Still, we have retained the WAT because it provides an especially useful method of distinguishing among pitchers at the bottom of the barrel. Very negative WATs indicate that the pitcher was much worse than his team, a clear-cut indictment of his ability. Statistical guru Pete Palmer agreed with our decision to use WAT as one of several criteria to select the worst pitchers of all time and provided us with WATs for pitchers from 1989 to 1991 (and modified WATs for some old-timers) to supplement the stats given in the first edition of *Total Baseball*.

The lifetime leader in the WAT statistic is Cy Young, whose WAT of +100.1 indicates that he won 100 games more than the average pitcher would have garnered pitching mostly for teams in Cleveland and Boston during the 1890s and 1900s; next on the career list are Walter Johnson

(+90.3) and Grover Cleveland Alexander (+81.9). Tom Seaver (+59.4) heads the list of pitchers from the most recent era (1969–92), easily out-distancing Phil Niekro (+36.9). At the bottom of the heap are Rube Walberg (−19.6), who pitched far more poorly than expected for the Athletics teams of the late 1920s and early 1930s, followed by Eddie Smith (−18.8) and Happy Jack Townsend (−18.3) — our nomination for the worst pitcher of the 20th century.

TOTAL PITCHER INDEX (TPI)

Like the adjusted ERA and WAT, the TPI takes into account fluctuating standards from year to year. It reflects a combination of three aspects of a pitcher's job: pitching, fielding, and hitting. It indicates the number of runs that a pitcher saved, over and above the number saved by the average pitcher in his league, via his pitching and fielding, and the number of runs he contributed by his batting prowess. All these "pitching runs" are reported as a function of what Palmer and Thorn referred to as the "runs per win" factor, a value that fluctuates from year to year. As with the WAT, zero is average, so the pitchers of interest to us appear at the bottom of the totem pole; they don't save runs, they squander them, and sport negative TPIs. Thanks to the Designated Hitter rule, the TPI reflects only runs saved (or squandered) by pitching and fielding by AL hurlers since 1973. Even though both the TPI and adjusted ERA take into account the number of earned runs yielded by a pitcher, we thought that both stats should be included among our criteria to give us the most well-rounded skunks possible.

Career leaders for the TPI are similar to the WAT leaders. Walter Johnson (+80.2) and Cy Young (+79.9) finished in a virtual dead heat for best ever, while Tom Seaver paced his era with a value of +50.4. The worst TPIs of the 20th century were turned in by Herm Wehmeier (−14.3), a journeyman pitcher form the 1940s and 1950s; old-timer Case Patten (−12.7); and Mike Kekich (−12.4).

The Worst Seasons and Worst Careers: 1876–1892

To choose the worst single season from 1876 to 1892 (see Chapter 2), we first limited the candidates to seasons in which a pitcher lost at least 15 games. Next, we listed the five worst single-season marks in four areas: losses minus wins, winning percentage, adjusted ERA, TPI. (As we stated previously, the WAT is not too appropriate for pre–1893 baseball.) These lists appear in a table at the end of Chapter 2.

We gave a pitcher five points if he had the worst stat in a category, four points for the second worst, three points for the third worst, and so forth. We added his points across the four categories, throwing in ten-point bonuses for each first-place ranking and five-point bonuses for each second-place finish. We also offered a ten-point bonus to pitchers who ranked among the worst in at least three categories, but no one qualified.

Regardless of point totals, we excluded pitchers who ranked among the worst in only a single category, as well as those who did fairly well in any category (for example, a pitcher with a winning record would have been declared ineligible regardless of a poor ERA and TPI).

John Coleman earned 30 points for his 1883 season (12–48) to come in first, followed by Art Hagan (1–16 in 1883) with 20 points, and Jack Neagle (5–23 in 1883) with 17 points. Dory Dean (4–26 in 1876) and George Cobb (10–37 in 1892) tied for fourth place with six points.

We followed the same point system and bonus system for determining the worst careers from 1876 to 1892 that we used to identify the worst single seasons. To compete for the worst career, a pitcher had to lose at least 50 games; we bent the rules only once, letting in George Keefe (20–48). John Coleman trounced the competition with 51 points, followed by Stump Weidman (24 points), Jack Neagle (18), Keefe (16), and John "Chicken-hearted" Kirby (5). Coleman finished in the top five in all four categories, while Keefe ranked among the leaders in three categories; both earned a ten-point bonus for their consistency (see the table at the end of Chapter 2).

The Worst Season and Worst Careers of the 20th Century

In Chapter 7 we listed the 25 worst single seasons and 25 worst careers of the 20th century (1901–91). We used statistical procedures that were similar to the techniques just described for 1876–92. First we listed the 25 worst single seasons of the 20th century (15 or more losses) in each of the five categories of interest to us: losses minus wins, winning percentage, adjusted ERA, WAT, and TPI (see the table at the end of Chapter 7). Kaiser Wilhelm (1905) had the worst WAT and ranked among the top 25 in every category, while Mike Parrott (1980) tied for worst adjusted ERA and was listed in four categories. A number of other pitchers ranked in the top 25 in three areas, the most notable being Joe Harris (1906) and Jack Nabors (1916), who each cracked three "top tens."

To determine the worst seasons of the century, we gave a pitcher 25 points for ranking first in a category, 24 points for ranking second, 23 points for ranking third, and so on, down to one point for a 25th-place finish. To reward the worst in each category, we tacked on a ten-point bonus for each pitcher who had the worst stat in any category and a five-point bonus for the second-worst stat. (Pitchers who tied for a ranking shared the points and bonuses. For example, Happy Jack Townsend and Ben Cantwell lost 21 games more than they won. They each earned 24.5 points by tying for the worst stat; plus they shared the ten-point and five-point bonuses, earning an extra 7.5 points apiece.)

To reward consistently bad pitching in several categories, we gave additional ten-point bonuses for ranking in *three* top tens, *four* top 20s, and *five* top 25s. Wilhelm accomplished all three, earning an extra 30 points for his efforts. Nabors and Harris were the only others to get a bonus for consistency.

We excluded pitchers from our final list of "worst seasons of the century" if their seasons were not uniformly bad. Regardless of their point totals, we disqualified pitchers who made only *one* top 25, had a winning percentage of .450 or better, had an adjusted ERA of 105 or higher, had a WAT higher than −2.0, or had a TPI of +1.0 or higher. We used such a stringent WAT rule because we did not want to penalize a pitcher if he was no worse than his team. The −2.0 WAT rule ensures that every pitcher on our worst-season list won at least *two* fewer games than the average pitcher on his team would have won. In a nutshell, pitchers made our final list of worst seasons on their own merits, not just because they pitched for lousy teams.

The rules that we used to exclude pitchers from our "worst" list did not eliminate any noteworthy Skunk Stearns winners. The highest-ranking pitcher eliminated was Hal Gregg (9–16 for Brooklyn in 1944), who would have tied for 12th place on the basis of his poor adjusted ERA and TPI; however, he was disqualified because his win total was about what you'd expect for any hurler on that terrible Dodger team. Matt Keough's 1982 season (11–18) was disqualified for the same reason; he wasn't much worse than expected, given his team's overall ability. Otherwise, Keough—who made the 25-worst list for his 2–17 record in 1979—would have been the only pitcher to make the list twice.

We applied identical rules for choosing the 25 worst careers of the century, limiting the candidates to pitchers with at least 50 defeats. We assigned the same bonuses and eliminated pitchers who failed to meet the minimum requirements of ineptness in each category. The lists of the 25 worst in each of our five categories appear in a table at the end of Chapter 7. Three hurlers—Jesse Jefferson, Kaiser Wilhelm, and Bill Bailey—earned ten-point bonuses for making all five lists. Jefferson earned an extra ten points for having four top-20 finishes, as did Happy Jack Townsend. And three pitchers took ten bonus points for three top-ten rankings: Townsend, Jay Hook, and Jack Fisher.

Rube Walberg had the worst WAT of the century (−19.6), but was disqualified from the 25-worst list because he posted a winning lifetime record. Similarly, TPI champ Herm Wehmeier (−14.3) was eliminated because he failed to make the list in any other category. The highest-ranking pitcher to be disqualified was Eddie Smith (73–113), whose lifetime WAT of −18.8 is the second worst in history. Smith would have tied for 16th in the worst pitcher sweepstakes, but his adjusted ERA of 108 and his TPI of +6.2 were too good.

INDEX